22 DAYS IN NORWAY, SWEDEN & DENMARK

THE ITINERARY PLANNER

BY RICK STEVES

Thanks to Dave Hoerlein and my wife Anne for research help
and support. Thanks also to our baby Andrew for making so
many Scandinavian friends and for graciously allowing us to
enjoy so many dinners. Thanks also to Thor, Berit, Hanne, Geir,
Hege and Kari-Anne, our Norwegian family.

Library of Congress Catalog No. 87-043133

Published by John Muir Publications
Santa Fe, New Mexico
Printed in U.S.A.

22 Days Editor   Richard Harris
Design   Mary Shapiro
Maps   Dave Hoerlein
Cover Map   Tim Clark
Typography   Copygraphics, Inc., Santa Fe, NM

ISBN 0-912528-83-4

CONTENTS

Southern Scandinavia

HOW TO USE THIS BOOK

This book is the tour guide in your pocket. It lets you be the boss by giving you the best 22 days in Scandinavia and a suggested way to use that time most efficiently.

Our 22 Day series is for do-it-yourselfers who would like the organization and smoothness of a tour without the strait-jacket. It's almost like having your "Danish" and eating it too.

This plan is maximum thrills per mile, minute, and dollar. It's designed for travel by rental car, but is adaptable to train (see train chapter later). The pace is fast but not hectic. It's designed for the American with limited time who wants to see everything but who doesn't want the "if it's Tuesday this must be Bergen" craziness. The plan includes the predictable "required" biggies (Tivoli Gardens, Hans Christian Andersen's house, and The Little Mermaid) with a good dose of "Back Door" intimacy mixed in—a bike tour of a sleepy remote Danish isle, a stranded time-passed fjord village and a look at a failed communal utopia.

The "22 Days" books originated (and are still used) as handbooks for those who join me on my "Back Door Europe" tours. Since most large organized tours work to keep their masses ignorant while visiting many of the same places we'll cover, this book is handy for anyone taking a typical big bus tour—but wanting also to maintain some independence and flexibility.

This *22 Days in Norway, Sweden and Denmark* plan is balanced and streamlined to prevent typical tourist burn-out by including only the most exciting castles and churches. I've been very selective. For example, we won't visit both the Elsinore ("Hamlet") Castle and the Frederiksborg Castle, but we will visit the best of the two. The "best," of course, is only my opinnion. But after twelve busy years of travel writing, lecturing and tour guiding, I've developed a sixth sense of what tickles the traveler's fancy. I love this itinerary. I get excited just thinking about it.

Of course, connect-the-dots travel isn't perfect, just as color-by-numbers painting ain't good art. But this book is your smiling Swede, your Nordic navigator, your handbook. It's your well-thought-out and tested itinerary. I've done it—and refined it—many times on my own and with groups (most recently in August and September 1987). Use it, take advantage of it, but don't let it rule you.

Read this book before you begin your trip. Use it as a rack to hang more ideas on. As you plan, study, travel and talk to people, fill this book with notes. It's your tool. The book is adaptable to any Scandinavian trip. You'll find 22 rearrangeable units, or days, each built with the same sections:

1. **Introductory overview** for the day.
2. An hour-by-hour **Suggested Schedule** recommended for that day.
3. List of the most important **Sightseeing Highlights** (rated: ▲▲▲Don't miss; ▲▲Try hard to see; ▲Worthwhile if you can make it).
4. **Transportation** tips and instructions.
5. **Food** and **Accommodations**: How and where to find the best budget places, including addresses, phone numbers, and my favorites.
6. **Orientation** and easy-to-read **maps** locating all recommended places.
7. **Helpful Hints** on shopping, transportation, day-to-day chores.
8. **Itinerary Options** for those with more or less than the suggested time, or with particular interests. This itinerary is *rubbery*!

Maps

My mapmaker and research assistant, Dave Hoerlein, knows a good map is worth a thousand words. His maps go hand in glove with my text. They are designed to orient you and direct you until you pick up something better at the tourist information office. Dave points out all the major landmarks, streets and accommodations mentioned in the book and indicates the best city entry and exits for our 22 day plan.

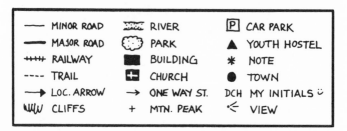

Travel Smart

Lay departure groundwork upon arrival in a town, read a day ahead in this book, use the local tourist info offices, and enjoy the hospitality of the Scandinavian people. Ask questions. Most locals are eager to point you in their idea of the right direction. Use the telephone, wear a moneybelt, use a small pocket notebook to organize your thoughts and make simplicity a virtue. If you insist on being confused, your trip will be a mess. Those who expect to travel smart, do.

Cost
Scandinavia is Europe's most expensive corner. Remember,
you're not getting less for your travel dollar. Up here there are
just no lousy or cheap alternatives to classy, cozy, sleek Scandinavia. Electronic eyes flush youth hostel toilets. Travel here
can be reasonable—but you'll have to be really on the ball to
keep your daily costs around $40 (plus transportation).

Trip costs break down like this: A basic round trip USA—
Copenhagen flight costs $500 to $900 (depending on the
season and where you fly from). Figure about $400 for a three-
week car rental (split between two people, including tax, insurance, and gas) or three weeks of rail and bus travel. For room
and board figure $40 a day, double occupancy—$880. This is
more than feasible, and if necessary, you can travel cheaper (see
Europe Through the Back Door for the skills and tricks of
budget travel). Add $200 or $300 fun money and you've got
yourself a great European adventure for under $2,400.

Sleeping
Accommodation expenses will make or break your budget.
There are plenty of good $10 to $15 per bed alternatives to
hotels, and an overall average of $40 per night per double is
easy using this book's listings. All accommodations I've listed
(unless otherwise noted) will hold a room with a phone call until 6:00 pm with no deposit, and the proprietors speak English.
I like places that are small, central, clean, traditional, and friendly. Most places listed meet four of these five virtues.

Tourist Offices: Every city we'll visit has an energetic and
well-organized tourist office whose room-finding service is a
great money saver, well worth the small fee. Be very clear about
what you want. (Say "CHEAP," and whether you have sheets,
will take a twin or double, don't require a shower, etc.) They
know the hotel quirks and private room scene better than
anybody. And they are working for you. Price listings are often
misleading since they omit cheaper oddball rooms.

To save substantial money, bring your own sheet and always
offer to provide it in cheap accommodations. Especially in rural
areas, this can save $5 per person per night. In general, places
that serve no alcohol enjoy tax advantages that translate into
cheaper prices for you.

Hotels: These are very expensive ($60 to $150 doubles) with
some exceptions. Business class hotels dump prices to attract
tourists in summer and on weekend (Friday, Saturday or Sunday) evenings. Certain hotel cards or passes do the same thing
in a more organized way. Norway's Fjord Pass, the Scandia
Bonus Pass and the Scandinavia Holiday Pass offer 15% to 50%

discounts at major hotels in summer only—ask your travel
agent for specifics. If you'll normally be using hotels, these can
be worthwhile although the local tourist offices can usually
match or even beat the special card or pass prices. Hotels are expensive but the bill includes a large (and otherwise expensive)
breakfast.

Hostels: Scandinavian hostels are Europe's finest. They offer
many classy facilities, members' kitchens, cheap and hot meals,
plenty of private "family" rooms, great people experiences, and
they have no age restrictions. Many are closed in the off season.
Buy a membership card in the U.S. or in Scandinavia. Non-
members are normally welcome for an extra charge. You'll find
lots of Volvos, Saabs and BMWs in the YH parking lots, as the
Scandinavians know hostels provide the best $10 beds in town.
(See the listing in the appendix.)

Camping: Again, Scandinavia offers some of Europe's top
campgrounds. It's a very practical, comfortable and actually
cheap way to go ($4 per person with camping card, available on
the spot). Each national tourist office has a fine listing and map
of all their campgrounds. This is the middle class family Scandinavian way to travel: safe, great social fun, no reservation problems. Free camping is permitted and is easy in Sweden and
Norway (but not allowed in Denmark).

Huts: Most campgrounds provide huts for non-campers who
want in on this cheap alternative to hotels. Huts normally sleep
four to six and charge one fee (around $20) plus extra if you
need sheets or blankets. Each hut has firm bunks and a
kitchenette.

Private Rooms: Throughout Scandinavia, people earn a few
extra crowns by renting rooms. While some put out a "Rum" or
"Hus Rum" sign, most operate solely through the local tourist
office. In some cases, the tourist information offices (T.I.s) put
you in contact with these homes only when all the hotels are
full. Prices are set by the T.I.—normally about $25 per
double—and these are a fantastic value as well as an opportunity to make some local friends. You'll get your own key and a
lived-in, clean and comfortable but usually simple, private
room with free access to the family shower and w.c.

Eating
The smartest budget travelers do as the locals do—avoid Scandinavian restaurants. Prepared food is heavily taxed and the
local cuisine just isn't worth trip bankruptcy. Of course, you'll
want to take an occasional splurge into each culture's high
cuisine, but the "high" refers mostly to the price tag.

I eat well on a budget in Scandinavia with this approach:
Breakfast is a huge and filling buffet when included in the hotel

room price. Otherwise, picnic (local meusli cereal with milk drunk out of a disposable plastic cup, orange juice and fruit) for a cheap, fast and enjoyable alternative. Scandinavians aren't big on lunch, often just grabbing a sandwich (smorrebrod) and a cup of coffee at their work desk. Follow suit with a quick picnic or a light meal at a sandwich shop or snack bar. Dinners are early and are the large meal of the day. Alternate between cheap, unmemorable but filling cafeteria or fast food dinners ($7) and atmospheric, carefully chosen restaurants popular with locals ($15).

Budget survival tips: Smorgasbord breakfasts are a good value (especially for unscrupulous people who never go to breakfast without a ziplock baggie to gather lunch). Alcohol-free cafeterias are taxed less and are reasonable, although the food is usually quite bland. In most Scandinavian restaurants you can ask for more potatoes or vegetables, so any restaurant entree is basically an all-you-can-eat deal. Fast food joints, pizzerias, Chinese food and salad bars are inexpensive. Booze will break you. Drink water, buy the liquor duty-free, or take out a loan. Waitresses are well-paid and tips are normally included, although it's polite to round up the bill.

Picnic! Scandinavia has colorful markets and even cheaper supermarkets. After hours you'll find mini-markets at gas stations most helpful. Some shopping tips: Wasa cracker bread ("Sport" is my favorite; "Ideal" flatbrod is ideal for in-the-car munchies), pre-packaged meat and cheese, goat cheese (geitost; "ekte" means pure and stronger), yogurt, freshly cooked fish in markets, fresh fruit and vegetables, lingonberries, mustard and sandwich spreads (shrimp, caviar) in a squeeze tube; boxes of juice, milk, ("lett" is light, like our 1%), pytt i panna (Swedish hash), rye bread (look for "rag," sweet as cake).

Most nations have one inedible dish that is cherished with a perverse but patriotic sentimentality. These dishes often originate with a famine and are kept in use to remind the young of their forefathers' suffering. Norway's penitential food, lutefisk (dried cod marinated for several days in potash and water), is used for Christmas and jokes.

When to Go
Summer is best. Scandinavia bustles and glistens under the July and August sun. Scandinavian schools get out around June 20, most local industries take July off, and the British and central Europeans tend to visit Scandinavia in August. You'll notice crowds during these times, but it's never as crowded as southern Europe and (especially if you call ahead and utilize local information sources) this tour is easily done without hotel reservations.

"Shoulder season" travel (May, early June, and September) involves minimal crowds, decent weather, sights and tourist fun spots still open—but without the vitality of summer. You can usually just grab a room almost whenever and wherever you like.

Winter is a bad time to explore Scandinavia. No crowds, but many sights and accommodations are closed or only open on a limited schedule. Winter weather can be cold and dreary, and nighttime will draw the shades on your sightseeing well before dinner time.

Prices & Times
To figure approximate prices in this book: 7 kr = $1.

I've priced things in local currencies throughout the book. While each of the Scandinavian countries' crowns (krona) have different values, they are close, at least in 1987. I have kept things simple by figuring one krone is worth 15 cents—about seven in a U.S. dollar. All krona are decimalized—100 ore equals 1 krona. The money is generally not accepted outside of its home turf (except, of course, at foreign exchange services and banks). Standard abbreviations are: Danish Krona—DKK, Swedish—SEK, and Norwegian—NOK. In this book we'll keep it simple and use the krona abbreviation, kr, for Denmark, Sweden, and Norway. To translate any prices in krona into U.S. dollars, simply divide by 7 (35 kr equals $5).

The Finnish markka, FIM, or mk, is worth about 25 cents (4 mk equals $1).

I have listed only normal full prices. Scandinavia is generous with student, youth and senior discounts. Students should travel with an International Student Identity Card (ISIC).

These countries are more stable than most European countries, but it's always smart to double-check hours and times when you arrive—especially when traveling between October and May. Prices, as well as hours, telephone numbers, and so on are accurate as of September 1987. Things are always changing and I've tossed timidity out the window knowing you'll understand that this book, like any guidebook, starts to yellow even before it's printed.

In Scandinavia—and in this book—you'll be using the 24-hour clock (or "military" time). After noon, instead of pm times, you'll see 13:00, 14:00 and so on. (Just subtract 12 and add pm to get "normal" time).

The hours listed are for peak season. Many places close an hour earlier in off season. Some are open only on weekends or are closed entirely in the winter.

The Language Barrier
I've written this book for people who speak only English—like me. Of course it would be great to speak the local language, but English is Scandinavia's foreign language of choice. Learn the polite words and a few very basic phrases (see appendix) and you'll manage fine with English.

Each country does have its own distinct language. Except for Finnish, they are very closely related (Norwegian kids enjoy Swedish cartoons on TV effortlessly) and have many similarities to English (a cousin of the Nordic tongues). The Scandinavians have several letters (**Æ**, **Å**, **Ø**) that we don't have. To keep things simple in this book, I have opted to spell Scandinavian words with only our letters. The only possible problem this could cause you is in alphabetizing. These extra letters follow "Z" in the Nordic alphabets. My apologies to these languages for my laziness.

Borders, Passports, Visas and Shots
Traveling throughout this region requires only a passport. No shots, and no visas. Border crossings between Norway, Sweden, Denmark and Finland are extremely easy. Normally you won't even have to stop. When you change countries, however, you do change money, postage stamps, and much more. Local sales taxes (10-15%) are refunded on the spot for souvenirs and gifts purchased. Ask local merchants for instructions.

Stranger in a Strange Land
We travel all the way to Europe to enjoy differences—to become temporary locals. You may find some frustrations. Certain truths that we find God-given or self-evident—things like cold beer, a bottomless coffee cup, long hot showers, and bigger being better—are suddenly not so true. One of the beauties of travel is the opportunity to see that there are logical, civil, and even better alternatives. Scandinavians are into "sustainable affluence." They have experimented aggressively in the area of socialism—with mixed results. To travel here tends to pry open one's hometown blinders. Fit in, don't look for things American on the wrong side of the Atlantic, and you're sure to enjoy a full dose of Scandinavian hospitality.

Scheduling
The overall plan and each daily suggested schedule is very carefully laid out. But you'll need to fine-tune it to plug in rest days, avoid closed days, and hit the most festivals and least traffic jams. Play with the calendar. Read through this book to troubleshoot problems before you leave home. Stretching the trip to 28 or 30 days would be luxurious. Minimize one-night stands.

Car Rental

If you plan to drive, rent a car through your travel agent well
before departure. Car rental for this tour is much cheaper when
arranged in the USA rather than in Scandinavia. You'll want a
weekly rate with unlimited mileage. Plan to pick up the car in
Copenhagen and drop it off there at the end of your trip.
Remember, if you drop it early or keep it longer, you'll be
credited or charged at a fair, pro-rated price. Each major car rental agency has a Copenhagen Airport office. Comparison shop
through your agent.

I normally rent the smallest, least-expensive model (e.g.,
Ford Fiesta). For a bigger, more roomy and powerful inexpensive car, move up to the Ford 1.3-liter Escort or VW Polo
category. For peace of mind, I splurge for the CDW insurance
(collision damage waiver) which gives a zero-deductible rather
than the standard $1,000-deductible, or get Travelguard In-
surance which includes the CDW at a more reasonable price.
Remember, mini-buses are a great budget way to go for 5 to 9
people.

Driving in Scandinavia

It's very difficult to keep your eyes on the road with all that
luscious scenery flying by. You'll see lots of broken guardrails.
Other than that, it's a great place to drive. All you need is a valid
driver's license and a car. Gas is expensive, $3 to $4 per gallon
(it's the worst in Denmark), roads are okay, traffic generally
sparse, drivers sober and civil, signs and road maps excellent,
local road etiquette nothing very different, seatbelts required.
Swedes use their headlights day and night. There are plenty of
good facilities, gas stations and scenic rest stops. Snow is a
serious problem off season in the mountains. Parking is a
headache only in major cities, where expensive garages are safe
and plentiful. Even in the Nordic countries, thieves break into
cars. Park carefully, use the trunk, and show no stealables.

Never drink and drive—*not even one!* The laws are very
severe.

Car vs. Eurail

While this tour is designed for car travel, a chapter in the back
of the book adapts it for train travel. With a few exceptions,
trains cover this entire itinerary wonderfully. A three-week first
class Eurailpass costs $370. A 21-day first class Nordtourist pass
costs $340 ($230 for a 2nd class pass). A train pass is best for
single travelers, those who'll be spending more time in big cities
and those who don't want to drive in Europe. While a car gives
you the ultimate in mobility and freedom, enables you to
search for hotels more easily and carries your bags for you, the

train zips you effortlessly from city to city, usually dropping you in the center and near the tourist office. Cars are great in the countryside but an expensive headache in places like Oslo, Copenhagen and Bergen. To go by car or train . . . that is the question. And for this itinerary, I'd drive.

Coming to Scandinavia from Europe

There are often cheaper flights from the USA into Frankfurt and Amsterdam than into Copenhagen. And you may be traveling in central Europe before or after your Scandinavian tour. It's a long, rather dull one-day drive to Scandinavia from Amsterdam, Frankfurt, and the castles of the Rhine region (with a two hour $50 per car and passenger ferry crossing at Puttgarten). By train the trip is effortless—overnight from Amsterdam or Frankfurt. The $90 ticket is included with your Eurailpass (but not the Nordtourist pass).

Compared to other parts of Europe, there's little to get excited about between Copenhagen and Amsterdam or Frankfurt. I'd do the trip overnight. Berlin is an easy connection (via Gedser) overnight by train from Copenhagen.

Recommended Guidebooks

This small book is only your itinerary handbook. To really enjoy and appreciate these busy three weeks, you should consider some supplemental information. I know it hurts to spend $20 or $30 on extra books and maps, but when you consider the improvements they'll make in your $2,400 vacation, the information is very valuable. In Scandinavia, one good budget tip can easily save the price of the extra guidebook.

Europe Through the Back Door (by me) gives you the basic skills, the foundations which make this demanding 22-day plan possible. Chapter topics include minimizing jet lag, packing light, driving vs. train travel, finding budget beds without reservations, changing money, theft, travel photography, long distance telephoning in Europe, ugly-Americanism, traveler's toilet trauma, laundry, and itinerary strategies and techniques. The book also contains special articles on 32 exciting nooks and undiscovered European crannies which I call "Back Doors."

Europe 101: History and Art for Travelers (by Rick Steves and Gene Openshaw) tells you about the cultures in a practical, fun-to-read 360 page package. Ideal for those who want to be able to step into a Gothic cathedral and excitedly nudge their partner saying, "Isn't this a great improvement over Romanesque!"

One reason I wrote this book is because, for my style, there is precious little in the way of good guidebook help available on the Scandinavian countries. Allow me to share a few opinions:

Arthur Frommer's Scandinavia on $50 a Day—This has been the only good budget guide to independent, do-it-yourself Scandinavian travel. The Scandinavia book has lots of helpful ideas and while it, like any mainstream guide, is short on guts, it's excellent for the less rugged, better financed traveler. Frommer himself writes the *Europe on $25 a Day* book, and the Oslo, Copenhagen, and Stockholm chapters in this book are great for the budget traveler.

Let's Go Europe—My favorite travel guidebook, written by Harvard students, is weak on Scandinavia. Still, its short Nordic chapters are very helpful for the more rugged budget traveler of any age.

There are other guides to Scandinavia published by Baedeker, Fodor, Rand McNally and guides to Norway and Sweden by Hunter. All are heavy on facts, low on personality and opinion.

Many travelers enjoy Karen Brown's *Scandinavian Country Inns and Manors*. This new book proposes interesting routes with a focus on elegant little hotels. Her recommended hotels are very charming—though not cheap.

Motoring in Norway, published and sold in Norway, is the best of the Norwegian-published English guides. It's very dry but gives you a running commentary on virtually every tourist route in Norway. Thumb through it in the Oslo tourist office.

Passport Books publishes *Just Enough Scandinavian*, a small phrase book covering Danish, Norwegian, and Swedish (ISBN-0-8442-9511-6). It's the best phrase book of its kind but the language barrier is very small here. A simple English-Norsk type dictionary is helpful but, frankly, you can get by fine with English.

Maps

I'd recommend one overall road map for southern Scandinavia (I used the Kummerly and Frey, 1:1,000,000 edition) and a map for "Southern Norway-North" (I used Sor Norge-nord, 1:325,000, by Cappelens Kart). Southern Norway-South is handy, but SN-N is essential. Excellent city and regional maps are available from local T.I.s, usually for free.

Freedom

The goal of this book is to free you, not chain you. Please defend your spontaneity like you would your mother. Use this book to sort Scandinavia's myriad sights into the most interesting, representative, diverse, and efficient 22 days of travel. Use it to avoid time- and money-wasting mistakes, to get more intimate with Europe by traveling without a tour—as a temporary local person. And use it as a point of departure from which to shape *your* best possible travel experience.

Anyone who has read this far has what it takes intellectually to do this tour on their own. Be confident, militantly positive, relish the challenge and rewards of doing your own planning. Judging from all the positive feedback and happy postcards we get from our traveling readers, it's safe to assume you're on your way to a great Scandinavian vacation—independent, inexpensive and with the finesse of an experienced traveler.

Send Me a Postcard, Drop Me a Line. . .

While I do what I can to keep this book accurate and up-to-date, things are always changing. If you enjoy a successful trip with the help of this book and would like to share your discoveries (and make my job a lot easier), please send in any tips, recommendations, criticisms or corrections to 120 4th N., Edmonds, WA 98020. All correspondents will receive a year's subscription to our "Back Door Travel" quarterly newsletter (it's free anyway. . .) and recommendations used will get you a free copy of my next edition.

Thanks, and happy travels!

22 DAYS IN SCANDINAVIA

DAY 1 Your Scandinavian adventure starts in wonderful Copenhagen, the most direct and least expensive Scandinavian capital to fly into from the USA and the gateway to Scandinavia from points south in Europe. After an evening orientation walk you'll be well acquainted with Denmark's capital.

DAYS 2 and 3 Copenhagen, Scandinavia's largest and most loved city, deserves two very busy days. Climb the church spire, cruise the harbor, follow a local historian on a walk through the old town, browse through Europe's greatest pedestrian shopping mall, enjoy a smorgasbord feast and spend a memorable night at the famous Tivoli Gardens, the Continent's ultimate amusement park. And that's just the beginning of what Copenhagen has to offer.

DAY 4 Pick up your rental car, or validate your railpass, before leaving Copenhagen to explore the highlights of North Zealand—a great castle and Scandinavia's top modern art museum. Then ferry to Sweden and travel deep into that pristine and woodsy land.

DAY 5 Today is for Smaland. You'll tour the best glass factory in Sweden, cross Europe's longest bridge to hike through the Stonehenge-type mysteries of the strange island of Oland, and bed down in atmospheric old Kalmar, historically the "key to Sweden" and home of a magnificent medieval castle.

DAY 6 Driving north along Sweden's east coast, picnic and take a walk along the romantic Gota Canal before finding your hotel in Stockholm. After going over your Stockholm plans with the very helpful tourist info people, join a local historian for a walk through Stockholm's lantern-lit old town, followed by dinner in an old world inn.

DAYS 7 and 8 Stockholm, one of Europe's most underrated cities, tempts many to toss out the itinerary and move in. Green, built on fourteen islands, surrounded by water and woods, energetic, efficient, and full of history, it demands a busy two days. Crawl through Europe's best preserved old warship, tour Europe's first and best open air folk museum and relax on a canal boat tour. A look at the modern side of this trend-setting city includes its futuristic planned suburbs, art galleries, city hall—host of the annual Nobel Prize banquet—and shopping. On your third Stockholm evening, take Europe's most enjoyable cruise with lovely archipelago scenery, a setting sun, and a royal smorgasbord dinner.

DAY 9 The boat is your hotel and you've got all day to see Finland's Neo-classical capital, Helsinki. Catch a half-day city bus tour or just wander through this compact town. Either way you can enjoy Helsinki's ruddy harborfront market, count goosebumps in her churches, and tour the national museum. By dinnertime you'll once again surround yourself with beautiful islands and lots of food. How about dancing and a sauna before crawling into your stateroom?

DAY 10 Back on Swedish soil you'll visit historic Uppsala. Its cathedral and university are the oldest, largest, tallest, etc., and the compact and bustling little city is a fine morning stop before making the long drive across Sweden and into Norway.

DAYS 11 and 12 Oslo's Viking spirit—past and present—has left sights that tell a thrilling story. Two days here allow plenty of time to prowl through the remains of ancient Viking ships, and more peaceful but equally gutsy modern boats like the *Kon Tiki, Ra* and *Fram*. You'll hear stirring stories of the local WWII

Nazi resistance and trace the country's folk culture at the Norwegian Open Air Folk Museum. For the modern side of Norway's capital, browse through the new yuppie-style harbor shopping complex, tour its avant garde city hall, get a good dose of Gustav Vigeland's sculpture and climb the towering Holmenkollen ski jump.

DAY 13 Heading for the Norwegian hills, tour the countryside manorhouse where Norway's constitution was signed, enjoy Norway's best folk museum and drive deep into the romantic Gudbrandsdal Valley—Peer Gynt country. Your destination is an ancient log and sod farmstead turned hotel, tucked in a quiet valley under Norway's highest mountains.

DAY 14 After a relaxed morning, drive over Norway's highest mountain pass, deep into Jotunheim ("giant's home") country. A long, rugged road takes you to the slow but fierce tongue of the Nigard glacier where a local expert will take you on a guided two-hour glacier walk. Then soften the scenery a bit by descending from Norway's highest mountains into its most picturesque fjord country.

DAY 15 While Norway has towering mountains, her greatest claim to scenic fame is her deep and lush fjords. To get intimate with the best, Sognefjord, do what is often called "Norway in a Nutshell." A fjord cruise will take you into towering narrow canyons, past isolated farms and villages steeped in the mist of waterfalls, and finally to Gudvangen where the road winds up and over more scenic mountain country to Bergen.

DAY 16 Bergen has a rugged charm. Norway's capital long before Oslo, she wears her rich Hanseatic heritage proudly. Enjoy her colorful market, stroll the small easy-on-foot old quarter, and ride the lift up a little mountain right downtown for a commanding city view. After a busy Bergen day, treat yourself to a grand Norwegian-style smorgasbord dinner.

DAY 17 Rounding the corner and beginning the return to Copenhagen, island-hop south from Bergen to get a feel for Norway's rugged Atlantic coast before heading inland along a frightfully narrow fjord and finally up and over a mountain pass into the remote—and therefore very traditional—Setesdal Valley.

DAY 18 Today is easy, with plenty of time for this cultural Easter egg hunt called Setesdal. Probably Norway's most traditional cranny, this valley is a mellow montage of derelict farmhouses, sod-roofed water mills, gold and silver smiths in action, ancient churches, yellowed recipes, rivers, forests and mountains. You'll spend the night sailing to Denmark.

DAY 19   Good morning, you're back in Denmark! Sand dunes, Lego toys, fortified old towns and moated manorhouses, this is Jutland and it's far from Copenhagen. Spend the morning in the wonderfully preserved old town of Arhus, Jutland's capital and Denmark's second largest city. By evening, nestle into the quiet and quaint island of Aero.

DAY 20   The sleepy isle of Aero is the perfect time-passed world to wind down, enjoy the seagulls and take a bike ride. Today is yours. Pedal a rented bike into the essence of Denmark. Lunch in a traditional "Kro" country inn. Settle in a cobbled world of sailors who, after someone connected a steam engine to a propeller, decided, "Maybe building ships in bottles is more my style."

DAY 21   For a grand finale and one last flurry of exciting sightseeing activity as you return to Copenhagen, spend the morning in Odense, the home of Hans Christian Andersen and a fine open air folk museum. After lunch on one last ferry ride, visit Roskilde, with its great Viking ships and royal cathedral before finding yourself back where you started—in that wonderful city. . .of Copenhagen.

DAY 22   Today your tour is over. The circle is complete and you've experienced the best 22 days Norway, Sweden and Denmark have to offer. Of course there's lots more to see and next year you may want 22 more days. But for now, go home, rest up, get your pictures developed and let your next travel dream off its leash.

BACK DOOR TRAVEL PHILOSOPHY
AS TAUGHT IN EUROPE THROUGH THE BACK DOOR

TRAVEL IS INTENSIFIED LIVING—maximum thrills per minute and one of the last great sources of legal adventure. In many ways, the less you spend the more you get.

Experiencing the real thing requires candid informality— going "Through the Back Door." Too much traditional travel writing comes from free trips. A guest of a country's tourist industry gains experience helpful only to other industry guests. I travel the way you will, making my share of mistakes so that you can learn from them. Here are some of the things I've learned:

Affording travel is a matter of priorities. Many people who "can't afford a trip" could sell their car and travel for two years.

You can travel anywhere in the world for $35 a day plus transportation costs. Money has little to do with enjoying your trip. In fact, in many ways, the less you spend the more you get. Money only builds a thicker wall between you and what you came to see.

A tight budget forces you to travel "close to the ground," meeting and communicating with the people, not relying on service with a purchased smile. Never sacrifice sleep, nutrition, safety or cleanliness in the name of budget. Simply enjoy local-style alternatives to expensive hotels and restaurants.

Many Americans are too "things-oriented" to travel well. Travel like Gandhi—with simple clothes, open eyes and an uncluttered mind. 'Tis a gift to be simple. If things aren't to your liking, don't change the things—change your liking. A culture is legitimized by its existence. Give a people the benefit of your open mind. Think of things as different but not better or worse.

Extroverts have more fun. If you don't enjoy a place, it's often because you don't know enough about it. Seek out the truth. Be fanatically positive and militantly optimistic.

Travel is addicting. It can make you a happier American, as well as a citizen of the world. Globetrotting destroys ethnocentricity and encourages you to understand and appreciate various cultures. Travel changes people. Many travelers assimilate the best points of different cultures into their own character.

The world is a cultural garden. We're working on the ultimate salad. Won't you join us?

DAY 1
ARRIVE IN COPENHAGEN

Start your Scandinavian adventure in Copenhagen, the most
direct and least expensive place to fly into from the USA, and
the gateway to Scandinavia from points south in Europe.
You'll land at Copenhagen's Kastrup Airport the day after you
leave the USA. After an easy bus connection downtown with
a quick stop at the tourist office, you'll check into your hotel.
Leave jet-lag in the room by enjoying an evening orientation walk.

Arrival at Kastrup Airport
If any airport tries harder to make your entry smooth and
stress-free, it's Copenhagen's Kastrup Airport. People pop out
into Denmark marvelling at its efficiency. You'll find a lavish
duty free shopping mall, a grocery store, bakery, cheap booze,
and a tourist information desk. English is spoken everywhere.
Do your banking here, the rates are fine.
  Once you're past customs, visit the tourist info desk. Pick up
a city map, "This Week in Copenhagen," and buy your
"Copenhagen Card." By the way, most USA-Copenhagen flights
(SAS, TWA, and Northwest Orient) arrive between 8:00 and
12:00 and depart from 12:00 to 14:00.

  Cheap Tricks—Get used to stretching lunch out of
breakfast. SAS serves easy-to-pack rolls and cheese. Also, their
inflight magazine has a good little Scandinavia map you may
want to "rip off." Drop by the airport's SAS info and reception
desk and pick up their free and very handy guides to all the

major cities you'll be visiting on this trip. If you want to buy liquor, buy it duty-free in the airport.

Getting Downtown—Taxis are fast and easy but fairly expensive. The SAS shuttle buses will zip you downtown in 20 minutes for 21 kr. City buses (#9 and #32) get you downtown in just 40 minutes for only 11 kr. Bus #9 leaves four times an hour across the street from the airport and takes you close to most of the accommodations I list. If you're going to Christianshavn, ride until you pass a lake and you're on Torvegade. Bus #32 takes you to the City Hall, T.I., and station.

Setting Up—If you haven't already reserved a room, find a phone booth at the airport and let your fingers do the walking with the places listed below. With the city map, the excellent bus system and so many friendly English speaking Danes, you should have no trouble. If you've already got your car, find a good place to park it and leave it there until Day 4.

Copenhagen (Kobenhavn)

Copenhagen is huge—with 1½ million people, Scandinavia's largest city—but the visitor rarely leaves the compact old town. The medieval walls that once circled this old center are now roads: Vestervoldgade (literally western wall street), Norregade and Gothersgade. The fourth side is the harbor and the island of Slotsholmen where "Koben" (merchants) "havn" (harbor) was born in 1167. The next of the city's islands is Amager, where you'll find the local "Little Amsterdam" district of Christianshavn—a never-a-dull-moment hodge-podge of chic, artistic, hippy and hobo. The former moat is now a string of pleasant lakes and parks, including Tivoli Gardens. To the north is the old "new town" where the Amalienborg Palace is surrounded by streets on a grid plan and the "Little Mermaid" poses relentlessly, waiting for her sailor to return and the tourists to leave.

It's a great walking town, bubbling with street life and colorful pedestrian zones. The place is superorganized for visitors and on a sunny day you'll very likely find yourself singing, "Wonderful wonderful Copenhagen."

Tourist Information

Coping with Copenhagen is easy if you take advantage of the local tourist services. The central tourist office, in the wax museum building facing the city hall (H.C. Andersen's Boulevard 22, tel. 01-111325, open May-September 9:00-18:00, Saturday 9:00-14:00, Sunday 9:00-13:00; October-April 9:00-17:00, Saturday 9:00-12:00, closed Sunday), is very helpful. Pick up brochures on Copenhagen (map, "This Week,"

"Copenhagen on Foot") and for all of Denmark (for this tour: Aero, Roskilde, Odense, Frederiksborg Castle, Louisiana Museum, Arhus, and ferry schedules). Confirm your sightseeing plans for the next three days and ask about any special events.

"Copenhagen This Week" is a free, handy and misnamed monthly guide to the city. It's worth reading for its good maps, list of museum hours, calendar of special events, and many illustrated "hey sailor" escort girl ads.

The train station's room-finding service can nearly always find you a bed. Open mid-May to mid-September, daily from 9:00 to 24:00. Off season, shorter hours and closed Sundays.

The Interail Center is a new service the station offers to young travelers. Your Youth Eurailpass, BIGE, Transalpino ticket or Interail pass is your ticket to free showers, lounge, luggage storage, maps, snacks, info and other young travelers. Open June-September, 7:00-24:00. Take advantage of it— unless you're too old.

"Use It" is another great service. This "branch" of Huset, a hip student-run cluster of cafes, theaters and galleries, caters to Copenhagen's young but welcomes travelers of any age. It's a friendly and energetic no-nonsense source of budget travel information, a free service with an excellent network of private bed-and-breakfast places, ride-finding board, free luggage storage, lockers, and good maps. Just plain very helpful. Open daily 10:00-14:00 mid-June to mid-September, Mon-Fri 10:00-17:00 the rest of the year. "Use It" is ten-minute walk from the station at Radhustraede #13, tel. 01-156518.

The Copenhagen Card covers nearly all public transportation and admissions to sights in greater Copenhagen, which stretches from Helsingor to Roskilde. It covers all the sights I list, Tivoli and the bus in from the airport. Available at any tourist office (including the airports) and the central station, 1 day—70 kr, 2 day—120 kr, 3 days—150 kr. With our plan, this card is probably not worth buying, but tally it up yourself to check.

(Note: All telephone calls in Denmark, even local ones, must include the area code prefix.)

Transportation in Copenhagen

While Copenhagen is a great walking town, don't hesitate to take advantage of its fine bus and subway (S-Tog) system. A joint fare system covers greater Copenhagen. You pay 7 kr for an hour's travel within two zones. Bus drivers are patient and speak English. City maps list bus and subway routes clearly. Locals are friendly and will help a lost traveler with a gracious smile. Taxis are plentiful and surprisingly reasonable. Just flag

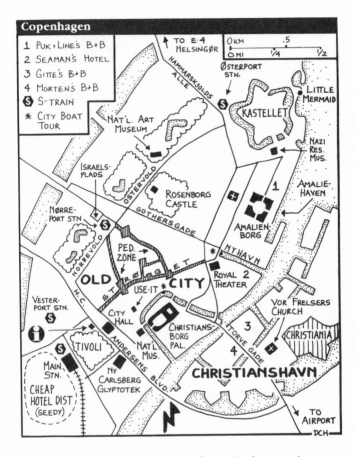

them down. Fares start at 12 kr and 4 people often travel cheaper by taxi than by bus.

Pedalling through Copenhagen on a rental bike is a great way to enjoy the town. The roads are biker-friendly, and "Use It" has a great biking guide brochure. Dan Wheel (3 Colbjornsens-gade, on the corner of Vesterbrogade, open 9:00-17:30, Sat & Sun 9:00-14:00, 30 kr per day, 50 kr for 2 days) and Christian-shavns Cykler (Bodenhoffs Plads 8, past the spiral church spire, open 9:00-17:30, Sat 9:00-13:00, Sun closed. 35 kr per day) rent bikes.

Planning Ahead
Now's the time to lay the groundwork for a smooth trip. Any travel agent can book your Stockholm-Helsinki-Stockholm and

Kristiansand-Hirtshals boat rides. Any hotels or rooms you know you want should be reserved by telephone now if you know for certain when you'll be there and don't think you'll need lots of flexibility. Also reserve your last night in Copenhagen now.

Norway and Sweden both have national tourist offices in Copenhagen where you can pick up maps and brochures covering each of your planned stops. The Scandinavian countries are generous with their tourist propaganda. Sweden's office is just across from the station at Vesterbrogade and Vester Farimags Gade, Norway's is out by the mermaid on Trondhjems Plads.

First Day Orientation Walk:
"Copenhagen's Heart and Soul"

After you're set up for the night, set out and get to know the lay of the land. This walk provides a good orientation and is a pleasant way to keep your jet-laggy body moving until a reasonable European bedtime. Whenever you run out of steam, just catch a bus or taxi back to your hovel. . .er. . .hotel.

Start from Radhuspladsen (City Hall Square), the bustling heart of Copenhagen, dominated by the spire of the City Hall. On a pedestal left of the City Hall, note the "Lur-Blowers" sculpture. The lur is a horn used over 3000 years ago. You can see the ancient originals in the National Museum. Over by the less-ancient Burger King you'll see Copenhagen's main pedestrian street, Stroget. Stroget is actually a series of colorful streets and lively squares that bunny hop right through the old town, connecting the City Hall Square with Kongens Nytorv (The Kings New Square, a 15-minute walk away) where you'll find the Royal Theater and Nyhavn, a recently gentrified sailors' quarter. This formerly sleazy harbor is an interesting mix of tattoo parlors, taverns and trendy (expensive) cafes lining a canal filled with glamorous old sailboats of all sizes. Any historic sloop is welcome to moor here in Copenhagen's ever-changing boat museum.

Continuing north, you'll pass a huge ship that sails to Oslo every evening. Follow the water to the modern fountain of Amaliehaven Park. The nearby Amalienborg Palace and Square is a good example of orderly baroque planning. Queen Margrethe II and her family live in the palace to your immediate left as you enter the square from the harbor side. Her son (and heir to the throne). Frederik recently moved into the palace directly opposite his mother's. The guards change at noon (only when Queen is in residence).

Leave the square on Amaliegade, heading north to Kastellet (Citadel) Park and a small museum about Denmark's WWII resistance efforts. Across the street is a great 3-D city map. See how oriented you're already getting. A short stroll past the Gefion fountain and along the water brings you to the overrated and over-photographed symbol of Copenhagen—the Little Mermaid.

You can get back downtown by foot, taxi or Bus #50 from the mermaid in summer, on Buses #1, #6 or #9 from the other side of Kastellet Park.

Accommodations—Copenhagen

Hotels
By far the expensive option in an expensive city with plenty of fine alternatives, hotels will generally run you over US$100 (700 kr) per double. Here are your best decent budget choices in the center:

Near the station—Behind the station on the edge of drugs, porno and prostidumpiness are two handy, friendly, safe and decent hotels. **Hotel Dania** is modern, bright, simple but comfortable (doubles in peak season 570 kr with shower and buffet breakfast, 440 kr without shower, Istedgade 3, tel. 01-221100). Across the street is the older, more traditional, stately but well worn **Missionshotellet Nebo** (doubles for 690 kr with buffet breakfast and shower, 460 kr without shower), Istedgade 6, tel. 01-211217.

The **Ladbroke Comfort Hotel**, very modern and hotel-esque, has a parking garage and not a hint of behind-the-station seediness. Doubles with a big breakfast and shower cost 800 kr. (Longangstr. #27, tel. 01-126570, one block past city hall, 6 minutes from station.)

Sofolkenes Mindehotel—This retired seaman's hotel is the cheapest real hotel in town. It's in a great, quiet, central location, one block off Nyhavn. The management is friendly. Rooms are small, a bit dingy but functional; the cafeteria is cheap. Doubles cost 325 kr with breakfast, singles 185 kr. Triples and quads cost less per person. (Peder Skrams Gade 19, D-1054, tel. 01-134882).

Youth Hostels
Copenhagen accommodates the student vagabond very nicely. The "Use It" office is your best source of info. Each of these places charges 40-50 kr per person.

The **Copenhagen Hostel**—IYHF. Sjaellandsbroen 55, tel. 01-522908, very modern, doubles and quads only, no curfew, excellent facilities, laundry, efficiently managed, on the edge of town, Bus #46 from station.

The **Bellahoj Hostel**—IYHF. Herbergvejen 8, tel. 01-289715, large impersonal, park setting, 8-12 beds per room, 20 minutes from station on Bus #2.

YMCA-YWCA, Kannikestraede l9 on Grabrodretorv just off Stroget, tel. 01-113031, closed 10:00-15:00 daily, great location in pedestrian center but musty and depressing rooms.

Sleep-In, Per Henriks Alle 6, tel. 01-265059, late June through August, huge co-ed rooms, no curfew, pretty wild, usually has room. For the desperate or adventurous. Free rubbers.

Private Rooms

Each Copenhagen room-finding service cultivates its own list of people who rent rooms to travelers. Here are a few le ds for Copenhagen's best accommodation values. By booking direct, you'll save yourself and your host the tourist office's fee. Always call ahead, each family speaks English and will hold your room until 18:00.

Rooms in Christianhavn, which is artsy, colorful and residential, with street people, lots of shops, cafes and canals, ten-minute walk to center, good bus connections to airport and downtown: **Gitte and Leif Kongstad**—Classy, sophisticated and friendly couple in a restored 1782 warehouse-turned-penthouse. Single—90 kr, Double—175 kr, Triple—240 kr, great breakfast worth Gitte's extra charge, Skt. Annaegade 1 B, fourth floor (no elevator); Bus #9 from airport, #2 and #8 from City Hall, just over Knippels Bridge or corner of Strandgade and St. Annaegade. If they are full, they can often find you a good place nearby. Tel. 01-572466. **Morten Frederiksen**—A very laid-back pony-tailed sort of guy runs this mod-funky-pleasant loft. Clean, comfy, good look at today's hip Danish lifestyle, great location right on Christianshavn's main drag (2 minutes from Gitte and Leif's). Torvegade 36, tel. 01-953273.

Near the Amalienborg Palace, a stately embassy neighborhood, no stress but a bit bland, very safe, you can look out your window to see the queen's place, a ten-minute walk north of Nyhavn and Stroget: **Line Voutsinos** (Amaliegade 34, 3rd floor, tel. 01-147142) and her friend **Puk La Cour** (pron: "pook," Amaliegade 34, 4th floor, 01-120468). Both of these young professional mod, bright, cheery, open and easy-going women keep busy with their families but love having guests. They charge 160 kr per double and 200 kr per triple for a three night stay (200 kr/double for shorter stays).

Other private homes: Inger Jensen has a large home with five doubles just off Gammel Kongevej (Bus #1 or #14) in a classy neighborhood. This is more subdued and private, with fewer stairs and a bit more expensive than the other listings. Hauchvej 9, tel. 01-240355. Friendly **Maria Gad** speaks just a little English and rents one small room (100 kr for single, 150 kr

as a double) in her bright, cheery apartment, a ten-minute walk
from station just past the lake called Skt. Jorgens So., Vodroff-
sveg 29, fifth floor (elevator), tel. 01-312481.

Eating

Copenhagen's many good restaurants are well listed by category
in the "This Week" publication. If your budget requires alternatives to restaurants, these survival tips for the hungry budget
traveler in Copenhagen are worth noting:

Picnic—Irma and Brugsen are the two largest supermarket
chains. Netto and Aldi are cut rate outfits with the cheapest
prices. The little grocery store in the central station (open daily
from 8:00 to 24:00) is great for picnic stuff. You'll find a
delightful outdoor fruit and vegetable market at Israels Plads.
Bakeries, found on nearly every corner, sell fresh bread, tasty
pastries, juice, milk, cheese and yogurt.

Smorrebrod—Denmark's famous open face sandwiches
cost a fortune in restaurants but the many smorrebrod shops
sell them for from 6 to 22 kr. Drop into one of these often no-
name, family run, open 11:00-15:00, budget-savers and get
several elegant OFS's to go. It makes for a classy—and cheap—
picnic. Downtown you'll find these handy local alternatives to
Yankee fast food chains: Centrum at 6 C.Vesterbrogade (long
hours), Smorrebrods Forretningen at 28 Gronnegade (8:00-
14:00), Domhusets Smorrebrod at 18 Kattesundet (7:00-14:30),
Sorgenfri just off the Stroget at 8 Brolaeggerstraede (Mon-Fri
11:00-14:00), one at the corner of Magstraede and Radhus-
straede (Mon-Fri, 8:00-15:00), and one on the corner next to
"Use It" (8:00-15:00). In Christianshavn you'll find Franske
Kokken on Torvegade near Wildersgade. And in Nyhavn, a
good sandwich shop is on the corner of Holbergsgade and
Peder Skram Gade.

The "Polse"—The famous Danish hot dog, sold in
"polsevognen" (sausage wagons) throughout the city, is one of
the few typically Danish institutions to resist the onslaught of
our global fast food culture. They are fast, cheap, tasty, easy to
order ("hot dog" is a Danish word for weenie), and almost
worthless nutritionally. Still the local "dead man's finger" makes
a great snack and by hanging around a polsevognen you can
study this institution. It's a form of social care: only difficult-to-
employ people, such as the handicapped, are licensed to run
these wienermobiles. As they gain seniority they are promoted
to more central locations. Danes gather here for munchies and
"polsesnak," (sausage talk), the local slang for empty chatter.

Cheap Restaurants: Cafeterias (in department stores, at the
Sofolknes Mindehotel, in the "Use It" complex, at the University Cafe—Fiolstraede 2), fast food joints (everywhere) and

pizzerias (look for salad bars and all-you-can-eat specials) offer Copenhagen's cheapest sit down meals.

The **Smorgasbord** (all-you-can-eat buffet) is a fine and fun budget way to stuff yourself with good Danish food. The best and handiest is the famous "Koldtbord" at the central station's **Bistro** Restaurant. Its 40 kr breakfast is served from 7:00 to 10:00 and the 97 kr dinner is from 11:00 to 22:30 daily. You'll enjoy a great variety. Study the menu options. Sometimes by skipping one course (dessert is the least exceptional) you'll save a lot. Tel. 01-141232. **Cafe Sorgenfri** also serves Copenhogs a good and traditional buffet dinner.

Good Eating in Christianshavn: The **Cafe Wilder** at Wildersgade and St. Annaegade serves good light meals to a trendy but very local crowd. For a special experience, walk past the hashish pushing welcome crew (or, for an extra special experience, stop) at the gate of the hippy commune of Christiania and climb to the renovated warehouse loft about 50 yards to your left. The **Spiseloppen** ("Eating Flea") restaurant serves fine meals in a classy candle-lit atmosphere for 70 kr. Open 12:00-22:00, closed Monday, tel. 01-579558. The **Franske Kokken**, right on Torvegatan near Wildersgade, serves great take-out sandwiches. The **Ravelin Restaurant** (Torvegatan 79) serves good food at good prices to happy local crowds on a lovely lakeside terrace.

DAYS 2 & 3
COPENHAGEN

You'll feel right at home in Scandinavia's largest (and most loved) city after a busy day of sightseeing, including a look at the royal palace, city views from a dizzy church spire, a relaxing canal boat ride, and a special look at Copenhagen through the eyes of a local historian who'll walk you right into the city's colorful past. Savor Copenhagen's two claims to fame, spending an afternoon on Europe's greatest pedestrian shopping street and the evening in the Continent's ultimate amusement park, the famous Tivoli Gardens.

Suggested Schedule	
	Day 2
8:00	Your first of many huge Scandinavian breakfasts.
9:00	Walk over to the Christiansborg Palace, explore the subterranean castle ruins under today's palace.
10:00	Take a guided tour of Denmark's royal Christiansborg Palace.
11:30	Catch the harbor tour boat, a relaxing trip out to the famous mermaid.
13:00	Wander over to Christianshavn for a smorrebrod picnic lunch.
14:00	Climb the Vor Frelsers church spiral tower. Consider a dip into the "hippy" communal world of Christiania.
15:30	Free afternoon to shop and stroll the Stroget pedestrian mall.
17:30	Meet Helge "Jack" Jacobsen for a city walking tour.
20:00	Spend the evening in Tivoli Gardens.
	Day 3
10:00	Trace Denmark's cultural roots in the National Museum.
12:00	Ny Carlsberg Glyptotek art gallery.
13:00	Lunch.
14:00	Free afternoon with many options including: Carlsberg Brewery tour, Rosenborg Castle and crown jewels, the Nazi Resistance Museum.
19:00	All-you-can-eat Danish smorgasbord at the station.

Wonderful Copenhagen requires a very busy second day. The National Museum is a must. After that, choose among a brewery tour (with plenty of free samples), great art including Rodin's "Thinker," a peek at Denmark's impressive WWII Nazi Resistance Movement, browsing through shops that specialize in Danish design, a look at the crown jewels and another fine palace, or more shopping. Whatever you do, you'll work up an appetite to justify the eternal buffet "koltbord" dinner at the very popular station Bistro restaurant.

Sightseeing Highlights

▲**Christiansborg Palace**—This modern "slot" or palace, built on the ruins of the original 12th century palace, houses the parliament, supreme court, prime minister's headquarters and royal reception rooms. Guided 40-minute tours (in English) of the reception rooms (June-August, Tues-Sun at 11:00, 13:00, 15:00 and sometimes 10:00, off season tours at 14:00 except on Monday and Saturday) cost 17 kr. You'll slip-slide on protect-the-floor slippers through 22 rooms and gain a good feel for Danish history and politics in this 100 year old, rather unremarkable palace. There are also guided tours of the connected Danish Parliament (daily except Saturdays in summer, 10:00-16:00, free).

▲**Christiansborg Castle Ruins**—A fine exhibit in the scant remains of the first castle built by Bishop Absalon, the 12th century founder of Copenhagen, lies under the palace. Go at 9:30, nothing else is open. (Open daily 9:30-16:00, closed Saturdays in off season, 7 kr).

▲▲▲**National Museum**—Focus on the excellent Danish collection, which traces this civilization from its ancient beginnings, laid out on the ground floor chronologically with English explanations. Highlights include passage graves, mummified bodies, the 2000 year old Gunderstrup Cauldron, original ancient lur horns, Viking gear, mead drinking horns and early Christian art. Good English brochures. This free museum is curiously enjoyable. (Open in summer, Tues-Sun 10:00-16:00; off-season, Tues-Fri 11:00-15:00, Sat 12:00-16:00).

▲**Ny Carlsberg Glyptotek**—Denmark's top art gallery, with an especially strong Egyptian, Greek and Etruscan collection and a fine small exhibit of French Impressionist paintings, is an impressive example of what beer money can do. One of the original Rodin "Thinkers" ponders the garden in the museum's back yard. Just behind Tivoli, open Tues-Sun 10:00-16:00, shorter hours off season, 15 kr.

▲▲▲**Tivoli Gardens**—The world's most famous amusement park is now 175 years old. It's 20 acres, 110,000 lanterns and countless ice cream cones of fun. You pay one small (18 kr) admission price and find yourself lost in a Hans Christian Andersen wonderland of rides, restaurants, games, marching bands, roulette wheels and funny mirrors. Tivoli is wonderfully Danish and doesn't try to be Disney. It's open from 10:00 to 24:00, May through mid-September (closed off season). Go at night on a full stomach or with a discreet picnic (the food inside is costly). Pick up a schedule or locate an English billboard schedule of events. Free concerts, mime, ballet, acrobats, puppets, and other shows pop up all over the park and a well organized visitor can enjoy an exciting evening of entertainment without spending a single krone. Rides are reasonable, but the all-day pass for 98 kr is best for those who may have been whirling dervishes in a previous life. On Wednesday, Friday and Saturday the place closes down with a midnight fireworks show. If you're taking an overnight train out of Copenhagen, Tivoli—just across from the station—is the best place to spend your last Copenhagen hours.

▲**Rosenborg Palace**—This impressively furnished Renaissance-style castle houses the Danish crown jewels and royal knick-knacks. The palace is surrounded by the royal gardens, rare plant collection and, on sunny days, sunbathing Danish beauties. Open daily 10:00-15:00 in summer, off season Tues, Fri & Sun only, 11:00-15:00. 20 kr.

▲**Denmark's Fight for Freedom (Nazi Resistance) Museum)**—The fascinating story of a heroic struggle is well explained in English. Located between the Queen's Palace and the Mermaid, open May to mid-September, daily 10:00-16:00 except Mondays, off season 11:00-15:00, free. Don't miss the 3-D city map across the street.

▲▲▲**"Stroget"'**—Copenhagen's experimental 25-years-of-age, tremendously successful and most copied pedestrian shopping mall—a string of serendipitous streets and lovely squares from the city hall to Nyhavn. Spend some time browsing, people-watching and exploring here and along adjacent pedestrian-only streets. The nearby Grabrodertorv (Grey Brothers Square) is probably Copenhagen's most charming square.

▲▲▲**Copenhagen on Foot**—Helge (Jack) Jacobsen is an inspirational local historian (possibly old H.C. Andersen himself reincarnated) who takes small groups on daily walks through different slices of Copenhagen. Pick up his "On Foot in Copenhagen" list of tours at the T.I. or see his walks in the "This Week" calendar, and take advantage of this best way to fall in love with Copenhagen. Helge charges 15 kr for his two-hour walk. He has six different tours, normally leaving at 17:30. Just show up (the schedule tells where) at any walk you can fit in—rain or shine.

▲**Harbor Cruise**—The 50-minute, 26 kr harbor tour leaves from Gammel Strand near Christiansborg Palace every half hour from 10:00, May through mid-September. It's a pleasant way to see the mermaid and take a load off those weary sightseeing feet.

▲**Vor Frelsers Church**—The unique spiral spire that you'll admire from afar can be climbed for a great city view and a good aerial view of the Christiania commune below. It's 311 feet high and, they claim (but I haven't counted), 400 steps. While you're there, the church's bright baroque interior is worth a look. Open daily 9:00-15:30, Sun 9:00-12:00, 10 kr.

Christiania—This is a unique on-again off-again social experiment—a counterculture utopia attempt which is, to many, disillusioning. A mish-mash of 700 idealists, anarchists, hippies, dope fiends and non-materialists have established squatters' rights in a former military barracks near the spiral church spire in Christianshavn. This communal cornucopia of dogs, dirt, drugs and dazed people—or haven of peace and freedom, depending on your perspective—is a political hot potato. No one in the establishment wants it—or has the nerve to get rid of it. Hash and pot are sold and smoked openly, while hard drugs are "out." Past the souvenir and hash-vendor entry you'll find a fascinating ramshackle world of moats and ramparts, alternative housing, unappetizing falafel stands, a fine restaurant (Spiseloppen), handicraft shops and filth. No photos, not safe at night—and, in some people's opinion, not safe ever.

▲**Carlsberg Brewery Tour**—Denmark's two beloved sources of *legal* intoxicants, Carlsberg and Tuborg, offer free brewery tours and tasting. Carlsberg's tour (Mon-Fri 9:00, 11:00 and 2:30, tel. 01-211221 ext. 1312, Bus #6 or #18 to 140 Ny Carlsberg Vej) is most popular.

Other sights to consider: The great Copenhagen train station is a fascinating mesh of Scandimanity and transportation efficiency. Even if you're not a train traveler, check it out. The noontime changing of the guard at the Amalienborg Palace is boring: all they change is places. Copenhagen's flea market (summer Saturdays 8:00-14:00 at Israels Plads) is small but feisty and surprisingly cheap. Nyhavn, with its fine old ships, tattoo shops and jazz clubs, is a wonderful place to "hang out."

Shopping

The city's top department stores (Illum at 52 Ostergade and Magasin du Nord at 13 Kongens Nytorv) offer a good, if expensive, look at today's Denmark. At Den Permanente (across from the station at 8 Vesterbrogade) you'll see sleek Danish design at its best. Shops are open Mon-Thurs 9:00-17:30, Friday 9:00-19:00, Saturday 9:00-13:00, closed Sunday.

DAY 4
NORTH ZEALAND AND INTO SWEDEN

Over jet-lag and ready to hit the road, you'll pick up your rental car and drive north to see Zealand's two top sights—the Frederiksborg castle (Denmark's best) and the renowned Louisiana modern art gallery. Then, after a quick ferry ride to Sweden, drive east for five hours through the forests to Vaxjo.

Suggested Schedule	
9:00	Pick up rental car, drive north to Hillerod.
10:00	Tour Frederiksborg castle.
12:00	Enjoy a picnic lunch marinated in modern art at the Lousiana art gallery.
14:00	Ferry to Helsingborg, Sweden and drive east.
20:00	Set up in Vaxjo (or Kalmar).

Transportation
To avoid driving in big cities, especially on my first day behind the wheel, I normally try to pick my rental car up at airports. Unfortunately, Copenhagen's is on the south side of town and we're heading north.

Wherever you pick up your rental car, don't rush the orientation. Study the basics: locate the car manual, know how to change a tire, what kind of gas to use, understand their breakdown policy and how to use the local automobile club membership—if one's included. Ask for advice and rules of the local road, a list of drop-off offices, any map they can give you and directions to Helsingor. Before leaving, drive around for five or ten minutes. Try everything. Distinguish emergency flashers from windshield wipers. Find problems before they find you.

I always get a second key made as soon as possible, jot down the license and vital info to store in my moneybelt, set up a backseat pantry and a trunk deep-storage box. This will be your home for three weeks. You might as well move in right away.

North Zealand by car: Follow signs for E4 and Helsingor north out of Copenhagen. The freeway is great and very soon it'll hit you: "This is a tiny country." Frederiksborg Castle (not to be confused with the nearby Fredensborg "slot" or castle) is clearly marked in the pleasant town of Hillerod. The Louisiana Museum is on the coast just south of Helsingor in the town of

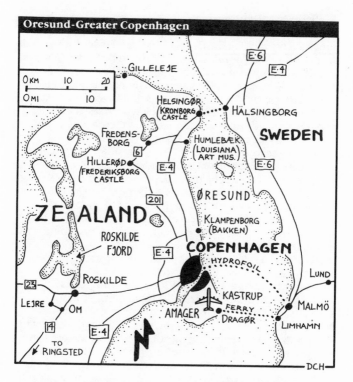

Oresund-Greater Copenhagen

Humlebaek. While the shortest distance between any two points is the autobahn (E4 in this case), the "Strand" coastal road (#152) is very pleasant, going by some of Denmark's finest mansions.

Getting to Sweden is easy but expensive. Just follow the signs to the "Helsingborg, Sweden" ferry. The freeway takes you right there. Boats leave every 15 minutes, you buy your ticket from the man as you roll on board (about $25 for car and driver), reservations are possible (tel. 02-211255) but rarely necessary. Gas is much more expensive in Denmark than in Sweden.

The 30-minute ferry ride gives you just enough time to enjoy the view of the Elsinore "Hamlet" castle and be impressed by how narrow this very important channel is. In Helsingborg (Swedish customs are a wave-through), follow signs for E4, Ljungby and Jonkoping. The road's good, traffic's light, you'll make good time. At Ljungby, Road #25 takes you to Vaxjo and Kalmar. It's about a six-hour drive from Copenhagen to Kalmar.

Sightseeing Highlights
▲▲▲**Frederiksborg Castle**—This grandest castle in Scandinavia is often called the Danish Versailles. Frederiksborg (built from 1602 to 1620) is the castle of Christian IV, Denmark's great builder king. You can almost hear the clackle of royal hoof beats as you walk over the moat through the stately cobbled courtyard, past the Dutch Renaissance brick facade and into the lavish interior. The English guidebook is unnecessary as each room has a handy English info sheet, and there are plenty of tours upon which to freeload. Listen for hymns on the old carillon at the top of each hour. The many historic paintings are a fascinating scrapbook of Danish history.

Savor the courtyard. Picnic in the moat park or enjoy the elegant Slotsherrens Kro cafeteria at the moat's edge. The castle is open daily 10:00-17:00 May-September. Off season it closes at 15:00 or 16:00. 20 kr entry. Easy parking. From Copenhagen, take the S-train to Hillerod, and then a pleasant 10-minute walk or catch the free Bus #701 from the station.

▲▲**Louisiana**—Beautifully situated on the coast 20 miles north of Copenhagen, this is Scandinavia's most raved-about modern art museum. It's a wholistic place—mixing its art, architecture and landscape masterfully. Wander from famous Chagalls and Picassos to more obscure art. Poets spend days here nourishing their creative souls with new angles, ideas and perspectives. The views over one of the busiest passages in the nautical world are nearly as inspiring as the art. The cafeteria (indoor/outdoor) is reasonable and welcomes picnickers who buy a drink. Open daily 10:00-17:00, Wednesdays till 22:00. 30 kr admission (or included in a special round trip tour's ticket). Train from Copenhagen to Helsingor, getting off in 36 minutes at Humlebaek. Then it's a free bus connection or a ten-minute walk through a park. From Frederiksborg there are rare Humlebaek buses but most will have to connect via Helsingor.

Helsingor—Often confused with its Swedish sister, Helsingborg, just 2½ miles across the channel, Helsingor is a small pleasant town with a medieval center and lots of Swedes who come over for lower-priced alcohol (the bar scene reminds me of *Gunsmoke*). This hamlet (Elsinore) is famous for a castle with bogus ties to Shakespeare. The "Hamlet" castle (Kronborg), darling of every big bus tour and travelogue, was built centuries after Hamlet died and Shakespeare never saw the place. Still hordes of tourists visit—"to see or not to see" it. It's much more impressive from the outside than inside and the view from the ferry is as close as you need to get. There's a fine beachfront hostel (Vandrerhjem Villa Moltke, tel. 02-211640) just a mile north of the castle. I've met people who prefer small

towns and small prices touring Copenhagen with this hostel as
their base.

Vaxjo—A pleasant, rather dull town of 50,000, Vaxjo is in the
center of Smaland—the Swedish province famous for its
forests, lakes, great glass and many emigrants to the USA. A
stroll through downtown Vaxjo is as purely a Swedish experience as I think you can have. Tourist office—Kronobergs-
gatan 8, tel. 0470/41410.

Accommodations
Hotel Esplanad is your best central hotel value. 250 kr
doubles from June 19 through August 9. More expensive other
times. No. Esplanad 21A, tel. 22580.

Sara Hotel Statt is very central, more traditional, and quite
luxurious. Doubles cost 800 kr (cheaper on weekends and in
the summer). 6 Kungsgatan, tel. 13400.

Kinnevaldsgardens Motel—Eva and Lasse Andersson (and
their two small children) run this homey place like a British
B&B. They have four doubles, 180 kr each, and are generous
with maps, info, evening cake and coffee. Breakfast is 20 kr extra. St. Vagen 9, Bergsnas (outside of town, take the "Morners
Vag" exit just before you reach Vaxjo and turn in the direction

of Ojaby.) It's across the street from the Q-8 gas station. Tel. 0470/60887.

The Bergsnas Motel, just across the street (no character and a bit musty, but cheap: 200 kr doubles) is run by the friendly man in the Q-8 gas station at Stora Vagen 11, tel. 60071.

Vaxjo has a fine **youth hostel** on a lake, 2½ miles out of town. STF Vandrarhem Evedal, 35590 Vaxjo, tel. 0470/63070. Open mid-April through mid-October, from 8:00-10:00 and 17:00 to 22:00, 2-4 bed rooms, 45 kr.

The tourist office (open 9:00-19:00, Sat 10:00-14:00, Sun 13:00-17:00) can find private rooms for 90 kr per person, 70 kr if you have sheets (plus a 20 kr fee), tel. 0470/41410. Best cheap meal—MacBest across from the station, is a fast, lively local hangout with good salads, pizzas and burgers.

DAY 5

VAXJO, KALMAR AND GLASS COUNTRY

Smaland is, outside of Stockholm, the most interesting region of Sweden. More Americans came from here than any part of Scandinavia and the immigration center in Vaxjo tells the story well. This is "glass country" and several prestigious glass works welcome curious visitors. Kalmar has a rare old world ambience and my favorite castle in Scandinavia. The strange island of Oland offers a mixed bag of beaches, bird watching, Stonehenge-type mysteries and windmills.

Suggested Schedule	
9:00	Tour Vaxjo, its Smalands folk museum and the impressive Emigrants Center. Drive to Orrefors.
11:30	Everybody seems to agree, Orrefors is Sweden's most interesting glassworks to tour.
14:30	Set up in Kalmar in time to see the castle and its new provincial museum (Lansmuseet).
18:00	Enjoy an easy evening in the old town.

Sightseeing Highlights
▲▲**House of Emigrants**—1,300,000 Swedes moved to the USA and most came from this neck of the Swedish woods. If you have roots here, this place is really exciting. If not, it's mildly interesting. The Dream of America exhibit tells the story of the 1850-1920s "American Fever." (At the emigration festival, second Sunday in August, thousands of Minnesotans storm the town.) Upstairs is an excellent library and research center. Root-seekers are very welcome. Advance notice is urged (write well in advance to Box 20l, S-351 04, Vaxjo for research form and info). Open Mon-Fri 9:00-16:00, Sat 11:00-15:00, Sun 13:00-17:00. tel. 0470/20l20. Research center open Mon-Fri only.

Vaxjo also has a fine cathedral, a lovely park with an arboretum and a pleasant pedestrian center. The tourist office, station and all sights are clustered very close together.
Smalands Museum—This cute small-townish museum (one of Sweden's oldest) offers a good look at local forestry, a prehistoric exhibit, a wonderful traditional costume display (top floor) and, most importantly, an introduction to the area's glass industry. Nothing is in English. Mon-Fri 9:00-16:00, Saturday 11:00-15:00, Sunday 13:00-17:00. 3 kr. Oh, go on, see it—it's just next to the Emigrants House.

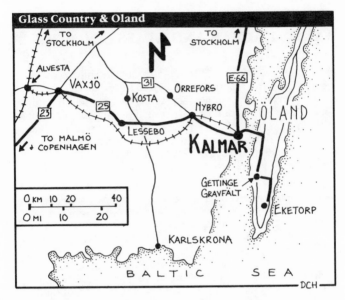

Lessebo Papermill— You'll pass right through Lessebo en
route to Orrefors (just after the Kosta turnoff you'll see a "hand-
papersbruk" sign). If you've never seen handmade paper pro-
duced, this is free and worth a stop. Pick up the English
brochure or ask for a tour. Wide open June-August, kind of
open in the off season.

▲**The Kingdom of Crystal**— This is Sweden's glass country.
Frankly, these glassworks cause so much excitement because of
the relative rarity of anything else thrilling in Sweden outside of
greater Stockholm. (Remember, I'm Norwegian). Of the several
renowned glassworks, Orrefors is the most famous and offers
the best tours. It's here that you'll actually see them blowing as
well as molding the molten glass. Free tours depart twice an
hour from 8:00 to l0:30 and 11:30 to 15:00 Mon-Fri, during the
summer. When there are no tours, visitors can observe the
work from platforms. The shop sells nearly perfect crystal sec-
onds at a fraction of the normal price—but it still ain't cheap.
(Open Mon-Fri 8:30-18:30, Saturday 8:30-16:00, Sunday
11:00-16:00.) Don't miss the dazzling "museum" (open
8:00-17:00, 9:30-15:00 on Saturday and 12:00-16:00 on Sunday.) It's wise to call (tel. 0481/30300) if you really want a tour.
The nearby Kosta (tel. 50300) and Boda (tel. 24000) glassworks
also give tours (Mon-Fri 10:00-15:00, closed July) and sell
crystal at cut-glass prices.

Kalmar
Kalmar feels formerly strategic and important. Its salty old center has a wistful sailor's charm. This, with its busy waterfront, fine castle and museum, make it an excellent last piece of small town Sweden before we plunge into Stockholm. In its day, Kalmar was called the gateway to Sweden. Today, it's just a sleepy has-been, "gateway" only to the holiday island of Oland.

Accommodations
"Sjofartsklubben" (seaman's club)—In June, July and August, old Mr. Persson opens his clean, salty dorm-like place up to tourists. (It's the home of student sailors during the school year.) He has one- to five-bedded rooms with kitchen privileges and a lively common room. He doesn't speak English but this place is worth the struggle. Only l00 kr per double plus l5 kr for sheets. Olaudsgaten 45, tel. 0480/10810, facing the harbor.

    Private rooms—The tourist office (0480/15350) can set you up in a private home. Try Britta Johanneson, who rents out four doubles for l20 kr each right downtown at Kaggensgaten 2 (near the T.I.), tel. 13440.

    Youth Hostel—A fifteen minute walk from the center, this is a wonderful hostel run by Annelise Knutsson. Two or four bed rooms, TV and sauna, lots of extra facilities. 50 kr per person. Closed from 10:00 to 16:30. Annelise also runs a "hotel" annex with 225 kr doubles including sheets and breakfast. STF Vandrarhem, Rappegatan 1, 39230 Kalmar, tel. 0480/12928. You'll see a blue and white hotel sign and hostel symbol at the edge of town on Angoleden St.

    Hotel Villa Lindo—Torsten and Monica Everbrand run this fine old wooden house with a big garden on the edge of town. 300 kr per double with shower. Lindolundsgatan 18, tel. 0480/14280.

    Hotel Villa Ango—This big old house on the water ten minutes out of town has great facilities and 300 kr doubles. Baggensgatan 20, tel. 0480/85415.

Food
Hotel Witt Vardshuset—This hotel's "backside" restaurant serves atmospheric budget meals with a salad bar, melt-in-your-mouth fresh bread and plenty of ice water. The very pleasant service, super minty toothpicks and bullseyes in the urinal all add up to make it my kind of place. 30 kr for lunch (with very cheap beers) and 70 kr for dinner. On the corner of Sodra Langgatan and Ostra Sjogaden, right downtown.

    The Domus Department Store's **4 Kok** cafeteria serves cheap meals right downtown. Open until 21:00 in summer, only until 18:30 off season.

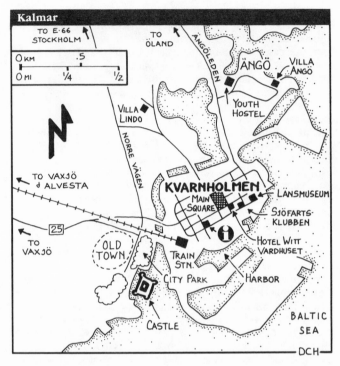

Byttan Restaurant—For a splurge, head out to the castle to enjoy a great waterfront terrace for a budget-wrecking meal or memorable cup of coffee.

Sightseeing Highlights
▲▲▲Kalmar Castle—This moated castle is one of Europe's great medieval experiences. The stark exterior, cuddled by a lush park, houses a fine Renaissance palace interior, which is the work of King Gustavus Vasa. The elaborately furnished rooms are entertainingly explained in English, and a more extensive guidebook is available for 13 kr. Notice how the electric candles "flicker." Open daily 10:00-18:00, Sunday 13:00-17:00 from mid-June to mid-August. Off-season—10:00-16:00, Sunday 13:00-16:00. 10 kr.

▲Kalmer Provincial (Lans) Museum—This new museum houses the impressive salvaged wreck of the royal ship *Kronan*, which sank nearby in 1676. Lots of interesting soggy bits and old pieces, but unfortunately no information in English. You still get a "here's the buried treasure" thrill. Upstairs you'll also find a good Swedish design exhibit. Right downtown on the waterfront, open Tues-Sat 10:00-18:00, Sunday 13:00-17:00, closed Monday, mid-June to mid-August. Shorter hours off season. 15 kr.

▲▲**The Island of Oland**—Europe's longest bridge (4 miles, free) connects Oland with Kalmar and the mainland. The island (90 miles long and only 8 miles wide) is a pleasant local resort known for its birds, windmills, flowers, beaches and prehistoric sights. Public transportation is miserable here, and the island is only worthwhile if you have a car and 3 extra hours. A 60-mile circle south of the bridge will give you a good dose of the island's windy rural charm. The **Gettlinge Gravfalt** (just off the road about ten miles up from the south tip) is a wonderfully situated boat-shaped Iron Age grave site littered with mono-liths, overseen by a couple of creaky old windmills. It offers a commanding view of the island's treeless steppe.

Farther south is the **Eketorp Prehistoric Fort**. Eketorp is a very reconstructed 5th century stone fort which, as iron age forts go, is fairly interesting. Several evocative huts and build-ings are filled with what someone imagines may have been the style back then, and the huge rock fort is surrounded by runty pig-like creatures that were common here 1500 years ago. ("'For your convenience and pleasure," the sign reads, "don't leave your children alone with the animals.") Open daily 9:00-17:00, English tours normally at 13:00. 15 kr.

Itinerary Option
We've got two nights and a day to explore this part of Sweden. The aggressive option is to spend the first night in Vaxjo, see its sights and tour the glassworks. Get to Kalmar early in the after-noon and skip Oland. The easy option gives you two nights settled in Kalmar and covers Oland and Kalmar rather than Vaxjo, glassworks and Kalmar. I like the first plan unless the im-migration center and the glass show don't interest you.

DAY 6
KALMAR TO STOCKHOLM

Today is basically a long drive. We'll leave early, stop for a
leisurely lunch and walk along the famous Gota Canal, then
drive into Stockholm in time to visit the tourist office, get comfortably set up, tour the charming old town and enjoy an atmospheric dinner.

Suggested Schedule	
8:00	Drive north along the coast.
12:00	Stop in Soderkoping for a picnic lunch and a walk along the Gota Canal.
14:00	Continue the trek north.
17:00	Arrive in Stockholm, visit tourist office to confirm plans and set up.
18:30	Catch the Gamla Stan (Old Town) walking tour.
20:30	Dinner at Kristina Restaurant in old town.

Transportation
Highway E-66 takes you from Kalmar right to Stockholm. It's
240 miles and takes about 5 hours. Sweden did a cheap widen-
ing job, paving the shoulders of the old two lane road to get
about 3.8 lanes. Still, the traffic is polite and sparse and there's
little to see or do, so stock the pantry (I call it my "auto-mat"),
set the compass on north, and home in on Stockholm.

You might consider three pleasant stops along the way: 15
miles north of Kalmar is Pataholm, a tiny port village with a
general store and more nicely painted wooden buildings (2
miles off E-66). Ninety miles north is Vastervik, with a pleasant
18th century core of wooden houses. Soderkoping (150 miles
north of Kalmar) is just right for a "lunch on the Gota Canal"
stop. After a look at the cuddly town center, have a picnic and
walk along the sleepy waterway to get a feel for the romance of
the popular three day Gota Canal cruise. You'll see locks and
cruise ships as you walk along the old hauling path.

Stockholm
If I had to call one European city "home" it would be
Stockholm. Green, clean, efficient and surrounded by as much
water as land, Sweden's capital is under-rated, landing just
above Bordeaux, Brussels and Bucharest on many tourist
checklists. I rank it with Amsterdam, Munich, and Madrid.

While progressive and frighteningly futuristic, Stockholm respects its heritage. Throughout the summer mounted bands parade daily through the heart of town to the royal palace announcing the changing of the guard and turning even the most dignified tourist into a scampering kid. The Gamla Stan (Old Town) celebrates the Midsummer festivities (late June) with the down-home vigor of a rural village, forgetting that it's the core of a gleaming 20th century metropolis.

Stockholm's 1.4 million residents live on fourteen islands but visitors need only concern themselves with five: Norrmalm (downtown, with most hotels, shopping areas and the train station), Gamla Stan (the old city of winding lantern-lit streets, antique shops and classy cafes clustered around the royal palace), Sodermalm (aptly called Stockholm's "Brooklyn," residential and untouristy), Skeppsholmen (the small, very central traffic-free park island with the Modern Art Museum and two fine youth hostels), and Djurgarden (literally "deer garden," Stockholm's wonderful green playground, with many of the city's top sights).

Tourist Info

Hotel Centralen—Basically a room-finding service (located downstairs in the central station), Hotel Centralen's friendly staff also handles your sightseeing and transportation questions. This is the place to arrange your accommodations, buy your Stockholm Card and pick up free brochures: city map, "Stockholm on a Shoestring," "This Week in Stockholm" (which lists opening hours and direction to all the sights and special events). Go over and confirm your sightseeing plans. They have a good but expensive (27 kr) transit map—the only one that shows bus lines. Long hours—June-August 8:00-21:00 daily, off season—Mon-Fri 8:30-16:45, tel. 08/240880.

Sweden House (Sverige Huset)—Europe's most creative and energetic tourist information office is a short walk from the station on Kungstradgarden. A patient local expert will answer all your questions. They've got pamphlets on everything, a "Meet the Swedes at Home" program, and an English library and reading room upstairs with racks of free info on various aspects of Swedish Culture. Tel. 221840 gets you their recorded "What's On Today" message. Open mid-June—mid-August, Mon-Fri 8:30-18:00, Sat-Sun 8:00-17:00, off season Mon-Fri 9:00-17:00, Sat-Sun 9:00-14:00. (Hamngatan 27, tel. 08/7892000, T-bana: Kuugstradgarden).

Transportation and the Stockholm Card

Stockholm is the complete hostess. She compliments her many sightseeing charms with great information services, a fine bus

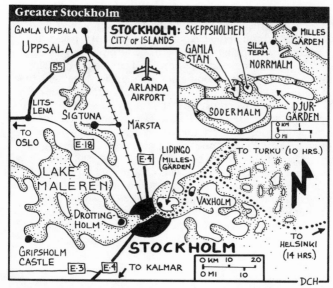

and subway system, and special passes to take the bite out of the cost (or at least limit it to one vicious budgetary gash).

Go-as-you-please passes, available at T.I.s, newsstands and subway stations, give you free run of all public transport for 24 hours (21 kr) or 72 hours (72 kr). This card includes the harbor ferry and admission to Skansen, Grona Lund and the Post Tower (Kaknastornet). If you decide to go by individual tickets, consider the cheaper ten-ride strip cards and remember, each bus ticket (around 8 kr) is valid for one hour. The subway, called T-bana or tunnelbana, gets you where you want to go very quickly.

Stockholm's new "Tourist Line" bus route, departing every 15 minutes, hits 14 major sights. This lets you get off and on as you please, to "do the circuit" at your leisure. The "Tourist Line" brochure explains exactly how this 30 kr, 24-hour pass works.

Be sure to take advantage of the exciting and expedient boat connections from Nybroplan and Slussen to Djurgarden landing next to the Wasa and Skansen. Busy sightseers save time and money with the Stockholm Card. This 24-hour (66 kr), 48-hour (ll2 kr) or 72-hour (168 kr) pass gives you free run of all the public transit, free entry to virtually every sight, a good map and sightseeing handbook. Pick one up at any T.I. or Pressbyra Kiosk (newsstand).

Parking: Only a Swedish meatball would drive his car in Stockholm. Park it and use the public transit. But parking here is a major hassle and expense. Unguarded lots generally aren't safe. Pay for a garage. The tourist office has a "Parking In Stockholm" brochure. Those with the Stockholm Card can park in a very big central garage for the duration of the ticket for only 10 kr (rather than the normal 60 kr rate). Get your parking ticket and specifics at the Sweden House. There is a big, safe and reasonable (10 kr per day) garage at Ropsten—the last subway station (near the Silja line terminal) and in the right end of town for your departure to Uppsala. If you'll be sailing to Finland, you can solve all your parking worries in a snap by long-term parking your car upon arrival in Stockholm at either terminal's safe and reasonable parking lot.

Accommodations

Hotel Centrallen in the central station, lower level, for a 15 kr fee, can nearly always find suitable rooms for those who arrive without reservations. They also have special discount possibilities and packages which can land you in an impossibly expensive hotel almost affordably. And they know exactly what's available in the realm of budget and "sleep-in" alternatives to hotels. The Stockholm Tourist Office at the Sweden House (tel. 789/2000, open daily) also books rooms—but not quite as well.

Stockholm's tourist offices refer people in search of a room in a private house to one of three agencies. **Hoteljanst** (Vasagatan 15, tel. 08/104467), **Allrum** (Brunnsgatan 15, tel. 08/213789) and **All Stockholm** (Norrtullsgatan 15, tel. 08/348153). Each can set you up for about 100 kr per night. Three people who rent out rooms privately are **Mrs. Lindstrom** (T-bana: Islandstorget, tel. 371608), **Mr. Jonasson** (near T-bana: Stanstull, tel. 847008) and **Mrs. Sallstrom** (near Karlaplan, tel. 675219).

Hotel Karelia—This stately old Finnish-run hotel is centrally located and a good value for a "normal" hotel. Swimming pool and sauna. Doubles 500 kr in summer, 800 in winter. 35 Birger Jarlsgatan, tel. 247660.

Jerum Hotell—This huge, sleek and clean university dorm offers 120 double rooms during the summer break (June, July and August only) for about 300 kr. It's not central but just ride the subway to Gardet and walk through the park. Studentbacken 21, tel. 635380.

Hotel Frescati—Another huge June-to-August-only hotel offering doubles with showers for around 150 kr. Professorslingen 13, T-bana: Universitetet, tel. 158742.

Pensionat Oden—This small, quiet pension is almost depressing and dingy but it's well located (subway stop Odenplan) and cheap with doubles for 350 kr. Odengatan 38, tel. 306349.

Hotel Gustav Wasa—Another cheap but well-worn place near Odenplan offering doubles with breakfast for 320-400 kr. Vastmannagatan 61, tel. 343801.

Youth Hostels—Stockholm has a tremendous selection of hostels offering good beds in simple but often interesting places for from 50 to 70 kr. If your budget is tight, these are great. Each has a helpful English-speaking staff, pleasant commons room, good facilities and will hold rooms for a phone call.

af Chapman—1988 is the centennial year of Europe's most famous youth hostel—the permanently moored cutter ship *af Chapman*. Just a five minute walk from downtown, this floating hostel has 140 beds—two to eight per stateroom. At least 50 beds are saved for unreserved arrivals each morning so if you call at breakfast time and show up before 10:00 you should land a bed even in summer. Open March to mid-December, 7:00-12:00, and 15:00-23:00, with a lounge and a cafeteria that welcomes even non-hostelers from 8:00 to 10:00 and 12:00 to 16:00. STF Vandranhem "af Chapman," Skeppsholmen, 11149 Stockholm, tel. 103715.

Skeppsholmen Hostel—Just ashore from the *af Chapman*, this hostel is open all year, better facilities and smaller rooms (many doubles), but it isn't as romantic as its sea-going sister. Tel. 202506.

Zinken Hostel—This is a big, basic, well-run hostel with nearly all doubles, a sauna, laudromat and the best hostel kitchen facilities in town. In a busy suburb (T-bana: Hornstull or Zinkensdamm). STF Vandrarhem Zinken, Zinkens Vag 20, tel. 685786. Open 7:00-23:00, all year.

Vandrarhemmet Brygghuset—A former brewery near Odenplan, open from June 9 to August 24 daily 8:00-12:00 and 15:00-22:00 (no curfew). Its two- to six-bed rooms are open to all. Norrtullsgatan 12 N., tel. 312424.

Columbus Hotel and Hostel—This plain, well run, no-smoking allowed hostel is an historic old building in a park next to a police station. Mostly four- and six-bed rooms with a few doubles. Near T-bana: Medborgarplatsen. Tjarhovsgatan 11, tel. 441717.

Camping—Stockholm has seven campgrounds which solve your parking and budgetary problems wonderfully. The T.I.'s "Camping Stockholm" brochure has specifics. The two most central places are Sodermalms (T-bana: Skanstull, tel. 439118) and Ostermalms (T-bana: #15 or #24 to Stadium, tel. 102903).

Food
Breakfast—Don't miss downtown Stockholm's budget miracle—the famous "Frukostbuffet" (smorgasbord breakfast) in the central station. Under the huge "Restaurang" sign in the

main hall, the **Centralens Restaurang** offers an elegant 37 kr all-you-can-eat feast every morning in Orient Express atmosphere. (Mon-Fri 6:30-10:00, Sat-Sun 8:00-10:30).

Lunch—Stockholm's major department stores, small corner groceries, the indoor market at Ostermalmstorg and the open-air market at Hotorget are all fine places to assemble a good picnic spread. Stockholm's elegant department stores (notably Domus and Ahlens near Sergelstorg) have cafeterias for the crown-pinching local shopper. Look for the daily specials called "Dagens ratt" (no, it doesn't mean "rodent of the day"). Monday through Friday the **City Hall Kalleren Restaurant** serves up a delicious 36 kr lunch (prepared by the same folks who prepare the Nobel Prize banquet).

Dinner—"Husmans Kost" means typical Swedish cuisine. Cafes serve the cheapest light meals. For an expensive but excellent authentically Swedish meal, try the **Diana** and the **Aurora** restaurants in Gamla Stan. **Lyktan** (just behind the Grand Hotel at Teatergatan 6) serves a salad bar and main course from 11:00 to 22:00 Mon-Fri, for 35 kr.

In the old town (Gamla Stan) don't miss the wonderfully atmospheric **Kristina Restaurang** (Vesterlanggatan 68, Gamla Stan, tel. 200529). In this 1632 building with a turn-of-the-century interior, you'll find good dinners from 40 to 80 kr (My Swedish meatballs, potatoes, salad and lingonberries dinner cost 42 kr). From 11:00 to 15:00 they serve a great 35 kr lunch—entree, salad bar, bread and drink.

DAYS 7 & 8
STOCKHOLM

Stockholm, one of Europe's most underrated cities, tempts
many to toss out the itinerary and settle in forever. Green, built
on fourteen islands, surrounded by water and woods, bubbling
with energy and history, it fills two days to the brim with

Suggested Schedule	
	Day 7
9:00	Confirm your plans at the Sweden House. Buy a picnic lunch in the basement of the NK department store across the street. Catch Bus #47 to the old warship, *Wasa*.
10:00	*Wasa*: see the 10:00 English-subtitled movie (30 min) and catch the English tour right afterwards.
11:30	Tour Skansen Open Air Folk Museum—guided one-hour walks in English at noon.
13:00	Picnic and wander in Skansen.
15:00	Nordic Museum, catch boat or Bus #47 back downtown. (Note: on Tuesday, Saturday and Sunday the museum stays open late, so you can get to this museum at 16:00 and spend an extra hour at the *Wasa* and Skansen.)
17:00	"Royal Canals" boat tour (from Grand Hotel).
Evening	Back at Skansen, or a cruise with dinner and jazz. Ask for timely advice at T.I.
	Day 8
10:00	Enjoy the city hall's entertaining guided tour.
11:00	Climb the city hall tower for Stockholm's best view.
12:00	Browse through the modern city center, around Kungstradgarden, Sergels Torg and Drottningsgatan area. Visit Kulture huset. Lunch at Ahlens department store cafeteria.
14:00	Free for an option: Art museums (National, Modern, Thiel, or Milles), the Drottningholm Palace, visit a planned suburb, sauna, or shopping in the Gamla Stan.
17:00	Board your boat, shower, rest.
18:30	Enjoy the island wonderland, smorgasbord dinner and a Scandinavian sunset.

memorable sights and experiences. On Day 7, we'll crawl through Europe's best preserved old warship, tour Europe's first and best open air folk museum and get a pleasant overview of the city during a canal boat tour.

Day 8 focuses on today's Stockholm with its marvelous city hall, modern department stores, art museums and futuristic planned suburbs. The city's "kulture huset," the royal family's palace and the many saunas are all very good at making us visitors feel welcome. You'll have some hard choices to make in order to catch the 18:00 boat to Finland. Europe's most enjoyable cruise begins with lovely archipelago scenery, a setting sun, and a royal smorgasbord dinner.

Sightseeing Highlights—Downtown Stockholm

▲Kungstradgarden—The "King's Garden" square is the downtown people-watching center. Watch the life-sized game of chess, enjoy the free concerts at the bandstand. Surrounded by the Sweden House, the HK department store, the harborfront and tour boats, grab the first blond you see and feel Stockholm's pulse.

▲Sergels Torg—The heart of skyscraper Stockholm, just between Kungstradgarden and the station, is worth a wander. Enjoy the colorful and bustling underground mall and the "Kulturhuset," a center for reading, relaxing and socializing designed for normal people but welcoming tourists. You'll enjoy music, exhibits, hands-on fun and an insight to contemporary Sweden. Free, daily from 11:00 to at least 17:00.

▲▲City Hall—The "Stadshuset" is a very impressive mix of 8 million bricks, 19 million chips of gilt mosaic and lots of Stockholm pride. One of Europe's most impressive modern (1923) buildings and site of the annual Nobel Prize dinner, it's particularly enjoyable and worthwhile for its entertaining tours (Mon-Fri at 10:00, Sat-Sun at 10:00 and noon, tel. 785-9000, just behind the station). Be sure to climb the 350-foot tower for the best city view possible (10:00-15:00, May-September).

Orientation Views—Try to get a bird's eye perspective on this wonderful urban mix of water, wood, concrete and people from: The city hall tower (see above), the Kaknas Tower (500 feet high, 9:00-24:00, 15 kr, Bus #69 from Nybroplan), or the top of the Katarina Elevator (near Slussen subway stop, 3 kr).

▲Royal Canal tour—For the best one-hour floating look at Stockholm—and a pleasant break—consider this cruise. Tour boats leave on the half hour from 10:30 to 19:30 from in front of the Grand Hotel, 40 kr. The open seats in the rear offer the most vibration and exhaust until the boat leaves. Then they become the best seats on board.

▲National Museum—It's mediocre by European standards

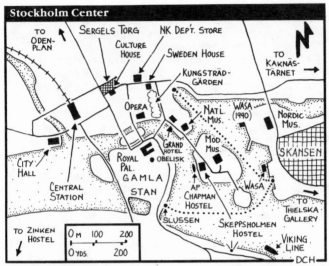

but small, central, uncrowded and very user-friendly. The highlights are several Rembrandts, a fine group of Impressionists and works by the popular and very good-to-get-to-know local artists Carl Larsson and Anders Zorn. Open Tuesday 10:00-17:00, Wed-Sun 10:00-16:00. In July and August, Tuesday till 17:00 because of special concerts. 20 kr (free on Tuesdays).

Mueseum of Modern Art—This bright and cheery gallery is as far out as can be, with Picasso, Braque, and lots of goofy "dada" art (such as the "urinal" and the "goat with tire"). In a pleasant park on Skeppsholmen. Tues-Fri 11:00-17:00, Sat-Sun 11:00-17:00, closed Monday, 20 kr (free on Thursday).

▲▲Gamla Stan—Stockholm's old island core is charming, fit for a film and full of antique shops, street lanterns, painted ceilings and surprises. Spend some time here, browse, enjoy a cafe, get to know a shop-keeper. The impressive Royal Palace is tourable—crown jewels and lavish apartments. A military parade culminates at the palace for the changing of the guard, a daily 12:00 thrill (13:00 on Sunday). The Riddarholm Church is the final resting place of Sweden's royalty (open 10:00-15:00).

▲Old Town Walking Tour—For an informal, chatty and historic walk, join gracious and eccentric (she'll take that as a compliment) Clara, or one of her fellow guides, on a two-hour Gamla Stan tour. Tours depart daily (rain or shine) at 18:30 from the "Obelisk" next to the palace. Groups are very small. Just show up. (If you're late, she talks for a while at the obelisk before heading into the palace courtyard.) She chatters on in a grandmotherly effervescent way. After a few doubtful moments, you'll feel good about the fluffy experience and leave with a better understanding of the remarkable Gamla Stan.

Djurgarden Sightseeing Highlights

▲▲▲**Skansen**—Europe's original—and best—open air folk museum, Skansen is a huge park gathering historic buildings (homes, churches, schoolhouses, etc.) transplanted from all corners of Sweden. Tourists can explore this Swedish culture on a lazy susan seeing folk crafts in action and wonderfully furnished old interiors. In the town quarter (top of the escalator), potters, glassblowers and other craftspeople are busy doing their traditional thing. Free and excellent one-hour guided walks paint a fine picture of old Swedish lifestyles (hourly from 12:00 to 16:00, June 15-Aug 15, from the Bollnastorget meeting place).

Skansen has much more, including a zoo (ride a Dalarna horse and stare down a hedgehog), folk dancing and other special events, several restaurants (the Solliden Vardhuset self-service offers uniformly good food, value, and a view) and lots of picnic benches (especially at Torshinden). Pick up the 5 kr map as you enter and drop by the Bollnastorget information desk to confirm your Skansen plans. Depart by the west entrance (Hazeliusporten) if you're heading for the Nordic Museum. Open June-August 9:00-22:00 (buildings 11:00-17:00), winter—9:00-17:00 (buildings 11:00-15:00). 20 kr entry (12 kr in winter). You can miss Grona Lund, the second-rate amusement park across the street.

▲▲▲**Wasa**—Stockholm turned a titanic flop into one of Scandinavia's great sightseeing attractions—and experiences. This glamorous but unseaworthy warship sank a few minutes into its maiden voyage in 1628. After 333 years, it rose again from the deep (with the help of marine archeologists) and today it's the best preserved ship of its kind anywhere. Catch the hourly intro movie first, then explore the old ship. The 30-minute English tours (on the half hour in summer and at 12:30 and 14:30 off season) are by far the best way to enjoy and understand the ship. Learn about "ship's rules—bread can't be older than 8 years," why it sank (heavy bread?), how it's preserved, etc. Note: The *Wasa* will be closed from September 5, 1988 to May of 1989 when it opens in its new and much improved home nearby. After being closed again for more work from September '89 to May '90, it'll have a grand opening in June of 1990. Otherwise it's open daily from 9:30-19:00, off season 10:00-17:00, 15 kr, take Bus #47 just past the big brick Nordic Museum, catch the boat or walk from Skansen.

▲▲**Nordic Museum**—Try hard to see this great look at Scandinavian culture. Highlights include the "Food and Drink" section with its stunning china and crystal table settings, the Nordic folk art (2nd floor) and the huge statue of Gustav Wasa, father of modern Sweden, by Carl Milles (top of 2nd flight of stairs). Open 10:00-16:00, Tuesdays till 20:00, Sat-Sun until 17:00, closed Fridays in winter. English tours daily at 13:00 in summer. 10 kr admission. The 20 kr guidebook isn't necessary, but pick up the free maps at the entrance.

▲**Thielska Galleriet**—If you liked the Larsson and Zorn art in the National Gallery and/or if you're a Munch fan, this charming mansion on the water at the far end of the Djurgarten park is worth the trip. Bus #69 from Karlaplan or boat from center. Mon-Sat 10:00-16:00, Sunday 13:00-16:00, 15 kr.

Sights Further from the Center

▲▲**Carl Milles Garten**—This is the home and major work of Sweden's greatest sculptor, situated on a cliff overlooking the city. Milles' entertaining, unique and provocative art was influenced by Rodin. Classy cafe, great picnic spot. T-bana to Ropsten, then Bus #221 to Torsvik getting off at Foresta. Daily 10:00-17:00, 15 kr.

▲**Drottningholm**—The queen's 17th century summer castle and present royal residence has been called Sweden's Versailles. It's great, but if you saw Denmark's Frederiksborg Palace and you are rushed in Stockholm, skip this. The adjacent uncannily well-preserved baroque theater is the real highlight here, especially with its guided tours (17 kr, English theater tours at 12:30, 13:30, 14:30, 15:30 May-September). Get there by pleasant but overpriced boat ride or take the subway to Brommaplan and the bus to Drottningholm. Palace and Theater open Mon-Sat 11:00-16:30, Sunday 12:00-16:30, May-August; in September, daily from 12:30-15:00. Palace tours in English Mon-Fri at 11:00 in June, July & August; at 13:00 in September. 10 kr.

The 17th century Drottningholm court theater performs (30 shows) perfectly authentic operas each summer. Tickets to these very popular and unique shows go on sale each March. Prices for this time-tunnel musical and theatrical experience are reasonable at 25 to 120 kr. Ten or fifteen seats are always held for sales at the door before the performance. For info, write in February to Drottningholm's Theater Museum, Box 27050, 10251 Stockholm or phone 08/608225.

▲**Futuristic planned suburbs**—Stockholm, the birthplace of cradle-to-grave security, is also a trendsetter in jukebox-orderly orbit towns. Farsta, a model of 1960s urban town planning, is most famous, but Skarholmen is a bit more interesting, with plenty of shopping and a flea market, as well as that frightening peek into our too-well-organized urban future.

▲**Archipelago**—24,000 of the world's most scenic islands surround Stockholm. Europeans who spend entire vacations in
and around Stockholm rave about these islands. If you cruise to
Finland you'll get a good dose of this island beauty. Otherwise,
consider the pleasant hour-long cruise (16 kr each way) from
the Grand Hotel downtown to the quiet town of Vaxholm.
▲**Sauna**—Sometime while you're in Sweden or Finland you'll
have to treat yourself to Scandinavia's answer to support hose
and a face lift. (A sauna is actually more Finnish than Swedish.)
"Simmer down" with the local students, retired folks and busy
executives. Try to cook as calmly as the Swedes. Just before
bursting, go into the shower room. There's no "luke cold," and
the "trickle down theory" doesn't apply—only one button
bringing a Niagara of liquid ice. Suddenly your shower stall
becomes a Cape Canaveral launch pad as your body scatters to
every corner of the universe. A moment later you're back
together. Rejoin the Swedes in the cooker, this time with their
relaxed confidence; you now know that exhilaration is just
around the corner. Only very rarely will you feel so good.

Any tourist office can point you toward the nearest birch
twigs. Good opportunities on our tour include: your
Stockholm-Helsinki cruise, any major hotel you stay in, many
hostels, or, least expensively, a public swimming pool. In
Stockholm, consider the Eriksdalsbadet at Hammarby Slussvag
8, near Skanstule T-bana. Use of its 50-meter pool and first rate
sauna costs 15 kr (Mon-Thur 6:30-15:00 and Tues 19:00-21:00,
Fri 12:00-15:00, Sat-Sun 8:00-13:00).

Shopping
Caution: shopping is a rich man's sport in Stockholm. Modern
design, glass, clogs and wood goods are popular targets for
shoppers. Browsing is a delightful, free way to enjoy Sweden's
brisk pulse. Cop a feel at the Nordiska Kompanient (NK) just
across from the Sweden House. Swedish stores are open from
8:00 to 18:00, only until 14:00 on Saturday, closed Sunday.

Sailing from Stockholm to Helsinki
Two fine and fiercely competitive lines, Viking and Silja, connect the capitals of Sweden and Finland daily and nightly. The
14-hour passage is very scenic, passing through a fair number of the countless islands that buffer Stockholm from the
open sea. Each line offers luxurious smorgasbord meals,
reasonable cabins, plenty of entertainment (discos, saunas,
gambling) and enough duty-free shopping to sink a ship.

The big and much discussed issue is, which line is best. You could count showers and compare shoeshines, but basically each line almost goes overboard to win the loyalty of the three and a half million duty-free-crazy Swedes and Finns who make the trip each year. I'd say it's too close to call.

For car travelers, the Viking Line offers very convenient Stockholm parking, more of the harbor to see on the cruise, a more centrally located terminal, bigger ships and a little cheaper fare. Those with Eurail passes should go Silja since the crossing is free with the pass (also, seniors, students with ISIC cards and Interrail pass travelers get 50% off, Nordtourist pass holders go to Turku free and pay 50% for the Helsinki trip). Viking offers lesser discounts to train travelers. (Deck class from Stockholm to Helsinki costs about $40 on both lines.)

Fares are reasonable and package mini-cruises are amazingly inexpensive. For instance, Viking offers a deal for about $100 (640 kr) that includes round trip boat fare, a berth in a 4-bed cabin each way, two buffet dinners and two all-you-can-eat breakfasts. You can stay over in Finland if you book your room through Viking (which is best anyway since they offer hard-to-beat discounts on Helsinki's best hotels). You can get a classier stateroom arrangement for more money. Silja offers similar packages, but not quite as cheap. Fares can vary a little from day to day. (Fridays most expensive, Sunday through Wednesday cheapest) and from summer (most expensive) to winter.

The fares are so cheap because they operate tax-free, and because the hordes of locals who sail to shop and drink duty-and tax-free spend a fortune on board. Last year, the average passenger spent more on booze and duty-free items than for the boat fare. It's a very large operation. Viking's big ships are 37,000 tons, nearly 200 yards long and, with 2500 beds, the largest (and some of the cheapest) hotels in Scandinavia.

Cruise Tactics and Miscellany
Both lines sail daily in both directions leaving at 18:00, arriving the next morning at 9:00. They also sail from Turku (21:30) to Stockholm (7:00) daily. There are morning departures, but for our purposes the night time is the right time. Remember, Finland is one hour ahead of Sweden.

Reservations—Never necessary for deck class "walk-ons." Summer (June-August) and Fridays are most crowded for staterooms. I'd book the whole package at a travel agency in Copenhagen or Kalmar. It's easy and costs no more than going direct.

Terminal Locations—In Stockholm, Viking is more central (free shuttle service on Bus #45 from the Slussen T-bana stop just past the Gamla Stan. You can normally see the huge red and white Viking ship parked in the harbor. For Silja, take the T-

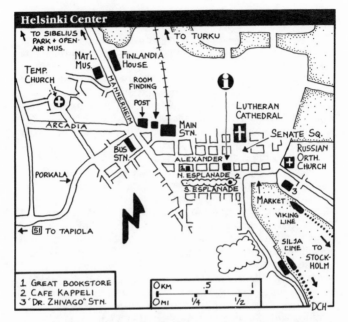

Helsinki Center

TO SIBELIUS PARK + OPEN AIR MUS.

TO TURKU

NAT'L. MUS.

FINLANDIA HOUSE

TEMP. CHURCH

ROOM FINDING

POST

MANNERHEIM

ARCADIA

MAIN STN.

LUTHERAN CATHEDRAL

SENATE SQ.

RUSSIAN ORTH. CHURCH

BUS STN.

ALEXANDER

PORKALA

N. ESPLANADE 2

S. ESPLANADE

MARKET

VIKING LINE

SILJA LINE

TO STOCKHOLM

51 TO TAPIOLA

3

1 GREAT BOOKSTORE
2 CAFE KAPPELI
3 "DR. ZHIVAGO" STN.

0 KM   .5   1
0 MI   ¼   ½

DCH

bana to "Gardet" and walk for about 10 minutes to the terminal. In Helsinki, both lines are perfectly central, just a few minutes' walk from the market, Senate Square and shopping district.

Parking—Both lines offer safe parking. Viking's lot, just behind the terminal in a caged and locked-at-night area, charges only 15 kr per day. (I'd even park it here upon arrival in Stockholm two days before I sail.) The ticket machine takes 10 kr notes and 5 kr coins. Put your money in until you see the date and time of your return on the meter. Then you hit the button and leave your ticket on your dashboard.

Terminal Buildings—These are well organized and functional, with facilities such as cafes, lockers, banks, tourist info desks, reserve-your-boat-meals desks, lounges and phones. Remember, two thousand passengers come and go with each boat. Customs is a snap—I have never shown my passport.

Meals—The cruise is famous for its smorgasbords—and understandably so. Board the ship hungry and prepare for a smorgasm. You'll pay about 80 kr for dinner and 38 kr for breakfast, each a great value for Scandinavia. These meals work out even cheaper with the mini-cruise package. Dinner is self-served at 18:00 and 20:30. The view is great from the table. Make a reservation in the terminal before boarding. Remember to set your watch ahead after leaving Stockholm or you'll eat your breakfast at the dock in Helsinki. Security is lax at breakfast and, if I don't stuff myself, I can rationalize packing a roll and cheese in my zip-lock baggie for lunch in very expensive Helsinki. There are also several classy a la carte restaurants on board.

Day Privileges—If you're spending two nights in a row on the boat you have access to your stateroom all day long. You can sleep in and linger over breakfast if you like long after the boat has docked. But, really, there's way too much to do in Helsinki to take advantage of these privileges (unless you take the $100 round trip passage twice, on four successive nights—a reasonable option given the high cost of hotels and meals on shore and the frustration of trying to see Helsinki in a day).

Free Beds—Those whose bruised and battered pocketbooks can't afford a berth in a stateroom can stake out one of a limited number of open and free bunks or a reclining seat. Board an hour early and ask for advice. If one bunkroom is full there's probably another with more space. Each ship has a safe locked-from-port-to-port luggage area.

Sauna—Each ship has a sauna. This costs about 35 kr extra and you should reserve a time upon boarding. On the Viking line they have a post-sauna weenie roast (or is that redundant?) with a beer—an atmospheric and traditional way to spend the evening with old or new friends (another 35 or 40 kr).

Banking—The change desk on board is actually a better deal than using a Helsinki bank. (There are about four marks in a U.S. dollar.)

Cruise Schedule	
17:00	Check in early. Pick up information about your ship and a Helsinki guide. Reserve dinner, sauna times, book Helsinki tour, change money into Finnmarks, find room, shower, set watch ahead one hour, and explore the boat. Notice the nautical chart on the wall with your circle route marked. (Boarding starts at 16:30).
18:00	Be on deck or near a window to enjoy two hours of incredible island scenery. The archipelago is one of Sweden's great sights.
18:00 or 20:30	Dinner. This is a sightseeing tour for your tongue. Take very small portions of everything in sight. More hot dishes often appear later. Don't miss the delicious dessert berries.
Late	Boogie, disco, waltz, or piano bar.

DAY 9
HELSINKI

The boat is your hotel and you've got all day to see the Neo-classical capital of Finland. Start with the two-and-a-half hour "Hello Helsinki" bus tour that meets the boat at the dock. Before de-boating, ask when is the latest you can board this evening before it sails. You'll have the afternoon to enjoy Helsinki's ruddy harborfront market, count goosebumps in her churches, tour the national museum or the open air folk museum. By dinnertime you'll once again surround yourself with beautiful islands and lots of food. How about dancing and a sauna before crawling into your stateroom?

Suggested Schedule	
9:30	Upon landing, catch the bus tour or take the city intro walk described below.
12:00	Mingle through the market, buy (and eat) a picnic, drop into the tourist office to confirm your plans.
13:00	Browse and people-watch through downtown to the National Museum.
15:00	Tour the National Museum or catch a bus to the Open Air Folk Museum to catching the 3:30 English walking tour.
17:00	Enjoy a cup of coffee in the Cafe Kappeli before boarding time.
17:45	Sail away. Another good dinner smorgasbord.

Helsinki
Helsinki feels close to the Soviet Union. It is. Much of it reminds me of Leningrad. It's no wonder Hollywood chose to film *Dr. Zhivago*, *Reds* and *Gorky Park* here. There is a huge and impressive Russian Orthodox church overlooking the harbor, a large Russian community, and several fine Russian restaurants. You'll see the "CCCP" (Soviet) train, which goes twice daily to Leningrad, in the station.

In the early 1800s when the Russians took Finland from Sweden, they moved the capital eastward from Turku, making Helsinki the capital of their "autonomous duchy." I asked a lady in the tourist office if a particular cafe was made for Russian officers. In a rare spasm of candor she said, "All of 19th century Helsinki was made for Russian officers."

Today Helsinki is gray and green. A little windy and cold, it looks like it's stuck somewhere in the north near the Russian border. But it makes the best of its difficult stuation and leaves the visitor impressed and glad he dropped in. It's a brisk walking and colorful shopping town which turns almost every guest into a fan of architecture.

Finland. Its buildings, its design and fashions, and its people, are whole-istic, fitting into their surroundings sensitively and fusing dissimilar elements into a complex but comfortable whole. It's a very intimate and human place.

History: Finland's history as far as the sightseer is concerned is Swedish (before the 1809 Russian takeover, very little remains physically), Russian (1809-1917, when most of Helsinki's great buildings were built), and independent, when Finland's bold trend-setting modern design and architecture blossomed. Since WWII, Finland has teetered between independence and the USSR. She treads very lightly on matters concerning her fragile autonomy and relations with her giant neighbor to the East.

Weather: They say the people of Helsinki spend 9 months in winter and the other 3 months waiting for summer. The weather dictates a brief (June-August) tourist season. February in Finland is not my idea of a good time. It gets so cold that for several months a year Bus #19 extends its route over the frozen bay to a suburban island!

Language: In Helsinki a man told me "Finnish isn't all that difficult. I mail my letters at the 'Posti,' put my money in the 'Pankki,' quench my thirst with a 'drinkki' at the 'baari,' eat a 'banaani' and sleep in a 'hotelli.' When I have a 'problemi,' I call the 'poliisi'." Very well, but after that it gets a bit trikki. Finnish is unrelated to Europe's Romance and Germanic tongues. Its cousins are Estonian and Hungarian—no help at all. Officially, the country is bilingual, with about 7% of Finns speaking Swedish. You'll see street signs etc. in both Finnish and Swedish. The Swedes call Helsinki "Helsingfors," and Turku "Abo." The people who live here call their country Suomi, not Finland. In past years English was rare but now most young people you meet, as well as those in the tourist trade speak English. The only essential word for your quick visit is "Kiitos" (pron: "key toes")—that's "thank you" and locals love to hear it.

Tourist Info
In Helsinki you'll find tourist info offices at the boat terminals, on the market square and next to the train station. They are uniformly friendly, very helpful, well-stocked in brochures, and blond. The best for our purposes is probably the market square office. Pick up the city map, the "Route Map" (public transit), "Helsinki on Foot" (six walking tours), the "Museums" brochure, and the quarterly "Helsinki Guide," with a great

primer for the city's architecture. Ask about the "3T" tourist tram and go over your sightseeing plans to be sure it'll all work today.

Public Transit
With the "route map" and a little mental elbow grease, you've got the city by the tail when you take advantage of the buses and trams. Each ticket costs 5.80 mk, is good for an hour of travel and is purchased from the driver. The "Helsinki Card"—free entry to city sights and use of all buses and trams all day for 55 mk—isn't worthwhile for our plans. It expires each midnight, not after 24 hours. Be sure to take advantage of the tourist tram, 3T, and its commentary.

Sightseeing Highlights
▲▲▲The Downtown Helsinki Walk—Harbor to Train Station—The colorful and compact city center is a great area to roam. Here are a few ideas on the area:

The Market Square, each day from 8:00 to 14:00 is a colorful outdoor market at the head of the harbor where your ship docked. Don't miss the busy two tone red brick indoor market adjacent. Across the street you'll see the City Tourist Office. Drop in to check out the huge aerial photo of downtown and ask questions.

One block inland behind the Tourist Office are the fine Neoclassical Senate Square and the Lutheran Cathedral. You'll pass the Schroder Sport Shop on Unioninkatu with a great selection of popular Finnish-made Rapula fishing lures—ideal for the fisherman on your gift list. Next to the Tourist Office step into the delightfully art nouveau "Jugendsalen," a free and pleasant info center for locals which offers interesting historical exhibits and a public w.c. The art deco interior is a knockout. (Open Mon-Fri 9:00-18:00, Sun 12:00-18:00, closed Sat, Pohjoisesplanadi 19.)

Across the street in the park facing the square is my favorite cafe in northern Europe, the Cafe Kappeli. When you've got some time, dip into this turn-of-the-century gazebo-like oasis of coffee, pastry, and relaxation. Built in the 19th century, it was a popular hangout for local intellectuals and artists. Today it offers the romantic tourist waiting for his ship to sail a great 6 mk cup of coffee memory.

Behind the cafe runs the park sandwiched between the north and south Esplanade—Helsinki's top shopping boulevard. Walk it. The north, tourist office side is most interesting for window shopping and people-watching. You'll pass the Marimekko store, the huge Academic Bookstore, designed by Alvar Aalto, nearby at 1 Keskuskatu, which has a great map and travel guide section (if we all request this book—maybe they'll stock it). Finally you'll come to the prestigeous Stockman's Department store—Finland's Harrods. This best, oldest and most expensive store in town has fine displays of local design. Just beyond is the main intersection in town, Esplanade and Mannerheimintie. Nearby you'll see the famous "Four Smiths" statue. (They say, "If a virgin walks by they'll strike the anvil." It doesn't work . . . I tried.)

A block to the right through a busy shopping center is the brutal but serene architecture of the central train station, designed by Saarinen in 1916. Wander around inside. Continuing past the "Hotelli keskus" room finding office and the "Posti," past the statue, return to Mannerheimintie which leads to the large white Finlandia Hall, another Aalto masterpiece. Normally it's not open, but ask at the T.I. about tours. Across the street is the excellent little Finnish National Museum (designed by Finland's first three great architects), and a few blocks behind that is the sit-down-and-wipe-a-tear beautiful rock church Temppeliaukio. Sit, enjoy the music. It's a wonderful place to end this Welcome to Helsinki walk.

From nearby Arkadiankatu Street, Bus #24 will take you to the Sibelius monument in a lovely park. The same ticket is good on a later #24. Ride to the end of the line—the bridge to the Seurasaari island and Finland's Open Air Folk Museum. From here, ride Bus #24 back to the Esplanade.

▲▲**Orientation Tour**—A fast and very good 2 ½ hour intro tour leaves daily from both terminals immediately after the ships dock. The rapid-fire three-language tour costs 75 mk and gives a good historic overview, a look at all the important buildings from Olympic Stadium to embassies with too-fast ten minute stops at the Lutheran Cathedral, the Church in the Rock (Temppeliaukio) and Sibelius Monument. It also swings through the planned "garden city" of Tapiola. You'll learn strange facts like how they took down the highest steeple in town during WWII so the Soviets in Estonia, just 55 miles over the water, couldn't see their target. You'll also see where they filmed the Moscow Railway Station scenes in *Dr Zhivago* (the low red brick building near the Viking Terminal). If you're on a tight budget, aren't interested in a look at Tapiola and don't care to get the general feel for Helsinki, you can do the essence of this tour on your own as explained in my city walk (above). But I thoroughly enjoyed listening to the guide—he sounded like an audio shredder which was occasionally turned off so English could come out. They'll return you downtown or to your hotel by noon. The same tour also leaves from downtown at 10:00 and 11:00, but I like the "pick you up at the boat and drop you at your hotel or back on the market square" efficiency of the

9:30 tour. Buy your ticket on board or at the tourist desk in the terminal.

▲▲Lutheran Cathedral—The dominant green dome overlooking the city and harbor, this is the masterpiece of Carl Ludwig Engel. Open the pew gate and sit savoring this Neo-Classical Nirvana. The interior is pure architectural truth. Open 9:00-19:00 daily, until 17:00 in winter. From the top of the steps, study Europe's finest Neo-Classical square. The Senate building is on your left. The small blue stone building with the slanted Mansart roof in the far left corner is from 1757, one of just two pre-Russian conquest buildings remaining in Helsinki. On the right is the University building. Czar Alexander II, a friend of Finland's, is honored by the statue in the square.

▲▲▲Temppeliaukio Church—Another great piece of church architecture, this was blasted out of solid rock and capped with a copper and skylight dome. It's normally filled with recorded music and awestruck visitors. I almost cried. Another form of simple truth, it's impossible to describe. Gawk upward at a 14-mile-long coil of copper wire. Open Mon-Sat 10:00-20:00, Sunday 12:00-14:00 and 17:00-20:00. Lutheran English service on Sundays at 15:00, 14:00 in the off season. You can buy the slides or the picture book.

▲Sibelius Monument—Hundreds of stainless steel pipes shimmer over a rock in a park to honor Finland's greatest composer. Bus #24 stops here (or look quickly from the bus) on its way to the Open Air Folk Museum.

Huvilak—This is the best Art Nouveau street in one of Europe's best towns for this organic, curvey, turn-of-the-century answer to Industrial Eiffel Tower-type art.

▲Seurasaari Open Air Folk Museum—Inspired by Stockholm's Skansen, also on a lovely island on the edge of town, this is a collection of 100 historic buildings gathered from every corner of Finland. It's wonderfully furnished and gives us rushed visitors a great opportunity to sample the far reaches of Finland without even leaving the capital city. In June, July and August there are free English tours at 11:30 and 15:30 except Wednesday, otherwise buy the 10 mk guidebook. Off season it's quiet, just you, log cabins and birch trees, and almost not worth a look. 5 mk entry, open daily 11:30-17:30 in June, July and August; 9:30-15:00 Mon-Fri, 11:30-17:00 Saturday and Sunday in May and September. Ride Bus #24 to the end of the line and walk across quaint footbridge. The boat from downtown is overpriced. Check at the T.I. for tour and evening folk dance schedules (tel. 484712).

▲▲National Museum—A pleasant, easy to handle collection covering Finland's story from A-Z with good English descriptions in a grand building designed by three of Finland's greatest early architects. I enjoyed the Neo-Classical furniture, portraits of Russia's last czars around an impressive throne, the folk costumes and the very well done Finno-Ugric exhibit downstairs (with a 20-page English guide to help explain the Finns, Estonians, Lapps, Hungarians and their more obscure Finno-Ugric cousins). Open 11:00-16:00 and 18:00-21:00 Thursdays, across the street from the Finlandia Hall.

Tapiola—This futuristic planned community created a real stir in the '50s. It mixes residential and business districts with nature, keeping the pedestrian world unstressed by mindless motor traffic. Getting well-worn and almost outgrowing its cuteness, it's still interesting. The city tour gives it a quick drive-through. Frequent buses, 9 mk, 15 minutes, a few miles out of town.

Accommodations

Helsinki is very expensive. The standard budget hotel double costs close to $100. But there are so many special deals on dorm and hostel alternatives that you'll manage easily. You have four basic options—cheap youth hostels, student dorms turned "summer hotels," expensive business class hotels at a special summer or weekend clearance sale rate, or just spend a wad and have fun.

Summer is "off season" in Helsinki, as are weekends (Friday, Saturday or Sunday). You can safely arrive in the morning and expect to find a budget room. Next to the train station (a pleas-ant 15 minute walk from your boat, or Tram #3B from Silja, Bus #13 from Viking) is the "Hotellcentralen" room finding service (Hotellikeskus). Open May to mid-September 9:00-21:00 (Satur-day until 19:00, Sunday until 18:00; off season, 10:00-18:00 Mon-Fri only. For 10 mk they'll book you a room in the price range of your choice. They know what wild bargains are available on this first day of the rest of your tour. Consider a lux-ury hotel clearance deal, which may cost $20 more than the cheapies. Ask about any Helsinki card "specials," which lowers prices from mid-June to early September and on Friday, Satur-day, and Sunday. Their 10 mk fee is reasonable, but they're happy to do the job over the phone for free. Call up from the harbor. Tel. 90/171133.

Hostels: Nuorisotoimiston Retkeilymaja (or NAK)— Cozy, cheery, central, well run and very cheap. Kitchen facilities, small (only 30 beds). 30 mk for dorm bed (boys), or bed in 5-bed rooms (girls). Closed 11:00-15:00. Open only June-August. Porthaniankatu 2. Tel. 70992590. From Market Square take Tram #1 or #2 to Hakaniemi Square Market.

Olympic Stadium Hostel (Stadionin Retkeilymaja)—Big, crowded, impersonal, last resort bed. 27mk, or 37mk with no YH card. Open all year. Tel. 496071. Take Tram #3T or #7B to the Olympic Stadium.

Summer Hotels: These are central, modern, college dorms put to good use as tourist hotels during the school holidays (June, July, Aug). These offer the cheapest doubles in town, including breakfast, with saunas and budget cafeterias.
Academica Hotel—216 doubles, private showers and toilets, 275 mk per double. They also have a hostel section with 100 mk doubles or triples. 14 Hietaniemenkatu. Tel. 440171. Bus #18 or Tram #3T. **Satakuntatalo Summerhotel.** 210mk/double. Lapinrinne 2A. Tel. 6940311.

Classy "Real" Hotels: Hotel Anna—Plush, very central (near Mannerheimintie and Esplanadi), 15 minute walk from boat. One of the best values in town with doubles, including breakfast, ranging from 260 to 420 mk depending on your luck. 1 Annankatu. Tel. 648011. **Hotel Klaus Kurki**—Classy, splurge-worthy pick of the town. Very central. Normal price is sky high but summer rates are as low as 320 mk per double. At 2 Bulevardi. Tel 602-322. **Hotel Olympia**—Not so central but on the T3 tram line, this is often about the least expensive hotel in town. At 2 Lantinen Brahenkatu. Tel. 750801.

Eating in Helsinki

Dining here is—you guessed it—expensive. But a good choice is worth the splurge. Most interesting is probably Russian food. While most places are very expensive, the **Kazbek Restaurant** in the Olympia Hotel serves great three-course Georgian meals for around 70mk. The **Troikka** serves good Russian food in a tsarific setting. Caloniukesenkatu 3, tel. 445229 for reservations.

The Palace Cafe overlooking the harbor and market square above the Palace Hotel is a good and not too exhorbitant place for lunch. For a meal with folk music ask at the tourist office about the dinner show at the **Seurasaari** Open Air Folk Museum.

The best food values are, of course, the department store cafeterias and a picnic assembled from the colorful stalls on the harbor. Don't miss the red brick indoor market on the edge of the square. At the harbor you'll also find several local fast food stalls and delicious fresh fish (cooked if you like), explosive little red berries, and sweet carrots. While the open air market is most fun, produce is cheaper in large grocery stores.

In the train station you'll find the **Eliel** self-service restaurant and a 25-35 mk mid-day special.

An Extra Day—Turku and Nantali

It's tempting to spend a second day in Finland. Turku, the

historic old capital of Finland, is just a 2 ½ hour train ride from
Helsinki (six times a day 55 mk, 12:42 departure works best,
free with Eurail or save 50% by getting RR connection with
boat ticket). The medieval town of Naantali is an easy bus ride
(30 minutes, 8 mk, 4 per hour) from Turku. Viking and Silja
boats sail each evening from Turku to Stockholm at 21:30 (and
the fare from here saves you enough money to pay for the extra
train ride).

Turku has a handicraft museum in a cluster of wooden houses
(the only part of town that survived a devastating fire in the
early 1800s), an impressive old cathedral and a busy market
square.

Nearby Naantali is a well preserved old wooden town with a
quaint harbor. These towns get good publicity, but I found the
sidetrip a little disappointing. The train ride is nothing special,
Turku (because of its fire) is a pale shadow of Helsinki, and
Naantali is cute, commercial, and offers little if you've seen or
will see Sigtuna near Stockholm.

DAY 10
UPPSALA TO OSLO

In some ways, Uppsala is more historic than Stockholm. Its cathedral and university win many "oldest, largest, tallest"-type awards, and the compact and bustling little city makes for a fine morning stop before the long drive across the green and wide open, but rather dull, spaces of Sweden to Oslo.

Suggested Schedule	
9:30	Dock in Stockholm, pick up your car and drive to Uppsala.
10:30	Sightsee in Uppsala, enjoying the river-straddling old town, the historic cathedral and the university flavor.
12:30	Picnic in the car as you drive, high-tailing it west to Oslo.
20:00	Arrive and set up in Oslo.

Transportation
From downtown Stockholm, signs direct you clearly to the E-4 highway and Uppsala, 40 miles to the north. Park as close to the twin cathedral spires as you can.

From Uppsala to Oslo it's about 325 miles of mostly clear freeway motoring. Leaving Uppsala follow signs for Route 55 and Norrkoping. When you hit E-18, just follow the Oslo signs past forests, lakes and prettily painted wooden houses. It's very pleasant but I'd stop only for gas. There are no border formalities unless you've got a tax refund to process for something you bought duty-free in Sweden. The ride from the border to Oslo is particularly scenic. The freeway butts you right up against downtown Oslo. Just follow the signs to "Sentrum," then "Sentral Stasjon" and "P-hus." The T.I. and room-finding service is in the station. There's short-term parking, but you may want to deep-store your car in the safe and most central garage. Look for the big blue "P" sign with a roof over it, 6 kr per hour, 66 kr per day.

Uppsala
Historic Uppsala's sights, along with its 40,000 students, cluster around the university and cathedral. Just over the river is the bustling shopping center and pedestrian zone. Its helpful tourist office has a branch in the cathedral, open May 23 to August 31, 9:00-17:00, Sunday 12:30-17:00. Off season use the

main office across the river near Stora Torget, tel. 018/117500.
Pick up their entertaining, helpful and free Uppsala guide. The
free and cute little Uppland Museum is on the river by the
waterfall. Nearby is the Carl Linnaeus Garden and Museum and
its mediocre 16th century castle on the hilltop overlooking the
town.

Sightseeing Highlights
▲▲**Uppsala Cathedral**—One of Scandinavia's largest and
most historic cathedrals has a breathtaking interior, the tomb of
King Gustavus Vasa and twin 400-foot spires. Excellent tours
leave several times daily (in English at 13:00 and 15:00 in 1987)
in summer. Otherwise, push the English button, sit down and
listen to the tape recorded introduction in the narthex opposite
the tourist info table.

The University—Scandinavia's first university was founded
here in 1477. Carl von Linnaeus and Anders Celsius are two
famous grads. Several of the old buildings are open to guests. A
very historic but not much to see, old silver-bound Gothic Bi-
ble is on display with many other rare medieval books in the
Carolina Rediviva (library). The anatomy theater in the Gusta-
vianum is thought-provoking. This strange theater's only show
was a human dissection.

Gamla Uppsala—Old Uppsala is rooted deeply in history but
now almost entirely lost in the sod of centuries. You'll see
several grass-covered ancient mounds marking the prehistoric
center of Sweden, the historic (but rebuilt) church and a colorful and touristy pub that serves mead—an "ancient" 14th century recipe for honey-and-hops wine—out of silver plated old
horns. A 21 kr horn serves a small group—it's fun if you like
history and mead like I do. Look at the postcards of Gamla Uppsala's grassy mounds from downtown—that's all you'll see if
you go out there. Easy by car, not worth the headache by bus
(#24 from station to the end of the line).

Lunch in Uppsala?—Browse through the lively Saluhallen,
the riverside indoor market in the shadow of the cathedral.
You'll find great picnic stuff and pleasant cafes. This entire
university district abounds with inexpensive eateries.

▲**Sigtuna**—Possibly Sweden's cutest town, but Sigtuna is
basically fluff. You'll see a medieval lane lined with colorful
wooden tourist shops, very pleasant tourist office with reading
room, cafe, romantic park, promenade along the lake, an old
church and some rune stones. The harborside cafe sells
delicious waffles with whipped cream and strawberries. (Just
one hour from Stockholm by train to Marsta and then bus to
Sigtuna. Buses leave Sigtuna for Uppsala at Mon-Fri 12:20 and

15:55. By car, leave Stockholm on the E-4 to Uppsala and take the clearly marked Sigtuna exit).

Sleeping in Sweden—The town of Arjang, just before the Norwegian border, is a good place to stop if you don't make it to Oslo. The main drag leads from the freeway through the center of town (hotels), past Mrs. Hyrcenter's B&B (look for the "Rum" sign on her lawn at the far end of town at 27 Storgatan. She speaks little English, but offers spacious, easy and quiet quiet doubles with kitchen for 140 kr; tel. 0573/11901) and on to the huge local campground (Sommarvik Fritidscenter, huts and good facilities, tel. 0573/12060). It would be a shame to do the scenic drive from Arjang to Oslo in the dark.

Oslo

Situated at the head of the 60 mile long Oslo fjord, surrounded by forests, and 500,000 people small, Oslo's charm doesn't stop there. Norway's largest city, capital, and cultural hub is a smorgasbord of historic sights, art and Nordic fun.

The city is easy to manage with nearly all its sights clustered around the central "barbell" (Karl Johan Street with the Royal Palace on one end and the new train station on the other), or in the Bygdoy Park, a ten-minute ferry ride across the harbor.

Oslo lacks the coziness of Copenhagen and the monumental grandeur of Stockholm. But it offers an exciting two day slate of sightseeing thrills, and it's well-organized with a very energetic tourist office. Even though it's very expensive, the organized visitor will leave feeling very good about the time and money he spent here.

Tourist Office

Oslo has two very helpful tourist offices—one in the city hall (Mon-Sat 8:00-19:00, Sunday 9:00-17:00, tel. 427170) and one in the central station (daily 7:00-23:00, tel. 416221). Be sure to pick up the free city map, guide, the Sporveiskart transit map, and "This Week in Oslo" publication (for museum hours and special events). They sell a 24 hour transit pass (30 kr) and the Oslo card (24 hours—70 kr, 48 hours—100 kr or 72 hours—130 kr) which gives you free use of all city public transit, entry to all sights, 50% off on city bus tours, many more discounts, and a handy handbook.

You'll have many occasions to use the buses and trains. Get and use the "Sporveiskart" transit map. Tickets cost 10 kr, mini-card gives you 4 trips at a discount—available as you board. Info tel. 417030.

Accommodations

Oslo is very expensive and, unlike its sister Scandinavian

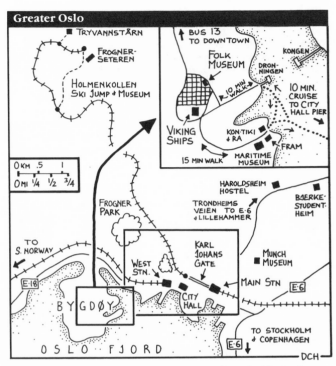

capitals, its hostels are few and fill up quickly. The T.I. in the
Central Station has a very hard-working room-finding service
(Innkvartering) that can set you up in a private home (200 kr per
double, at least two nights, not central) or sort through all the
confusing hotel "specials" and get you about the best bed
possible for your budget. July and early August are easy, but
early June and September can be tight. October-April is very
slow. The Innkvartering people are your advocates. They are
notified each afternoon which hotels have dropped their prices
to fill up, and they can find deals you'd never get on your own.
Always be clear about what you want (e.g., central, without
shower, cheapest possible).

Hotels
Each of these places is within a two minute walk of the station
in a neighborhood your mom probably wouldn't want you
hanging around in at night. The hotels themselves, however, are
secure and comfortable. The only really safe place to park your
car in this station area is in the park house (P-hus), handy but
not cheap—66 kr per 24 hours.

City Hotel—This clean, basic, very homey place originated 100 years ago as a cheap place for Norwegians to sleep while they waited to sail to their new homes in America. Well-run by the Salvation Army, its alcohol-free status earns it a special tax exemption that means cheaper rooms for us. Wonderful lounge, breakfast included. Doubles—360-450 kr, Singles 250-300. This is the best of Oslo's cheap hotels. Skippergatan 19, tel. 413610.

Hotel Fonix—Another basic, clean, breakfast-included place, it lacks the City Hotel's comfyness but is a good value in Oslo. Doubles 370-480 kr depending on plumbing, a few small singles for 175 kr. Dronningensgt 19, tel. 425957.

Sjomannshjem—This "retired seaman's hotel" is one of Oslo's great bargains. Plain, clean, no-nonsense doubles for only 230 kr, singles 170 kr. Big breakfast 30 kr extra. Some rooms include a shower. Tollbugt 4, tel. 412005.

Pensions and Hospits

Unfortunately, Oslo's many fine pensions, which used to provide a great alternative to costly hotels, are mostly taken over by the small flood of illegal immigrants who sneak into Norway from the Third World via East Berlin and Sweden, which has no border formalities with Norway. The government keeps these new arrivals off the streets by housing them in this long-term temporary manner. Here are three decent places that still accept tourists.

Ellingsen's Pensjonat—Run by a friendly lady whose name is actually Mrs. Viking, this is a very pleasant place with fluffy down comforters and a great location four blocks behind the Royal Palace. She has 18 singles (130 kr) but only 3 doubles (230 kr). Call well in advance for doubles. Holtegt 25, tel. 600359. On the corner of Uranienborg veien and Holtegatan, Train #1 from the station.

Cochs Pensjonat—Plain rooms, stale wet-noodle atmosphere but right behind the palace (Train #11 to Parkveieu 25, tel. 604836) and **Lindes Pensionat** (near Frogner park, Train #2 to 41 Thomas Heftyes Gate, tel. 553282) are nothing special but have doubles for around 250 kr.

The Secret Stateroom: The **MS Hakon Jarl Hotel**, a refurbished steamer, retired after 30 years on the coastal run up to Nordkapp, is now permanently moored as central as you can be in Oslo—directly in front of the City Hall. All its doubles cost 600 kr except for one—the "Writers Room"—which does not have a sink or shower (use the one two flights up) and rents for 300 kr including a lavish breakfast. Hotel guests get free and safe parking right on the dock. This budget anomaly isn't advertised in the tourist office and if you call ahead, they'll happily hold your stateroom. Radhusbrygge 3, 0160 Oslo, tel. 424345.

St. Katarinahjemmet—Dominican sisters run this summer guesthouse. It's very clean, modern and comfortable with doubles for 250 kr. Open for men and women from mid-June through early September. Train #1 or #11 to Valkyrie Plass or Vibesgate, Majorstuveien 21B, tel. 601370.

Haraldsheim Youth Hostel—Oslo's huge, modern, well-run hostel is open all year, situated far from the center on a hill with a grand view. Its 300 beds (6 to a room) are often completely booked. About 100 kr, including breakfast. 4 Heraldsheimveien, Tram #1 or #7 from station to Sinsen, tel. 155043.

Bjerke Studentheim—This high rise university dorm offers 70 kr beds in modern doubles and triples from mid-June to mid-August (may close in '88). Bus #30 or #31 to Bjerkebanen, Trondheimsveien 271, tel. 648787.

Eating in Oslo

I lose much of my appetite when a simple open face sandwich (which looks and tastes like half of something I can make, with an inedible garnish added) costs $5 and a beer is nearly as much. Nevertheless, one can't continue to sightsee on post cards and train tickets alone.

My strategy is to splurge for a hotel that includes breakfast. A Norwegian breakfast is fit for a Viking. Picnic for lunch—There are plenty of grocery stores (**Rimi** just off the harbor between the city hall and the castle has great prices), and picturesque spots to give your feast some atmosphere. I eat dinner at a cafeteria (cheapest places close at 18:00) or at a place with a salad bar. Pizzerias and salad bars are the new trend—you'll find them near any hotel—ask your receptionist for advice. Many pizzerias have all-you-can-eat specials. Try **Den Roede Moelle** at #9 Brugata.

The Aker Brygge development has some cheery cafes, restaurants and markets. **Smor Petersen** is a classy deli with seafood and fixings for a first class picnic. Aker Brygge also has a late hours grocery store (open till 22:00, 20:00 on Saturday, 19:00 on Sunday).

Oslo has several Kaffistova cafeterias. They are alcohol-free, clean (check out the revolving toilet seats) and serve simple, hearty and typically Norwegian (read "bland") meals for the best price around. My favorite, at 8 Rosenkrantzgate, gives you your choice of an entree and all the salad, cooked vegetables and "flat bread" you want (or at least need) for 35-55 kr at lunch (11:00-14:00) and 60-85 kr at dinner. It's open from 11:00-22:00 (19:00 Saturday and 20:00 Sunday) in summer and 11:00-20:00 (18:00 on Saturday and Sunday) in off season. The **Torgstova Kaffistova** at 13 Karl Johans Gate closes at 18:00.

Other cafeterias are found in department stores. The **Norrona Cafeteria**, also central at 19 Grenson, is another budget-saver that closes at 18:00.

Of course, there are plenty of wonderful and atmospheric ways to dine in Oslo—but not for under $20. For classy splurges (about $25 a meal) that work well into our sightseeing plans consider these two restaurants:

At Bygdoy, in the Maritime Museum, next to the *Fram*, is the very popular **Najaden Restaurant** (tel. 438180). Each evening from 17:00 to 21:00 for about 200 kr they serve a huge and impressive seafood buffet. You'll fill your plate as many times as you like from over 30 different dishes. Lunch buffets are less expensive.

At Holmenkollen Ski Jump, **The Frognerseteren Hovedrestaurant** (tel. 143736) is a traditional old lavishly-decorated Norwegian lodge perched high above Oslo. The house specialties are game—reindeer, elk, chuckers, pheasant, and fallen ski-jumpers. You'll find it under the big flagpoles, about 500 yards from the Forgnersteteren train stop or a short hike up from the ski jump. Its self-service cafeteria on the terrace offers a staggering view with less staggering prices.

DAYS 11 & 12
OSLO

Sights of the Viking spirit—past and present—tell a thrilling story. Day 11 includes looks at the remains of ancient Viking ships, and more peaceful but equally gutsy modern boats like the *Kon Tiki*, *Ra* and *Fram*. Then you'll hear stirring stories of the local WWII Nazi resistance and trace the country's folk culture at the Norwegian Open Air Folk Museum.

Oslo is the smallest and probably least earth-shaking of the Nordic capitals. But brisk and almost brittle little Oslo offers

Suggested Schedule

Day 11

9:00	Visit the T.I. to confirm sightseeing plans, pick up maps and other info.
10:00	Tour Nazi Resistance Museum at Akershus Castle.
11:00	Guided tour of Akershus Castle. Explore ramparts and harbor view.
12:00	Buy picnic (Rimi grocery store two blocks west of city hall, shrimp from boats at harbor), catch ferry to Bygdoy and eat with a city harbor view on the waterfront near the museums.
13:30	Tour Fram and Kon Tiki Museums. Walk to Viking ships (15 minutes).
15:30	Tour Viking Ships Museum.
16:00	Tour Open Air Folk Museum (ask about any crafts demonstrations or folk music scheduled). Bus #30 or boat home. (Or dinner in the popular old restaurant above the stave church).

Day 12

10:00	City Hall Tour.
11:00	Free time to browse and stroll in city center, Aker Brygge (new "Festival Market" mall on the harbor) and walk Karl Johans Gate from palace to station.
16:00	Visit Vigeland Park, then see Vigeland Museum.
18:00	Subway to Holmenkollen, climb the ski jump for city view, tour ski museum. Hike up to traditional Norsk dinner and a great sunset at Frognerseteren Hovedrestaurant, or return downtown for cheap Koffistova dinner.

many more sightseeing thrills than you would expect. On Day 12, you'll get a feel for the modern town as you browse through the new yuppie-style harbor shopping complex, tour Oslo's avante garde city hall, get a good dose of Gustav Vigeland's sculpture and ride the scenic commuter train to the towering Holmenkollen ski jump and ski museum.

Sightseeing Highlights

▲▲▲**Bygdoy**—This is an exciting cluster of sights on a pleasant peninsula just across the harbor from downtown. The museums listed below are reached by Bus #30 from the National Theater or by a special little ferry that leaves at least twice an hour from in front of the city hall (Museums are at the second stop). In the summer a shuttle bus connects these sights. Otherwise, all four listed below are within a 15-minute walk of each other.

▲▲**Norwegian Folk Museum**—170 buildings brought from all corners of Norway are reassembled on these 35 acres. You'll find crafts people doing their traditional things, security guards disguised in cute, colorful, traditional local costumes, endless creative ways to make do in a primitive log-cabin-and-goats-on-the-roof age, a 12th century stave church, as well as a museum filled with toys, musical instruments and fine folk costumes. The place hops in the summer but is quite dead off season. Unfortunately, there aren't daily guided walks so it's just you, the 15 kr guidebook and guards who look like Rebecca Boone's Norwegian pen pals. Open May 15-August 31 daily from 10:00 to 18:00, off season—11:00-16:00, Sundays it opens an hour late. 15 kr. Ask about the folk dance performances, usually at 16:00 on Tuesday and Thursday in summer.

▲▲**Viking Ships**—Three great 9th century Viking ships and plenty of artifacts from the days of rape, pillage, and—ya sure betcha—plunder. Don't miss the old cloth and embroidery in the dark room you turn on by simply stepping into. There are no museum tours but it's hard not to hear the bus tour guides explaining things to their English-speaking groups. There was a time when much of a frightened Europe closed every prayer with "and deliver us from the Vikings, Amen." Gazing up at the prow of one of these sleek time-stained vessels, you can almost hear the screams and smell the armpits of those redheads on the rampage. 10:00-18:00 daily in summer, 11:00-16:00 or 15:00 in the off season.

▲▲**The Fram**—This great ship took modern day Vikings Amundsen and Nansen deep into the Arctic and Antarctic, further north and south than any ship before. For three years the *Fram* was part of an arctic ice drift. The exhibit is fascinating.

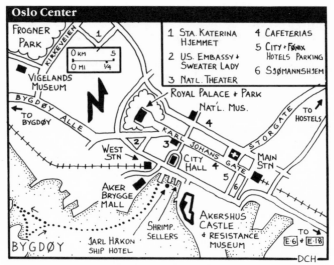

Oslo Center

FROGNER PARK
1
VIGELANDS MUSEUM
TO BYGDØY
BYGDØY ALLE
WEST STN
AKER BRYGGE MALL
JARL HÅKON SHIP HOTEL
BYGDØY
SHRIMP SELLERS
ROYAL PALACE + PARK
NAT'L. MUS.
CITY HALL
AKERSHUS CASTLE + RESISTANCE MUSEUM
MAIN STN
TO HOSTELS
TO E-6 + E-18
DCH

1 STA. KATERINA HJEMMET
2 US. EMBASSY + SWEATER LADY
3 NATL. THEATER
4 CAFETERIAS
5 CITY + FØNIX HOTELS PARKING
6 SJØMANNSHJEM

Read the ground floor displays, then explore the boat,
10:00-17:45 daily in summer, 11:00-16:45 daily off season. 7 kr.
▲The Kon Tiki Museum—Next to the *Fram* are the *Kon Tiki*
and the *Ra II*, the boats Thor Heyerdahl built and sailed, 4000
and 3000 miles respectively, to prove early South Americans
could have sailed to Polynesia and Africans could have populated
Barbados. 10:00-18:00 daily, 10:30-17:00 off season. 10 kr.
▲Norwegian Maritime Museum—Next to the *Fram*, the
museum provides a fine look at the maritime heritage of this
very seafaring land. If you're at all salty, don't miss this. Daily
10:00-20:00, off season 10:30-16:00. 7 kr.

Downtown Sights
▲▲City Hall—Oslo's richly decorated "Radhuset" was built in
1950 to celebrate her 950th birthday. Norway's leading artists all
contributed to what was an avant garde thrill in its day. The interior's 2000 square yards of bold and colorful murals take you
on a voyage through the collective psyche of Norway, from its
simple rural beginnings through the scar tissue of the Nazi occupation and beyond. Guided tours, given free at 10:00, 12:00
and 14:00 in the summer, make the place meaningful. Entry on
the Karl Johan side (the tourist office is on the harbor side).
Open Mon-Sat 10:00-15:00, Sunday 12:00-15:00, free.
▲Akershus Castle—One of the oldest buildings in town, this
castle overlooking Oslo's harbor is mediocre by European
standards but worth a look. Its grounds make a pleasant park
with grassy ramparts, pigeon-roost cannons and great city

views. Tours of the interior (free, daily in summer at 11:00, 13:00 and 15:00, 50 min. long) are interesting. Without a tour, you can read the English info sheets in each room. Open daily 10:00-16:00, Sunday 12:30-16:00, May to mid-September, Sundays only in the off season, 5 kr.

▲▲**Norwegian Resistance Museum**—A stirring story about the Nazi invasion and occupation is told with wonderful English descriptions. This is the best look in Europe at how national spirit can endure total occupation by a foreign power. Located in the Akershus Castle. Open daily in summer, 10:00-16:00, Sun 11:00-16:00, closing one hour earlier in the off season. 10 kr.

▲**National Gallery**—Located right downtown (13 Universitets Gata), this easy-to-handle museum is nothing earth-shaking, but if you're into art it's worth a look for its Impressionist collection, its Romantic Norwegian art, and a roomful of Munch paintings. Open Mon-Fri 10:00-16:00, Saturday 10:00-15:00, Sunday 12:00-15:00, and Wed-Thur evenings 18:00-20:00. Free.

▲▲**Browsing**—Oslo's pulse is best felt along the central Karl Johans Gate (from station to palace) and in the trendy new harborside Aker Brygge Festival Market Mall (a glass-and-chrome collection of sharp cafes and polished produce stalls just past the west station).

▲▲▲**Vigeland Sculptures** in **Frogner Park** and the **Vigeland Museum**—The 75-acre park contains a lifetime of work by Norway's greatest sculptor, Gustav Vigeland. 175 bronze and granite statues—all nude and each one unique—surround the 60-foot-high tangled tower of 121 bodies called "the monolith of life." The small blue "Guide to the Vigeland Park" booklet is worthwhile. The park is more than great art. It's a city at play. Enjoy its urban Norwegian ambience. Then visit the wonderful Vigeland Museum to see the models for the statues and much more in the artist's studio. Don't miss the photos on the wall showing the construction of the monolith. The museum is open daily 12:00-19:00, closed Monday. The park is always open. Both are free. Take Train #2 or Bus #72, #73 or #20 to Frogner Plass.

▲▲**Edvard Munch Museum**—The only Norwegian painter to have a serious impact on European art, Munch is a surprise to many who visit this fine museum, where his emotional, disturbing, and powerfully expressionist art is arranged chronologically: paintings, drawings, lithographs and photographs by a strange and perplexing man. Don't miss "The Scream," which captures the fright many feel as the human "race" does just that. Tues-Sat 10:00-20:00, Sunday 12:00-20:00, closed Monday. 10 kr.

▲▲**Holmenkollen Ski Jump and Ski Museum**—Just out of town is a tremendous ski jump with a unique museum of skiing. A pleasant subway ride (to Holmenkollen) gets you out of the city and into the hills and forests that surround Oslo. Ride the elevator and climb the stairway to the thrilling top of the jump for the best possible view of Oslo—and a chance to stand looking down the long and frightening ramp that has sent so many tumbling into the agony of defeat. The ski museum is a must for skiers—tracing the evolution of the sport from 4000-year-old rock paintings to crude 1500-year-old skis to the slick and quickly evolving skis of our century. The ski jump and museum are open daily from 9:00 or 10:00 to 17:00, 19:00 or 22:00 depending on the month. 12 kr.

A 45-minute hike or a few more stops to the end of the subway line is the "Tryvannstarnet" observatory tower, offering a lofty 360-degree view with Oslo in the distance, the fjord and endless forests, lakes and soft hills. It's impressive, but not necessary if you climbed the ski jump, which shows you Oslo much better.

Evenings—They used to tell people who asked about nightlife in Oslo that Copenhagen was only an hour away by airplane. Now Oslo has sprouted a nightlife of its own. The scene is always changing. The tourist office has info on Oslo's many cafes, discos and jazz clubs.

Shopping—For good values in sweaters and other Norwegian crafts, shop at **Husfliden** (Den Norske Husflidsforening, 4 Mollergate behind the cathedral, daily 9:00-17:00, Saturday until 14:00), the retail center for the Norwegian Association of Home Arts and Crafts. If you like to "buy direct" and "patronize the little person" do your sweater shopping at **The Sweater Lady's**. Mrs. Lulle Otterstad runs a little shop with top quality handknit sweaters for about 100 kr less than the bigger stores. She's near the US Embassy at Solligt 2, tel. 554709. A good handknit sweater costs about 650 kr. Shops are generally open from 9:00 to 17:00 (or 16:00 in summer). Many close early on Saturday and completely on Sunday.

DAY 13

LILLEHAMMER AND GUDBRANDSDALEN, NORWAY'S HEARTLAND

Leaving Oslo, drive north, stopping for a look at the Norwegian Philadelphia, Eidsvoll, where Norway's constitution was hammered out and signed. Then, after a picnic and tour through Norway's best folk museum at Maihaugen near Lillehammer, drive up the romantic Gudbrandsdal Valley—Peer Gynt country. Your destination is the ancient log and sod farmstead turned hotel called Roisheim.

Suggested Schedule	
9:00	Drive out of Oslo to Eidsvoll.
10:00	Tour museum at Eidsvoll, then drive along Norway's largest lake.
12:00	Picnic at Maihaugen.
13:00	Walking tour through the traditional buildings and homes of this part of Norway.
15:30	Drive into scenic Gudbrandsdal Valley.
19:00	Check into hotel.

Transportation
Leave Oslo following signs for "E6, Hamar, and Trondheim." In a few minutes you're in the wide open pastoral countryside of Eastern Norway. Norway's Constitution Hall is actually a little south of Eidsvoll in Eidsvoll Verk. You'll see a sign for "Eidsvoll Bygningen" and a large parking lot on the right side of E-6 three miles south of Eidsvoll town. Then E6 takes you along Norway's largest lake, Mjosa, through the town of Hamar, over a toll bridge (12 kr), and past more nice lake scenery into Lillehammer. Signs direct you uphill from downtown Lillehammer to the Maihaugen museum. You'll find plenty of free parking near the entrance. Then E-6 enters the valley of Gudbrandsdalen. Follow signs to "Dombas."

Sightseeing Highlights
▲**Eidsvoll Manor**—During the Napoleonic period, Denmark was about to give Norway to Sweden. This shifted Norway's Thomas Jeffersons and Ben Franklins into high patriotic gear and in 1814 the Norway's constitution was written and signed in this stately mansion. It's full of elegant furnishings and stirring history—well worth a stop and 2 kr. The friendly ticket lady is a

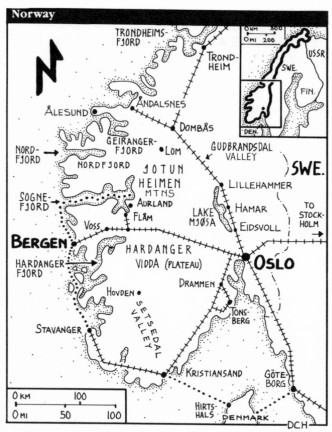

source of information, and there's a good 12 kr guidebook.
Open daily 10:00-15:00, 12:00-14:00 off season.

Skibladner—The world's oldest operating lake steamer takes
sightseers the length of Lake Mjosa from Eidsvoll to Lillehammer.
You'll find more thrills further west, but this makes for a very
pleasant day. If you're driving, one person can drop and pick up
the group at whatever ports work with your schedule.

▲▲▲**Maihaugen Open Air Folk Museum**—Founded by a
"visionary dentist" around the turn of the century, this
wonderfully laid out look at the local culture gets my "we try
hardest" award. Dr. Anders Sandvig started the collection in
1887. It now has 100 old buildings from the Gudbrandsdalen
region and a fascinating indoor museum showing the interior of
the shops of 60 crafts and tradesmen (such as a hatter, cooper,
bookbinder, and Dr. Wandvig's old dental office). In summer it

bustles with activities like weaving and baking. There's a thorough English guidebook (25 kr), English descriptions at each house and loving (and free) 45-minute guided tours daily in English at 11:00, 13:00, and 15:00 (and sometimes on request). The museum welcomes picnickers and has a good cafe and an outdoor restaurant. 25 kr entry, open daily 9:00-19:00 June-August, 10:00-16:00 shoulder season, 11:00-14:00 from Sept 15-May 15, (tel. 062/50135—call to be sure you arrive for a tour—especially outside of summer). Ask upon arrival about special events, crafts or music, and don't miss the indoor museum. (Steep 15-minute walk up from train station).

▲**Lillehammer**—The pleasant winter and summer resort town, with a happy old wooden pedestrian zone, has several interesting museums including a popular transportation museum, but its Maihaugen Open Air Folk Museum is our reason to stop here. As you drive north of town you'll see two interesting but tacky sights: just past the dam, over the river, a huge 40-foot-tall green troll—the entry to a children's park (you walk under his legs) with 50 rides and activities associated with Norwegian fairy tales. It's a favorite with local children. (40 kr, open 10:00-20:00 June 15 to September 15.) Farther up the road, on your right this time, you'll pass "Lilleputthammer," a ¼-size downtown Lillehammer (25 kr, open 12:00-17:00, mid-June to mid-August . . . half price for very short people).

▲**Gudbrandsdalen**—This "Queen of Valleys" has connected north and south Norway since ancient times. You'll pass hills, farms, and lots of riverside campgrounds. This is Peer Gynt country, and two scenic side trips give visitors a good dose of the wild beauty associated with this Norwegian Huck Finn. Peer Gyntveien is a 30 kr troll road that leaves E6 at Tretten, looping west for 25 miles and rejoining E6 at Vinstra. This trip sounds romantic, but it's basically a windy, windy dirt road over a high desolate heath and scrub brush plateau with fine mountain views: scenic, but so is E6. The second, lesser known but more rewarding scenic side trip is the Peer Gynt Setervei. For another toll you'll loop east from E6 from Vinstra to Kvam via Rondablikk, climbing to 3,500 feet and passing very close to old Peer Gynt's farm.

▲**Lom**—This isn't much of a town—except for its great stave church. Drop by the church (you'll see its dark spire just over the bridge) and take advantage of the tourist info booth before leaving Route 15 for Route 55.

Accommodations

I've listed a variety of places here stretching from Kvam to Roisheim, past Lom, depending on your style, budget and speed. This is a very popular vacation valley for Norwegians and you'll find loads of reasonable small hotels, campsites with huts for those who aren't quite campers. These huts normally cost around 140 kr and can take from 4 to 6 people. They are simple but you'll have a kitchenette and access to a good w.c. and shower. Sheets cost 30 to 40 kr extra per person.

Kvam—The **Kirketeigen Ungdomssenter**, literally "church youth center", just behind the Old Kvam church is run by friendly Katrina and Hakon Olsen, who welcome travelers like us. They have camping places (35 kr per tent or van), huts (140 kr per four-person hut) and very simple 4-bed rooms (110 kr per room). They also have a rustic old chalet near Rondablikk in Peer Gynt country. Sheets (40 kr) and blankets (10 kr) can be rented. I stayed in a very old sod-roofed log cabin hut and enjoyed fine clean facilities. Their address is 2650 Kvam i. Gudbrandsdalen, tel. 062/94082. Be sure to call in advance. 100 meters away is the **Sinclair Vertshuset Motel, Cafeteria, Pizzeria** (basic doubles—280-360 kr, good cheap pizzas, tel. 285365).

Mysuseter Fjellstue—At the entrance to the high and mighty Rondane National Park, at the end of an 8-mile dead-end mountain road from Otta (turn right at the Texaco station) is a remote and comfy mountain hotel in an area that looks like (and is) a ski resort without the snow. Jorunn and Arne offer doubles for 210-250 kr, serve hearty meals (85 kr, 3-course dinner, 50 kr breakfast) and can help you enjoy some lovely walks around this hiking and skiing center. Pb 58, 2671 Otta, tel. 062/33925, open June 15 to September 30. Note: a dirt road leads back to E-6 via the "Kvitskrinprestene"—three dirt pinnacles that have eroded to look like "Three priests" walking.

Roisheim—In a marvelously remote mountain setting is a storybook hotel comprised of a cluster of centuries-old sod-roofed log farmhouses. Roisheim, filled with antiques and friendliness by its gracious owners, Unni and Wilfried Reinschmidt, is a cultural end in itself. Each room is rustic but elegant with doubles from 350-400 kr. Some are in old log huts with low ceilings and heavy beams. The honeymooners special has a canopy bed. Wilfried, a chef, serves memorable meals. Breakfasts are 55 kr and a full three-course traditional dinner is served at 19:00 (160 kr, call ahead so they'll be prepared). Arrive early enough to enjoy the living room, library, old piano and a peaceful walk—a very memorable splurge. Open April-September, 6 miles south of Lom on the Sognefjell Road (#55) in Boverdalen, about a three hour drive from Maihaugen. tel. 062/12031.

Youth Hostels in the area: Lillehammer (tel. 062/51994), Sjoa (tel. 062/36037), Boverdalen (tel. 062/12064).

DAY 14
JOTUNHEIM COUNTRY—
THE GIANT'S HOME

After a relaxed morning, drive over Norway's highest mountain pass, deep into Jotunheim (the "giant's home") country. A long and rugged road takes you past Norway's highest mountains to the slow but fierce tongue of the Nigard Glacier, where a local expert will take you on a guided 2-hour glacier walk. Soften the scenery a bit by descending to the famous Sognefjord for the evening.

Suggested Schedule	
9:00	Easy morning exploring Norway's highest mountain road.
11:30 or 14:00	Two-hour guided glacier hike.
18:00	Find a hotel on romantic Sognefjord.

Sightseeing Highlights
▲▲**Sognefjell**—Norway's highest mountain crossing (4600 feet at the summit) is a thrilling drive through a can-can line of Northern Europe's highest mountains. In previous centuries the farmers of Gudbrandsdalen took their horse caravans over this difficult mountain pass on their necessary treks to Bergen. Just a shade more comfortably, you'll follow the same route. Today the road (route 15), still narrow and windy, is usually closed from October 15 to June 1. The descent from Sognefjell, with ten hairpin turns between Turtagrø and Fortun, is an exciting finale. Be sure to stop, get out, and enjoy the lavish views.

Lustrafjorden—After the mountains you'll drive along an arm of the famous Sognefjord called Lusterfjord. This is still rugged country. Only 2% of the land here is fit to build on. At Nes, be sure to look back at the impressive Feigumfoss Waterfall. Drops and dribbles come from miles around for this 200-yard tumble.

In Dale, the 13th century stone Gothic church with 14th century frescos is unique and worth a peek. A very friendly man named Thomas Dalsoren runs a combo campground/flower shop just down the street if you have a need for a kiosk, campground hut, potted peony, or any information on the fjord or glacier hike.

From the peaceful Victorian village of Solvorn (see Walaker Hotel recommendation) you can catch the fjerry across the

fjord to Urnes, where a pleasant 20-minute walk takes you to
Norway's oldest stave church (1150). Ferries leave Solvorn between 10:00 and 16:30.

▲▲**Jostedalsbre**—Your best chance for a hands-on glacier experience is to visit the Jostedalsbre's Nigardsbreen "tongue."
This branch of Europe's largest glacier (185 square miles) is an
exciting drive up Jostedal from Lustrafjorden. From Gaupne,
drive up road #604 23 miles to Elvekrok where you take the
private toll road (10 kr) for 2 ½ miles to the lake. From here, hike
along the trail or take the special boat (10:00-18:00, June 20 to
August 20, 10 kr round trip) to within 30 minutes' walk of the
glacier itself. There are 2-hour guided walks of the glacier (daily
at 11:30 and 14:00) for 20 kr. The glacier is a powerful river of
ice, and last year five tourists were killed by it. The guided walk
is safest, and exciting enough. Use the Gaupne T.I. (tel.
056/81211) to confirm your plans and the rather complicated
timing.

Sogn Folkemuseum—Between Sogndal and Kaupanger is
this fine look at the region's folk culture. English tours are
available—sometimes upon request. (Open June-August,
10:00-18:00, Sunday 12:00-18:00, September closing at 15:00,
tel. 78206). This is a great place to kill time if you're waiting for
the Kaupanger-Revsnes ferry.

Kaupanger-Revsnes-Aurland Option

Our basic plan is to ferry from Kaupanger to Gudvangen tomorrow. For extra mountain and fjord credit consider ferrying to
Revsnes (15 minutes, at least hourly departures including 15:00,
15:45, 17:00, 17:50 and 19:00, 40 kr for car, driver and
passenger, call 056/78116 on summer weekends for free reservation). Leave E-68 at Erdal to make the wildly scenic and
treacherous 90-minute drive to Aurland over 4,000-foot high
Hornadalen. This summer-only road is Norway's highest. You'll
see remote mountain huts (stop at Nalfarhogdi for best view of
summer farms), terrifying mountain views, and survive a
twelve-hairpin zig-zag descent into the Aurland fjord with the
best fjord views I've seen anywhere in Norway. As I write this, I
wonder why it's not in the basic plan. There's simply not
enough time to do it and the glacier walk comfortably. You
choose, or add another day. This could also be done tomorrow
morning. Be careful! A surprise summer snowstorm on the Hornadalen Pass nearly made this the first of my books to be
published posthumously.

Accommodations on Sognefjord

Walaker Hotel—For 300 years (tri-centennial in 1990) the
Walaker family has run this former inn and coach station. Tradi-

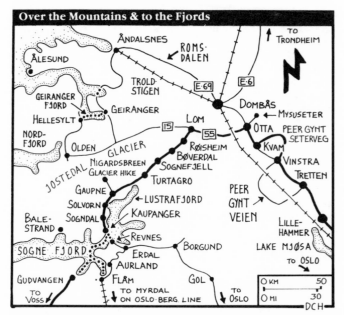

Over the Mountains & to the Fjords

tion drips like butter through the halls and living rooms. The rooms are simple but good, and a warm family feeling pervades. The Walaker, set in a lovely garden right on the Lusterfjord, is open May through September. Oda and Hermod Walaker serve fine food and are a wealth of information and help. Doubles range from 360 to 580 kr including breakfast. This is the only hotel in Solvorn, a sleepy little Victorian town, a two-mile dead-end off route 55, ten miles east of Sogndal. The town's tiny ferry crosses the fjord regularly to Urnes and Norway's oldest stave church.

Kaupanger—This town is a ferry landing set on the scenic Sognefjord—and little more. To spend the night consider one of two "husrom"s (room in a private home-type options). Both are funky, right on the water left of the dock, with seagulls and a view. The Ylivisaken family (loft in a boat house, key in main house above, tel. 056/78360) and Mrs. Lund (farther down the coast in a house with a porch you could fish from, she speaks no English, tel. 056/78366) each charge about 130 kr for their simple double rooms.

Aurland Accommodations
Aabelheim Pension—Located right in the town center, friendly old Gurid Stigen runs far and away Aurland's best "cozy like a farmhouse" place. You'll pay 220 kr for one of five

doubles, and a very traditional award-winning living room. (Open June 16 to September 6, breakfast 50 kr extra, little English spoken, tel. 056/33449).

Vangen Motel—Also nestled in downtown Aurland, this simple old hotel offers very basic rooms (all with private showers). Doubles 250 kr or only 150 if you provide the sheets. There's a big self-serve kitchen, dining and living area. Open all year. The Motel has four bed huts right on the beach for 200 kr. Tel. 33580.

Aurland Fjordstu—This is a modern place with more comfort and less traditional coziness. Good restaurant, central location, friendly, the only pub in town. Doubles cost 460 kr, singles 340, including shower and breakfast. Tel. 33505.

Flam Accommodations
Solhammar Pension and Hostel—Incredible value, 23 beds, free showers and self-serve kitchen in the blue building just 200 yards inland from station. Simple doubles cost 90 kr without sheets, 150 kr with sheets provided. Beds in a quad without sheets are 35 kr each. This private hostel is ignored by the thriving Flam chamber of touristic commerce. Tel. 056/32129.

Heimly Lodge—This place is doing its best to go big time in a small-time town. Clean, efficient, trying very hard, best normal hotel in town, 500 kr doubles with breakfast and shower. Sit on their porch with new friends and watch the clouds roll down the fjord. 400 yards along the harbor from the station. Tel. 056/32241.

Youth Hostel—Run by the Heimly Lodge people, just behind the Heimly Lodge. 53 kr per dorm bed, 6 kr for a shower. Tel. 056/32241.

DAY 15

SOGNEFJORD CRUISE, "NORWAY IN A NUTSHELL"

While Norway has great mountains, her greatest claim to scenic fame is her deep and lush fjords. A series of well organized and spectacular bus, train and ferry connections, appropriately called "Norway in a Nutshell," lays Norway's most beautiful fjord country spread-eagle on a scenic platter. This is the seductive Sognefjord—tiny but tough ferries, towering narrow canyons, isolated farms and villages steeped in the mist of countless waterfalls. The day ends with the road, in Bergen.

Suggested Schedule	
9:00	Enjoy fjord country, "Norway in a Nutshell," possible Hornadalen/Aurland trip.
14:00	Cruise to Gudvangen.
17:00	Coffee and a good strong view at the Stalheim hotel.
20:00	Late arrival in Bergen. Drop by the tourist office to plan for tomorrow and find your room.

Transportation

Post and express boats connect towns along the Sognefjord and Bergen. Ferries go where you need them and cost roughly $3 per hour for walk-ons and $12 per hour for a car, driver, and passenger. Reservations are generally not necessary but in summer, especially on Fridays and Sundays, I'd get one to be safe. Ask locally for advice. Reservations are free and made easily by telephone. Since most of today is joy riding, I've worked transportation specifics into the sightseeing notes.

Sightseeing Highlights—"Norway in a Nutshell"

▲▲▲Sognefjord—Aurlandsfjord—Everything up to now has been merely foreplay. This is it: the ultimate natural thrill Norway has to offer. The entire west coast is slashed by stunning fjords, but the Sognefjord, Norway's longest (120 miles) and deepest (over a mile), is tops. Aurlandsfjord, a remote, scenic and accessible arm of the Sognefjord, is possibly the juiciest bite in the scenic pomegranate of Norway. The local weather is actually decent, with about 24 inches of rain per year compared to over 6 feet annually in nearby Bergen.

Flam, at the head of the Aurlandsfjord, is on the "Norway in a

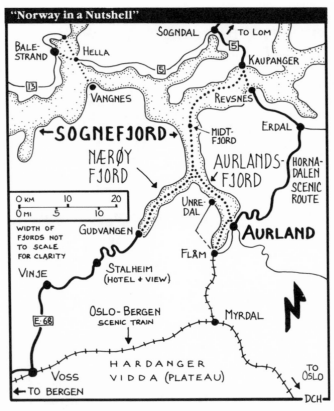

"Norway in a Nutshell" route. Very scenic and fairly touristed, it's little more than a train station, ferry landing and cluster of hotels and hostels.

Aurland, a few miles down the coast, is more of a town and less of a tourist depot. Nothing exciting, but it's a good easy-going homebase from which to feel the fjord. You can rent a bike, hike up the valley, or tour the electrical works (public tours show visitors the source of most of Oslo's electricity daily from mid-June to mid-August, Mon-Sat at 13:00, Sunday at 16:00, tel. 33292). The harborside public library is a pleasant refuge, and the 800-year-old church is worth a look. The area has as many goats as people (two thousand). The one who runs the tourist office (mid-June to mid-August) speaks English and can be phoned at 056/33313. The local geitost (goat's cheese) is sweet and delicious. (Note: every train arriving in Flam connects with a bus to Aurland. Nine buses and four ferries connect the towns daily.)

Unredal is an almost impossibly remote community of 52 families that, until the road from Flam was opened in 1985, was reached only by boat. It has Norway's smallest stave church (12th century). If you're looking for remoteness, this is it. You'll sail by it on your boat trip to Gudvangen.

▲▲▲**Flam-Aurland (or Kaupanger)-Gudvangen fjord cruise**—The post boat takes more tourists than mail on this breathtaking voyage. For 90 minutes camera-clicking tourists scurry on the drool-stained deck like nervous roosters scratching fitfully for the photo to catch the magic. The boat stops at whichever isolated farm has mail, sometimes two ferries hook up at the junction of two fjords to let passengers change over. Waterfalls turn the black rock cliffs into a bridal fair and you can nearly reach out and touch the sheer cliffs of the awesome Naeroyfjord. This ride is the ultimate fjord experience (Geiranger doesn't begin to compare). It's one of those fine times, like when you're high on the tip of an Alp, at which a warm comraderie spontaneously combusts between all the strangers who came together for the experience.

Starting from Kaupanger (2-hour trips depart daily at 8:50, 11:40, and 14:45) or Aurland (90-minute trips daily, 9:10 and 15:00 departures, 84 kr for car and driver, 26 kr for passenger or walk-on, call 056/78116 for reservations if you have a car) you get equal scenery. The ferry starts in Flam a few minutes before Aurland, but cars must board at Aurland. The scenic express boat to Bergen leaves Flam daily in June, July, and August at 15:00, stopping in Aurland and covering most of the Sognefjord before it arrives in Bergen at 21:30 (340 kr or 170 with a train pass or hotel card, per person).

From Gudvangen to Bergen

Gudvangen-Stalheim-Voss-Bergen—From the boat dock in Gudvangen, you'll continue by car or bus up the Naeroydalen ("narrow valley") past a river bubbling excitedly about the plunge it just took. You'll see the two giant falls just before the road marked "Stalheimskleiva." Stop to see the falls before taking the Stalheimskleiva road. This incredible road worms its way doggedly up into the ozone. I overheated my car in a few minutes. Take it, but take it easy. (The other road gets you there easier—through a tunnel.) At the top, stop for coffee at the friendly but very, very touristy Stalheim Hotel. This huge eagle's nest hotel is an overnight stop for every tour group that ever saw a fjord. Genuine trolls sew the pewter buttons on the sweaters here, but a cup of coffee is only 8 kr and the priceless view is free.

The road continues into a mellower beauty past lakes and farms to Voss. Here the road to Bergen forks. The big road (E68) is the more congested, but less treacherous, major route into Bergen. But since we're still high on Norwegian scenery, let's take the small, windy one, lucky #13. The road to Dale is very narrow (all the heavy traffic takes E68), the land barren but scenic, lots of summer cabins, nothing much more. The switch-backs into Dale are thrilling. From Dale to Bergen the road is better and the landscape is fjordic.

The Oslo-Bergen Train—This is simply the most spec-tacular train ride in northern Europe. You'll hang out the win-dow with your camera smoking as you roar over Norway's mountainous spine. The barren, windswept heaths, glaciers, deep forests, countless lakes, and a few rugged ski resorts create a harsh beauty. The line, an amazing engineering feat completed in 1909, is 300 miles long, peaks at 4266 feet which—at this latitude—is far above the tree line, goes under 18 miles of snow sheds, over 300 bridges, and through 200 tunnels in just under 7 hours. (400 kr, departures each morning and night in both directions.)

Myrdal-Flam Train—This little 12 mile spur line leaves the Oslo-Bergen line at Myrdal (2800 feet) and winds down to Flam (sea level) in 50 thrilling minutes. It's party time on board as everyone there is doing the same thing—living well. The con-ductor even stops the train for photos at the best waterfall. This line has 20 tunnels (over three miles worth) and is so steep that the train has five separate breaking . er, braking . systems. Hikers can get off at Berekvam or Dalsbotn and enjoy the last half of the trip alone on foot. It takes two hours.

"Norway in a Nutshell"—The most exciting single day trip you could make from Oslo or Bergen is this circular train-boat-bus-train trip through the chunk of fjord country I've been rav-ing about. Rushed travelers zip in and out by train from the big cities. Those with more time do the "nutshell" segments at their leisure. It's famous, everybody does it and, I'm afraid, if you're looking for the scenic grandeur of Norway, so should you.

The all-day trip goes by train every morning from Oslo and Bergen. Tourist offices have brochures with exact times. It's a handy round trip or an exciting way to connect the two cities. The trip includes (as described above) the Oslo-Bergen train, the spur Myrdal-Flam train, the Flam-Gudvangen cruise, and the Gudvangen-Voss bus trip (on E68).

Voss—An ugly town in a lovely lake and mountain setting. It does have an interesting folk museum, a 13th century church and a few other historic sights, but it's basically a homebase for summer or winter sports. The tourist office (tel. 05/511716) can find you a room but I'd drive right through or stay in its lux-urious youth hostel. They say "Vossing Town" is the ancestral home of our first president.

Accommodations in Voss—Voss hotels are modern and expensive. Its pensions are modern and a bit less expensive. If you simply refuse to hostel, the **Vang Pensjonat** (tel. 512145) and the **Kringsja Pension** (tel. 511627) offer good doubles for 400 kr including a large traditional breakfast. Both are very central.

The Voss Youth Hostel—This modern (automatic sliding doors), luxurious, lakeside, all-are-welcome place almost redefines hosteling. Just a ten-minute walk on the Bergen Road from the station, the charges are 72 kr per bed (plus 10 kr for non-members, 20 kr for sheets, 35 kr for breakfast, family rooms with two or four beds rent for 261 kr). Voss YH, Postboks 305, 5701 Voss, tel. 05/512017, open May through October.

The "Golden Route" Option—Two extra days and a swing farther north.
To cover the west of Norway more thoroughly, seeing more wild fjord and mountain beauty plus the interesting city of Alesund, consider this two-day extension to the north.

Leave our 22-day plan near Lom and continue up the Gudbrandsdalen Valley. At Dombas follow Romsdalen past the 3000-foot sheer rock face of the "Troll's Wall" to Andalsnes, where you'll either detour to the Art Nouveau town of Alesund or climb south over the famous switchback Trollstigvegen mountain pass.

You'll cruise the very popular and impressive Geiranger Fjord and either rejoin the basic tour at Lom or continue south to the Jostedals Glacier and along more fjords to the prestigious resort of Balestrand. From here you'll cruise the Sognefjord to Gudvangen and on in to Bergen.

Andalsnes—This town is nothing to stop for, but nearby are two spectacular natural sights. The Trollveggen (Troll's Wall) at the end of the Romsdal Valley is a 3000-foot sheer rock face— one of the world's toughest rock climbs and, until a few years ago when it was outlawed, very popular with cliff diving parachuters (you'll see one of these daredevils featured on postcards). The Trollstigvegen is an incredible road built in 1936 with a 1:12 incline ratio rising 3000 feet in eleven dramatic hairpin curves.

Those spending the night here can choose the boring **Pension Rauma** (250-300 kr doubles, tel. 072/21233, right downtown), or the fine youth hostel, which has pension-style private rooms with bedding for much less (1 mile out of town toward Alesund, tel. 072/21382).

Alesund—This town of 35,000 makes the most intriguing photo in any picture book of Norway. Blanketing several islands on the rugged Atlantic coast, Alesund burned down in 1904 and

was rebuilt with German aid in 1905 in the prevailing style—
Jugend, or Art Nouveau. The downtown is an amusing stew of
towers, pinnacles, and fun painted facades. The T.I. (tel.
071/21202) has a handy walking tour brochure. The famous
view is from "Mount" Aksla. The best budget beds are in the
Centrum Pensjonat (Storgata 24, tel. 071/21709), clean, central,
260 kr doubles. The final verdict, though, is that it's probably
not worth the time and miles if you have less than a month
in Scandinavia.

Geiranger Fjord—Every major cruise line stops here giving
this fjord more fame than it deserves. It's mighty and good, but
the Sognefjord is better and more accessible. The fjord is
bounded by two towns—Geiranger and Hellesylt. Seventy-
minute ferry rides connect these towns regularly from May
through September (44 kr for car and driver, 20 for walk-on,
departing Geiranger at 7:40, 10:15, 13:10, 16:00, and 18:40 and
leaving Hellesylt at 9:00, 11:45, 14:30, 17:30, and 20:10, reservations not necessary). They sail by trumped-up waterfalls and
stranded farms. Hellesylt, a sleepy little place at the far end of
the fjord with two cafes and a tiny harbor is the best overnight
stop (T.I. tel. 071/65052). Its **Grand Hotel**, an old stately place
right on the fjord, charges 400 kr for a double with breakfast
(tel. 65100). The youth hostel is a hike up the hill (trail by the
waterfall) with huts or dorms for 60 kr per person. The huts are
open all year, tel. 63657 or 65128.

Bergen

Bergen, Norway's most historic city, is permanently salted with
robust cobbles and a rich sea-trading heritage. Norway's capital
in the 12th and 13th centuries, its wealth and importance was
due to its membership in the heavyweight medieval trading
club of merchant cities called the Hanseatic League. It's a
romantic place with a colorful harborside fish market, old atmospheric "Hanseatic" quarter, and great people watching.
Famous for its lousy weather, Bergen gets an average of 80
inches of rain annually (compared to 30 in Oslo). That's about
200 wet days per year. With just over 200,000 people, it has its
big city tension, parking problems and high prices. But visitors
stick mainly to the old center—easily handled on foot—and,
with the help of the friendly tourist office, you'll manage just
fine. Bergen is just seven scenic hours (240 miles) from Oslo by
train. Any visit to Norway needs a stop here.

Tourist Office—Right downtown (two blocks past the fish
market) this energetic office will handle all your Bergen and
West Norway information needs. For a 15 kr fee they'll set you
up in a private room or hotel (often finding special hotel deals
you'd never get on your own.) Pick up any sightseeing

brochures you need, confirm your sightseeing plans and ask about town and fjord tours. At Torgalmenning, tel. 05/321480, open May 18 to September 6, Mon-Sat 8:30-22:00, Sunday 9:30-22:00, off season Mon-Sat 10:00-15:00. Pick up their free "Bergen Guide" which lists all sights, hours and special events. Also consider their special 48-hour "Tourist Ticket" (35 kr) which gives you free use of the city buses—otherwise 9 kr per ride.

Accommodations
Hotel Hordaheimen—The best budget hotel in town, this is very central, just off the harbor. Run by the same alcohol-free, give-the-working-man-a-break organization that brought you the Kaffistova restaurants, their prices are 300 to 660 kr for doubles (depending on the room and the season—weekends and summer are cheaper) including a big breakfast. If you want the cheapest room, you must ask for it. Their cafeteria, open late, serves traditional, basic (drab) inexpensive meals. 18. C. Sundts Gate, tel. 232320. The Hordaheimen runs an "annex" (newly refurbished, one block inland on small quiet street) that offers doubles with breakfast for only 250 kr—a real deal in Bergen!

Mycklebust Pension—This homey family-run place offers better rooms than the Hordaheimen, but it's less central and offers pension rather than hotel services. Friendly, 5-minute walk to market, kitchen and laundry service, doubles from 300-330 kr, great family room—480 kr for four. Breakfast extra. Call at 9:00 or 10:00 the day you'll arrive to see what's available. 19 Rosenberggate, tel. 311328.

Kloster Pension—In a funky cobbled neighborhood four blocks off the harbor. Basic 300 kr doubles including breakfast. 12 Klostergade. tel. 318666.

Fagerheim Pension—Open only mid-May to mid-September, this place offers some of the cheapest doubles in town—200 kr, breakfast extra. 49 Kalvedalsveien (up King Oscar's Gate half a mile), tel. 310172.

Park Pension—Very classy, nearly a hotel, in a wonderful neighborhood—central but residential, the Park charges 500 kr for doubles with shower and breakfast. 35 Harold Harfagres Gate, tel. 320960.

Shalom Pension—Just around the corner from the Park Pension, nearly as nice, 365-420 kr doubles with breakfast. Run by the Park Pension from May 20 to September 20 (tel. 320960). Off season it runs itself—tel. 326993.

YMCA—Open July 7 to Aug. 5, 7:00-10:30 and 17:00-23:30 only, the Y offers the cheapest mattresses on the floor in town—only 50 kr. They also are the only people in town who rent bikes. Kalfarsveien 8, tel. 313275, near the train station.

Montana Youth Hostel—Possibly Europe's best hostel, it's drawbacks are its remote location and relatively high price. Still, the bus connections (#4, 20 minutes from the center) and the facilities (modern 5-bed rooms, classy living room, no curfew) are excellent. 85 kr per bed (plus 20 kr for non-members), family rooms for 225 kr. Open mid-May to mid-October, breakfast not worthwhile, no members' kitchen, picnic in lounge, very well run and friendly, huge parking lot. 30 Johan Blydts Vei, tel. 292900.

Private homes—the T.I. sets people up in local homes for about 190 kr per double. These are normally friendly, comfortable and central or with easy bus access. In summer they are usually all taken by noon. Here are a few you can book direct (if you do, you save the booking fee and your hosts save the T.I. commission):

Alf & Elizabeth Heskja are a young couple with four good double rooms, a kitchen and facilities down the hall. Located just 3 minutes from the train station on a steep cobbled lane. This is far better than the hostel for budget train travelers. Call in advance. Skivebakken 17, tel. 315955. On the same street is **the Olsnes** home, with very comfortable doubles, 24 Skivebakken, tel. 312044.

The Vagenes family has four doubles in a large comfortable house on the edge of town. Not so central, but 10 minutes from downtown on bus #19. From downtown cross the Puddefjordsbroen bridge (road #555), go through tunnel, turn left on J.L. Mowinckelsvei until you reach Helgeplasset street just past the "Hogesenter."

Eating in Bergen

Cafeterias: As in Oslo the **Kaffistova**, facing the fish market, is the best basic food value. Fine atmosphere (ground floor—fast food, 1st floor—self-service cafeteria, 2nd floor—cafe serving meals), open until 22:00, cafe only 19:30, closed earlier off season. For a more traditional Norwegian fare, eat at the **Hordaheimen Hotel**'s cafeteria—great prices and lots of lefse, but a bit dreary.

For pleasant vegetarian eating, the **"White Cloud"** next to the funicular station, 2 blocks off the market, is good.

Bryggeloffet and **Bryggestuen**—The two restaurants at #6 in the Bryggen harborfront offer great (but smokey) atmosphere, good value for Norway, and good seafood meals for around 90 kr. Small servings but more potatoes upon request. Dagens Menu—50 kr.

Hotel Norge's "Kaltbord" buffet—Bergen's ritziest hotel is famous for its daily (12:00-18:00) all-you-can-eat spread. Serv-

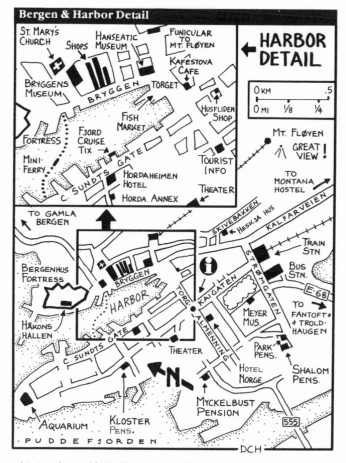

ed in its classy Ole Bull restaurant, this is your one required meal in Norway—hot dishes, seafood, desserts rich in memories and calories. 120 kr. Their breakfast is also a worthy splurge. Just past the tourist office.

The **Augusta Conditori and Lunchsalon** (next to Hotel Hordaheimen) serves good lunches at reasonable price in cheery-classy atmosphere. Open 10:00-18:00, at C. Sundtsgate #24.

Bergen's "in" cafes are stylish, cozy, small, open very late, and a great place to experience the "Ynuppie" scene. The **Cafe Opera**, **Cafe Chagall**, and **Cafe Henrik** are all on Vasker Elven near the theater.

DAY 16
BERGEN

Bergen has a rugged charm. Norway's capital long before Oslo, she wears her rich Hanseatic heritage proudly. The town seems made for a tourist, with a colorful market, a small easy-on-foot old quarter, and a little mountain right downtown that comes complete with a handy lift to zip visitors up for the view. This busy Bergen day works up an appetite to justify splurging for for a grand Norwegian-style smorgasbord dinner.

Suggested Schedule	
9:00	Shop, explore the center around the tourist office, open 8:30.
10:00	Fish market and Hanseatic Quarter.
11:00	Walking tour of old town from Bryggens Museum.
12:30	Buy picnic and ride the funicular for a view and lunch.
14:30	Shop, spend more time in Hanseatic Quarter or go out to Gamle Bergen.
17:00	Buffet dinner at the classy Hotel Norge (closes at 18:00).

Sightseeing Highlights
▲▲▲**Hanseatic Quarter**—Also called "Bryggen," this is the city's old German trading center. In 1550 it was a German city of 2000 workaholic merchants—walled and surrounded by 8000 Norwegians in Bergen. Bryggen, which has burnt down several times, is now gentrified and boutiquish but still lots of fun and color. Explore. You'll find plenty of shops, restaurants, planky alleys, leaning old wooden warehouses, good browsing, atmospheric eating and two worthwhile museums.

The Hanseatic Museum is a very atmospheric old merchant house furnished with dried fish, old ropes, sagging steps and cupboard beds from the early 1700's. This wonderful little museum is open daily 10:00-16:00, May and September 11:00-14:00, 6 kr. Drop in and ask when the next sporadic but very good English tour is scheduled.

Bryggens Museum, a new modern museum on the archeological site of the earliest Bergen (1050-1500), with interesting temporary exhibits upstairs, offers almost no English information. You can see the actual excavation—half the museum—for free from the window just below St. Mary's Church. Summer Mon-Wed-Fri 10:00-16:00, Tues-Thurs 10:00-20:00, Sat-Sun 11:00-15:00; September-April Mon-Fri 11:00-15:00, Sat-Sun 12:00-15:00, 10 kr. There is a good cafeteria with soup and bread specials.

St. Mary's Church is Bergen's oldest building and one of Norway's finest churches from about 1150. Summer, Mon-Sat 11:00-16:00.

Bergen's famous fish market bustles nearby, Mon-Sat from 10:00 to 15:00, offering lots of smelly photo fun. Don't miss it. All of these sights are within 2 minutes walk of each other.

▲▲**Floybanen**—Just two blocks from the fish market is the steep funicular ride to the top of "Mount" Floyen (1000 feet up) for the best view in town of the town, surrounding islands and fjords all the way to the west coast. There are endless hikes on top and a pleasant walk back down into Bergen. It's a popular picnic perch.

▲▲**Wandering**—Bergen is a great strolling town. Good areas to explore are around Klostergate, Knosesmanet, Ytre Markevei, and the area behind Bryggen. The modern town, around the T.I., also has a pleasant ambience. For a musical interlude, most Norwegian record shops have a bank of earphones so browsers can "sample" the records of their choice. The best buses for a city joyride are #1 and #4. A little red ferry chugs across the harbor every half hour for 5 kr. It's a handy short cut with great harbor views.

▲**Aquarium**—This aquarium is small but great fun if you like fish. Wonderfully laid out and explained in English, it claims to be the second-most-visited sight in Norway. Pleasant ten-minute walk from center. Cheery cafeteria (with very very fresh fish sandwiches). Daily 9:00-20:00, 18 kr.

▲**Old Bergen**—"Gamle Bergen" is a Disney-cute gathering of thirty-five 18th and 19th century shops and houses offering a pleasant cobbled look at "the old life." Open daily from mid-May to mid-September from 12:00 to 18:00 with English guided tours on the hour, 15 kr, Bus #1 or #9, from the post office (direction Conborg) to Gamle Bergen (first stop after tunnel).

▲**Walking Tours**—Every day at 11:00 and 13:00 from mid-May through August, a local historian takes visitors on a 90 minute walk through the old Hanseatic town. This is a great way to get an understanding of Bergen's 90 years of history. Tours cost 35 kr and leave from the Bryggens Museum (fee includes entry to both the Hanseatic and Bryggens museums, call 316710 to confirm schedule).

Other City Tours—The tourist info center organizes two other tours—a daily 75-minute intro at 9:30 for 40 kr and a daily 2-hour intro at 11:00 for 70 kr. They leave from Hotel Norge next to T.I. These are barely worthwhile for a quick orientation. Info tel. 05/299543.

▲**Fantoft Stave Church**—The most impressive stave church I've seen in Norway, this 12th century wooden church is situated in a quiet forest next to a mysterious stone cross with a beautifully decorated interior. It's difficult to really understand without a tour. It's worth a look, even after hours, for its evocative setting. Open mid-May through mid-September, 10:30-13:30 and 14:30-17:30. 6 kr.

▲**Grieg's Home, Troldhaugen**—Norway's greatest composer spent his last years here (1885-1907) soaking in inspirational fjord beauty and composing many of his greatest works. In a very romantic Victorian setting, the place is pleasant even for non-fans and essential to anyone who knows and loves Grieg's music. The house is full of memories and his little studio hut near the water makes you want to sit down and write a song. May-September 10:30-13:30, 14:30-17:30, 7 kr. Ask the tourist office about concerts (Wednesdays at 20:00, Sundays at 13:00 and 20:00, and other days sporadically).

Fantoft and Troldhaugen are both a headache to reach without a car (it's possible—well explained in the T.I.'s free "Bergen Guide" pamphlet). The daily bus tour (15:30-18:30, 100 kr) is worthwhile for the very informative guide and the easy transportation. If you've seen other stave churches and can't whistle anything by Grieg—I'd skip them. Drivers will pass both sights as they enter and leave Bergen on E68. When you see a campground, "Tennis Paradise" center and a Kro restaurant at the edge of town, you're close. Stop and ask for help.

Shopping—The Husfliden Shop just off the market at 3 Vagsalmenning is a fine place for handmade Norwegian sweaters and goodies. Mon-Fri 9:00-16:30, Thursday evening until 19:00, Saturday 9:00-14:00.

Folk Evenings—The "Fana Folklore" show is Bergen's most famous folk evening. It's a very touristy collection of cultural cliches with unexciting food, music, dancing and colorful costumes on an old farm. Many think it's too gimmicky—but many others think it's lots of fun. 140 kr includes the short bus trip and dinner. Most nights from late May to early September, 19:00-22:30, tel. 915240.

The Bergen Folklore show is a smaller, less gimmicky program featuring a good music-and-dance look at rural and traditional Norway. Performances are right downtown at the Bryggens Museum every Wednesday (20:30) and Sunday (18:00) from mid-June through mid-August. Tickets for the one hour show are 50 kr at the T.I. or at the door. Tel. 248929 or 134506.

An Atlantic coast sidetrip? Dotted with villages, the nearby rugged Atlantic coast of Norway is a brisk switch from all the fjord beauty. You can tour a tidal electric plant at Toftay Bolgehrafuerh (call 338881 for a key and/or a tour, specifics at T.I.) The small windswept town of Bloomvort (with the Pension Makeu, at the head of the bay) is a fine retreat.

Boats from Bergen: The T.I. has several brochures on tours of the nearby Hardanger and Sogne fjords. There are plenty of choices. "Norway in a Nutshell," if you skipped the days before Bergen in this 22-day plan, can be done in a day from Bergen, explained in Day 15. Ask about the special Fyksesund fjord and old farm tour.

Itinerary Option

Bergen is an efficient place to end your tour. You can turn in your car and fly home from here. (Ask your travel agent about the economic feasibility of this "open jaws" option.) If you plugged in Days 20 and 21 after Copenhagen at the start of this trip, you'd miss nothing essential and save substantial time and piles of miles.

To travel directly from Bergen to Copenhagen, you can fly— occasionally there are very cheap (500 kr) flights available only locally. Ask around—but don't count on it—or sail. The Fred Olsen Line sails from Bergen to Hirtshals, northern Denmark, twice a week, but not at all from mid-June through the end of August, for about 300 kr. By the way, don't worry about missing Stavanger. I don't know what it's like to live there—but it's a dull place to visit.

The Norway Line sails from Bergen to Newcastle, England two or three times weekly from May through mid-October. Fares range from 385 kr to 825 kr. (Summer and Friday, Satur- day and Sunday departures are most expensive, cars cost 500 kr or are free with four paying passengers. The cheapest tickets get you a "sleeperette" to stretch out on overnight.) Tel. 322780 in Bergen, or 91/2587643 in Newcastle.

DAY 17
SOUTH TO SETESDAL VALLEY

Today is a long drive as you round the corner and begin your
return to Copenhagen. There are several scenic options. My
choice is to island hop south from Bergen, getting a feel for
Norway's rugged Atlantic coast before heading inland along a
frightfully narrow fjord and finally up and over a mountain pass
into the remote—and therefore very traditional—Setesdal
Valley.

Suggested Schedule	
9:00	Drive south, island-hopping, then inland to Setesdal Valley.
18:00	Set up in Hovden, a ski resort at the top of Setesdal

**Transportation: Driving from Bergen to Setesdal—
two options:**
For speed and maximum fjord beauty (and traffic), drive E68
from Bergen to Kvanndal, then ferry to Utne and drive #550
along the Sorfjorden to Odda. Head east on E76 to
Haukeligrend, the Gateway to Setesdal.

More interesting, relaxing, time consuming and expensive—
but I think worthwhile—is the island-hopping route down the
south coast. Rather than fjords you'll see stoney rugged islands
and glimpses of the open sea. Leave Bergen on E68, past the
stave church and Grieg's home (you could see these on your
way south, but, unfortunately they don't open til 10:30), follow
route 14 to Osoyro and Halhjem, where you'll catch the ferry to
Sandsviksvag (60 minutes, 90 kr for car, driver and co-pilot). If
you drive the speed limit for 20 miles across the island of Stord,
staying on route #14, you'll catch the connecting ferry from
Skersholmane to Utbjoa It takes 35 minutes, 64 kr for car and
two bodies. From Skersholmane you'll see a small town which
assembles the huge North Sea oil rigs.

From Utbjoa, drive to E76 and follow the very scenic cliff-
hanging road along the Akrafjord and up into the mountains (30
kr toll). You'll pass mountain lakes, broad vistas and long
tunnels—all quite majestic—before descending into a heavily
forested but lightly populated area and finally to Haukeligrend,
where you'll leave the main drag to head south into the Setesdal
Valley.

In Bergen, the T.I. has a pamphlet called "Kyst Vegen" which gives you all the ferry connections and a handy chart. Normally the Halhjem ferries leave on the hour all day and the Skersholmane ferry leaves for Utbjoa every 90 minutes (11:00, 12:30, 14:00, 15:30, 17:00, 18:30 and 20:00). Reservations (except maybe summer Fridays) aren't necessary.

Hovden
Hovden is a full day's drive from Bergen putting you right at the top of the Setesdal Valley and ready for a full and fascinating day of sightseeing as you work your way south to the coast tomorrow. Hovden is a ski resort (2500 feet high), barren in the summer and painfully in need of charm. But it has plenty of places to eat and sleep and it's just the right place to end today and start tomorrow. There are good walks offering a chance to see reindeer, moose, arctic fox and rabbits—so they say. Every other day a chairlift takes summer visitors to its nearby 3700-foot peak.

Accommodations
Haugly Gjesteheim—This is the only old house with character in town; it also has mountain views and double rooms for 150 kr (cheaper if you have a sleeping bag or sheets). Birgit Lidtveit runs the place and speaks very little English (get help when you call in advance). She serves no meals, but you're

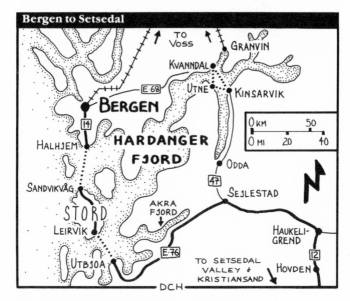

Bergen to Setsedal

welcome to use the kitchen. It's an easy-to-find big white house on Hovden's main drag, just past the Shell Station. Tel. 043/39527.

Hovdehytta—This large modern ski chalet with a lively ski-lodge atmosphere (large dining room, open fire in the living room) offers clean modern bunkbed doubles with a large breakfast for 300 kr. Tel. 043/39522.

Triangel Feriesenter Youth Hostel—Another modern resort-like complex with a lodge, member's kitchen, pub, disco, and fancy huts, this fine youth hostel rents double rooms for 75 kr per person. Sheets are 60 kr extra—they have to send laundry 80 miles away for cleaning! Those without YH cards pay 10 kr extra. It's often full, so call in advance. Tel. 043/39501. You'll see their sign on the right just as you enter Hovden.

The Bergtun Hotel, 20 miles south of Hovden in Valle, run by Gunnar Oiestad, is the first real cozy, old time lodging you'll see in Setesdal. It's full of traditional furniture, painting and carvings—and four-poster beds in each charming room. A double with breakfast costs 400 kr. Located in the center of the town of Valle, the problem with this place is that it's too far south for our plan. If you want a memorable evening, and don't mind the expense or the backtracking to see Bykle, this is for you. Otherwise, it's a good place for lunch tomorrow—daily specials (Dagens Ratt) for 50 kr from 12:00—19:00. Valle i Setesdal, tel. 043/37270.

DAY 18
SETESDAL

After all the miles you covered yesterday, today is easy, with
plenty of time for this cultural Easter egg hunt called Setesdal.
Probably Norway's most traditional cranny, it joined the 20th
century only with the construction of the valley highway in the
1950s. This valley is a mellow montage of derelict farmhouses,
sod-roofed water mills, gold and silver smiths in action, ancient
churches, yellowed recipes, rivers, forests and mountains.

Suggested Schedule

9:00	Depart Hovden.
10:00	Tour old farmstad of Bykle.
13:00	Lunch and browsing in Valle, see silver smiths in action.
14:00	Explore your way to the coast.
18:00	Evening and dinner in port of Kristiansand.
22:00	Sail to Jutland, Denmark.

Sightseeing Setesdal
The most interesting route from Bergen to Norway's south
coast is down Setesdal Valley ("dal" means valley but I'll be
redundant just to be doubly clear for sure). One of Norway's
most traditional, undeveloped and scenic valleys, Setesdal
follows the Otra River for 140 miles south to the major port
town of Kristiansand. You'll turn south off of E76 at
Haukeligrend and wind up to Sessvatn at 3,000 feet. From here,
road #12 takes you comfortably through ski resorts, past great
steep mountains and much traditional architecture. The road is
good and scenic. Skip the few smaller secondary routes. All
along the valley you'll see the unique two-storied "stabburs"
(the top floor stored clothes, the bottom, food) and many sod
roofs—even the bus stops have roof tops the local goats would
love to munch.

This is a valley of traditional costumes, fiddlers, mouth
organs, rose painting, whittling and silversmiths. The famous
Setesdal filigree echoes the rhythmical design of the Viking and
Medieval ages.

This is an easygoing stretch of sightseeing—nothing earth-
shaking. Let's just pretend you're on vacation and dilly-dally
downhill all day long. Here are some interesting excuses to get
out of the car:
Ekte Geitost—In the high country, just over the Sessvatn sum-

mit (3,000 ft) you'll see goat herds and summer farms. If you see an "Ekte Geitost" sign, that means homemade goat cheese is for sale. Get some. Some people think it looks like a decade's accumulation of ear wax—I think it's delicious.

Dammar Vatnedalsvatn—Just south of Hovden is a two-mile side trip to a 200-foot-high rock pile dam. Great view, impressive rockery.

Bykle—The most interesting Setesdal church is the teeny Bykle church. The 17th century interior has two balconies—one for men and one for women.

Bykle has two small open air folk museums. Across the street from the church is the Henriksen collection (12 buildings, handicrafts in action and for sale, open Mon-Sat, 10:00-18:00). More interesting is the "Huldreheimen" Museum. Follow the sign up a road to a farm high above the town—fine view, six houses, good English info sheet, open mid-June through mid-August, 10:00-18:00, Sat-Sun 12:00-18:00, 5 kr. Off season, ask the friendly old lady who lives on the farm if you can have a look. She gave me a great private tour. Following her up the hill and through these ancient huts was a rich experience.

Trydal—Just along the main road, on your left you'll see an old water mill (1630). A few minutes further south is a WC sign on the right. Exit onto that little road. You'll pass another old water mill. At the second picnic turnout (just before this roadlet returns to the highway) turn out and frolic along the river rocks.

Flateland—One mile to the left, off the main road, is the Setesdal museum, offering more of what you saw at Bykle (daily from mid-June to mid-August 10:00-18:00 in July, 11:00-17:00 otherwise).

Valle—Setesdal's prettiest village, (but don't tell Bykle), you'll find a pleasant "husflid" (traditional homemade crafts) shop, fine silver and gold work at Grete and Ornulfs Sylvsmie, good traditional lunches in the cozy Bergtun Hotel (daily specials, 50 kr from 12:00-19:00) and a fine suspension bridge for little boys of any sex or age who still like to bounce and for anyone interested in a great view of the strange mountains over the river that look like polished petrified mud slides. (Tourist Info tel. 043/37312.)

Nomeland—"Sylvartun"—The silversmith with the valley's most aggressive publicity department whistles while he works in a traditional log cabin from the 17th century.

Ose—"Storstogo" is a charming cafe and gift shop with lots of tourist info (pick up a map of Kristiansand) and a friendly, knowledgeable proprietor. Just south is the impressive Reiarsfoss waterfall.

Bygland Fjord—Along these two lakes that call themselves a fjord (don't accept any substitutes, but they are scenic) you'll

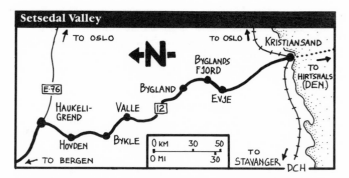

see the Bygland church (1838), with pre-Christian era runic stones in its yard.

Grendi—The Ardal Church (1827) has a runestone in its yard too. And, for good measure, 300 yards south of the church is an oak tree said to be 900 years old.

Evje—A huge town by Setesdal standards (1400 people), Evje is famous for its gems and mines. Fancy stones fill the shops here. Only rock hounds would find the nearby mines lots of fun (for a small fee you can hunt for gems). The Thulitten Stein (rock) and Souvenir Shop (just north of the town center past the Esso Station, on a small road parallel to #12) is run by a friendly and knowledgeable Englishman named Paul. There's a rock museum across the bridge on the south side of Evje. The road south from Evje to Kristiansand passes through a land of glassy lakes. It's a pleasant non-stop drive.

Setesdal—Kristiansand—Denmark

Kristiansand—This "capital of the south" with 60,000 inhabitants has a pleasant grid plan Renaissance layout (the Kvadraturen), a famous zoo with Norway's biggest amusement park (6 miles towards Oslo on E-18) and lots of big boats going to England and Denmark. It's nothing worth writing home about, but a pleasant place to stroll through your last few hours in Norway before sailing to Denmark.

The "Kvadraturen" center around the bustling pedestrian market street is the shopping, eating, people-watching and browsing town center. You'll find plenty of Kafeterias, and a Peppe's Pizza (open until 23:00, 100 kr pizzas for two, 45 kr salad bar, on Gyldenloves).

Overnighting

Evje—Those who spend more time in Stetesdal than they planned can sleep in Evje. A wonderful "husrum" is in the **Alfred Falleras** home (tel. 043/30086 or 043/30151—little

English spoken, you might get someone to call for you). They have just one room but it's a huge suite sleeping from two to four people. It rents for 150 kr plus 20 kr per person for sheets. It's across the street from Paul's rock shop, just past the Esso station, north of the town center on the small road that runs along #12.

Kristiansand—Hotels here are expensive and nondescript. The cheapest ones, **Bondeheimen** (tel. 042/2440) and **Metropole** (tel. 042/21465), lie somewhere between cozy old world and musty. They both charge around 450 kr for a double with breakfast and shower and are very central. **The Hotel Norge** (042/23320) is a little more modern and a little more expensive. Ask for weekend prices (Fri-Sat-Sun). The new **youth hostel** (042-94947) isn't so central but offers beds for 85 kr. There are several beachside campgrounds with huts available.

Sailing to Denmark
The Fred Olsen Line sails daily and nightly from Kristiansand to Hirtshals. The trip takes just over four hours (the overnight ride is slower) and there are usually several departures daily. Passengers pay about 160 kr and 220 kr for a car. This ride is nothing classy like the ride to Helsinki (Fred Olsen buys its boats used from the Viking line) but it's too cold to swim and you've got to get to Denmark somehow. As soon as you're ready to commit yourself to a firm date, drop by a Norwegian travel agency to get your ticket and exact schedule information. Fred Olsen is at tel. 02/192218 in Oslo and 042/70501 in Kristiansand.

Sleep on the boat. I'd enjoy the evening in Kristiansand, board the night boat and sail while I sleep to Denmark. Beds on board are reasonable. For around $10 you'll get a simple curtains-for-privacy couchette, for $15 a bed in a four-berth room and for $20 per person, a private double with shower. You owe yourself this comfort if you're doing something as efficient as spending this night traveling. While there's no problem getting on the boat and you're welcome to sprawl freely on the floor, cabins book up, especially on Friday night departures, and should be reserved in advance.

DAY 19
JUTLAND, ARHUS, AND ACROSS DENMARK TO AERO

Sand dunes, Lego toys, fortified old towns and moated
manorhouses, Jutland—the part of Denmark that's connected
to the rest of Europe—is far from Copenhagen. After your boat
docks, spend the morning in the wonderfully preserved old
town of Arhus, Jutland's capital and Denmark's second largest
city. By evening, after a long drive, you'll nestle into the quiet
and quaint island of Aero.

Suggested Schedule	
7:00	Arrive in Hirtshals, Denmark, find breakfast.
8:00	Drive south to Arhus.
10:00	Tour Den Gamle By (the old town), picnic lunch.
14:00	Drive to Svendborg via Middelfart and Assens.
18:00	Catch the ferry to Aero, leaving your car in Svendborg.

$3a \rightarrow 45$

Transportation
Denmark is a small country, but today you'll drive nearly its entire length—and that's a long way. From the dock in Hirtshals
(you'll arrive very early), drive highway 13 to the freeway E-3,
and continue south 110 miles to Arhus. Break your fast and
journey wherever you feel like it.

E-3 brings you right into central Arhus. Those skipping Arhus
will skirt the center, turning right on Nordre Ringgade to follow
E-3 south. To get to the Old Town (Den Gamle By) circle
around the center on Nordre and Vestre Ringgade and turn left
off E-3 at Viborgvej (look for signs to Botanisk Have and Den
Gamle By).

From Arhus you'll continue south on E-3 another 50 miles to
E-66 where the Middlefart bridge takes you to the Island of Fyn
(Funen in English). At Odense, take highway 9 to Svendborg.

Leave your car in Svendborg at the easy long-term parking
lot two blocks from the ferry dock and sail for the little isle of
Aero. The Svendborg—Aeroskobing ferry (one hour crossing,
leaving every 30 minutes, 165 kr for car and driver, 35 kr for
walk-ons) has plenty of room for passengers. Cars often get on
only with reservations. The town of Aeroskobing is tiny and
everything is just a few cobbles from the ferry landing.

Remember, it's wise—especially in this age of overbooking—to
call and reconfirm your flight home 72 hours before departure.

Arhus
Denmark's second largest city (250,000 people), Arhus is the
cultural hub of Jutland. Its Viking founders, ever conscious of
aesthetics, chose a lovely wooded where-the-river-hits-the-sea
setting, and today it bustles with a lively port and an important
university. It's well worth a stop. The Arhus Tourist Office
is in the town hall (tel. 06-121600, open daily 9:00-21:00, mid-
June through August, 9:00-17:00, closed Sundays off season).
Ideally, you picked up the very helpful Arhus tourist info
brochure and map in Copenhagen. If not, get it here. They run
a fine city intro bus tour (daily in the summer at 10:00 for 2 ½
hours from the T.I.) for 30 kr. That tour ticket also gives you 24
hours of unlimited city bus travel.

Sightseeing Highlights: Arhus
▲▲▲**Den Gamle By**—"The Old Town" open air folk museum
puts Arhus on the touristic map. This is a unique gathering of

60 half-timbered houses and 40 working crafts shops, all wonderfully furnished just like when they were new back in the days of Hans Christian Andersen. Unlike other Scandinavian open air museums, which focus on rural folk life, Den Gamle By recreates old Danish town life. 25 kr. Open daily in June, July and August from 9:00 to 17:00, May and September 10:00 to 17:00, with shorter hours off season. Take Bus #3 to the "Old Town." Tel. 06-123188.

▲**Forhistorisk Museum Moesard**—This prehistory museum at Moesgard, just south of Arhus, is famous for its incredibly well-preserved Grauballe Man. This 2000-year-old "bog man" looks like a fellow half his age. He's amazingly intact. You'll see his skin, nails, hair and even the slit in his throat that they gave him at the sacrificial banquet. The museum has fine Viking, Stone, Bronze and Iron Age exhibits. 20 kr. Open Daily 10:00-17:00, closed Mondays in the off season. Take Bus #6 from the Arhus station to the last stop. Behind the museum, a prehistoric open air museum ("'trackway") stretches two miles down to a fine beach (good 3 kr guidebooklet) where, in the summer, Bus #19 takes you back downtown.

Arhus Cathedral—Denmark's biggest at over 300 feet long and tall, this late-Gothic (from 1479) church is open to tourists daily except Sundays from 9:30-16:00 (shorter hours off season).

Other Arhus attractions—There's lots more to see and do in Arhus including an art museum, a Viking museum and a "Tivoli" amusement park. Two-hour walking tours through the old center and the Viking museum are given daily in the summer at 2:00 from the T.I. (15 kr). A popular "Meet the Danes" program puts interested visitors in touch with locals for an evening of talk, coffee and cake. This is arranged through the T.I. (at least a day in advance).

Accommodations in Arhus
Missionshotellet Ansgar—This huge traditional hotel at 14 Banegardsplads, near the town hall, charges from 400 to 500 kr for doubles with a small breakfast. Tel. 06-124122. Their restaurant serves good soup and salad. Try their reknowned "soup with balls."

   Ericksen's Hotel—This is a clean and very simple shower-down-the-hall place, also very central, with doubles for around 300 kr. Banegardsplads 6-8, tel. 06-136296.

   The T.I. can set you up in a private home for around 90 kr per person. Also, the local Youth Hotel is a good one, situated near the water two miles out of town on Ostreskovvej, tel. 06-167298, Bus #1 or #2 to the end and follow the signs.

Other Jutland Sights

Jutland is the large chunk of Denmark that is attached to Germany. The rest of the country consists of islands. The land of the Jutes has vast beaches, lots of sand dunes, forests, soft hills, rather desolate moors, and a few interesting sights. Arhus, as we've seen, is the only blockbuster sight, but here are a few others to consider.

▲▲**Legoland**—Legoland is Scandinavia's top kids' sight. If you have one (or think you might be one), it's a fun stop. Thirty-three million Lego bricks (European tinker toys) are creatively arranged into Mt. Rushmore, the Parthenon, "Mad" Ludwig's castle, the Statue of Liberty, wild animals, etc. and combined with lots of rides, restaurants, trees and smiles into one big park. It's a Lego world here, as everything is cleverly related to this very popular toy. Surprisingly, however, the restaurants don't serve "Legolamb." The park has a great doll collection and a toy museum full of mechanical wonders from the early 1900s, many ready to jump into action as soon as you push the button. There's a Lego playroom for some hands-on fun for your kids—and a campground across the street if they refuse to move on. East of E3 on highway 28, one hour from Arhus or Odense in the otherwise unremarkable town of Billund. Open May through mid-September 10:00-20:00 daily, tel. 05-331333. 36 kr entry, 18 kr for kids, special price for 8 rides, 24 kr.

Jelling—If you've always wanted to see the hometown of the ancient Danish Kings Gorm the Old and Harold Bluetooth, this is your chance. Jelling is a small village (12 miles from Legoland just off E3 near Vejle) with a small church that has Denmark's oldest frescos and two very old runic stones in its courtyard—often called "Denmark's birth certificate."

▲**Ribe**—A Viking port a thousand years ago, Ribe is the oldest and possibly loveliest town in Denmark. An entertaining mix of cobbled lanes and leaning old houses with a fine church (3 kr, bright modern paintings under old Romanesque arches). A smokey, low-ceiling, very atmospheric inn, the Weis Stue, serves great meals across the street from the church. Drop by the T.I. for its handy walking tour brochure, or better yet, catch one of the guided town walks (daily, 11:30, 15 kr).

▲▲▲**Aero**—This small (22-by-6-mile) island on the south edge of Denmark is salty and sleepy as can be. Tombstones here say things like "Here lies Christian Hansen at anchor with his wife. He will not weigh until he stands before God." It's the kind of island where baskets of new potatoes sit in front of houses—for sale on the honor system. Being so close to Germany you'll see plenty of smug Germans who return regularly to this peaceful retreat.

Aeroskobing is Aero's town in a bottle. Temple Fielding said it's "one of five places in the world that you must see." It's the only entirely protected town in Denmark. Drop into the 1680s, when Aeroskobing was the wealthy homeport of over a hundred windjammers. The many Danes who come here for the tranquility—washing up the cobbled main drag in waves with the landing of each boat—call it the "fairy tale town."

Accommodations

Pension Vestergade—Bent and Phyllis Packnass run this pleasantly quirky old place (1784) located right on the main street in the town center. They take very good care of their guests with a homey TV room and a library with Aero guidebooks you can use. They charge 160 kr per double, 210 kr for doubles with a kitchen, breakfast is extra. The loft rooms have great views. Ask to borrow a bike. Vestergade 44, 5970 Aeroskobing, tel. 09/522298.

Det Lille Hotel—Friendly and chatty Erling and Lis Jensen run this former 19th century captain's home. It's warm, tidy and modern—like a sailboat. Their rooms (305 kr per double, 180 per single) include a huge breakfast and loaner bikes. Open May through October. Just one street off the harbor at Smedegade 33, 5970 Aeroskobing, tel. 09/522300. Call the morning of your arrival to ask for a room.

The Aeroskobing Youth Hostel is a glorious place, an easy walk out of town, equipped with a fine living room, members' kitchen, family rooms with two or four beds (50 kr each) or dorms (44 kr per bed). Dinner costs 35 or 45 kr and breakfast is available for 30 kr. The place is normally booked solid in July and September. June and August are much less busy. Smedevejen 13, tel. 09/521004.

The Tourist Office (several blocks up from the ferry on Torvet, open in summer Mon-Fri 10:00-17:00, Saturday 10:00-12:00 and 13:00-15:00, Sunday 10:00-12:00, tel. 09-521300), can find you a room in a private home (doubles for 150 kr).

Dunkaer Kro—Set quietly far from town in the center of the island, this traditional old inn with great food, a classy dining room and a rowdy pub has lovely doubles with down quilts for 215 kr, breakfast extra. 5981 Dunkaer, tel. 09/521554.

Camping—This first-class campground (follow the waterfront, a short walk from the center) is on a fine beach, has a lodge with a fireplace, windsurfing, and cottages for 4 or 5 people for 165 kr plus 28 kr per person. It's open from May through mid-September and always has room for campers (26 kr each). Tel. 09/521854.

DAY 20
THE ISLE OF AERO

After the staggering beauty of Norway's fjord country and all you've seen so far, the sleepy isle of Aero will lack luster. But this is the perfect time-passed world in which to wind down, enjoy the seagulls and take a bike ride. Today is yours. Pedal a rented bike into the essence of Denmark. Lunch in a traditional kro country inn. Settle in a cobbled world of sailors who, after someone connected a steam engine to a propeller, decided "maybe building ships in bottles is more my style."

Suggested Schedule	
Morning	Sleep in.
10:00	Bike tour with lunch at an old-fashioned kro inn.
15:00	Explore little Aeroskobing, pop into the Bottled Ship museum.

Sightseeing Highlights
▲▲**The Town of Aeroskobing**—It's just a pleasant place to wander. The post office dates to 1749, cast iron gas lights still shine each evening, the harbor now caters to holiday yachts, and on midnight low tides you can almost hear the crabs playing cards. The Hammerich House is full of old junk which you can see daily in the summer from 10:00 to 12:00 and 14:00 to 16:00. The "Bottle Peter" museum on Smedegade is a fascinating house of 750 different bottled ships. Old Peter Jacobsen died in 1960 (most likely buried in a glass coffin) leaving a lifetime of tedious little creations for us visitors to marvel at.
▲▲**The Aero Island bike ride**—This 18-mile trip will show you the best of this remote island's many charms. If your hotel can't loan you a bike (ask), rent one from the Esso Station (Pilebaekken 7, go through the green door to the right of the T.I., past the public WC and garden to the next road) for 30 kr per day. On Aero there are no deposits and no locks. If you leave in the morning, you'll hit the Kro Inn in time for lunch. Ready to go? "May the wind always be at your back."
   Leave Aeroskobing to the west on the road to Vra. You'll see the first of many U-shaped farms, typical of this island. The three sides block the wind and are used for storing cows, hay, and people. "Gaard" (meaning "farm") shows up on many local

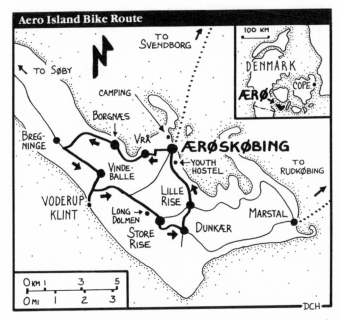

names. Bike along the coast in the protection of the dyke which made the once salty swampland to your left farmable. You'll see a sleek modern windmill and, soon, a pleasant cluster of mostly modern summer cottages called Borgnaes. (At this point wimps can take a shortcut directly to Vindeballe.)

Next you'll pass a secluded beach, the best you'll see on Aero, and then climb uphill over the island's summit to Bregninge. Unless you're tired of thatched and half-timbered cottages, turn right and roll through Denmark's "second longest village" to the church. Take a peek inside. (Public WC in the church yard). Then roll back through Bregninge past many more U-shaped "gaards," heading about a mile down the main road to Vindeballe, taking the Vodrup exit.

A straight road leads you (with a slight jog to the right) to a rugged bluff called Voderup Klint. If I were a pagan, I'd worship here—the sea, the wind, the chilling view. Then it's on to Tanderup. You'll roll past the old farm with the cows with the green hearing aids, a lovely pond, and right past a row of wind-bent stumps. At the old town of Olde you'll hit the main road. Turn right toward Store Rise the next church spire in the distance. Just after the Stokkeby turnoff, follow the very rough tree lined path on your right to the Tingstedet Long Dolmen, just behind the church spire. Here you'll see a 5000-year-old

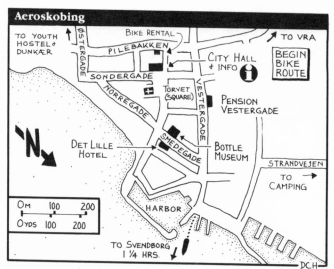

early neolithic burial place. Aero had over a hundred of these—but few survive.

Carry on to the Store Rise church. Inside, notice the little boats hanging in the nave, the fine altar piece, and Martin Luther in the stern. Continue down the main road with the impressive—and hopeful—forest of modern windmills on your right until you get to Dunkaer. How about lunch at the "Kro" Inn here ("mid-day plate" special is about 60 kr) or a drink and a snack in the rowdy and atmospheric pub.

For the homestretch, take the small road past the topless windmill. Except for "Lille Rise," it's all downhill from here as you coast past great seaviews back home to Aeroskobing.

DAYS 21 & 22
ODENSE, ROSKILDE AND BACK TO COPENHAGEN

Okay, enough resting. You'd think this was a vacation, or something. Let's have one last flurry of sightseeing activity as we return to Copenhagen. Catch the early ferry—breakfast on board—to get to Odense in time to see the home of Hans Christian Andersen and Odense's fine open air folk museum. Roskilde, with its great Viking ships and cathedral is the last stop before you find yourself back where you started—in that wonderful city. . .of Copenhagen.

Suggested Schedule	
	Day 21
6:10	Breakfast on the early ferry.
7:30	Pick up your car in Svendborg, buy a picnic lunch, and drive to Odense.
8:30	Tour Odense's folk museum and Hans Christian Andersen's home.
13:00	Picnic on the ferry from Funen to Zealand.
15:00	Tour Roskilde's Viking ships and cathedral.
18:00	Drive "home" to Copenhagen where your room is reserved and waiting.
	Day 22
	Copenhagen. Tour is over.

Transportation: Aero—Copenhagen
Today we need to catch the early (6:10) ferry back to Svendborg. (tel. 09-521018 for info, reservations for walk-ons never necessary. On Saturday and Sunday there are normally no early trips.) By 7:30 you'll be driving north on highway 9 past the Egeskov castle to Odense. Just south of town at Hojby leave route 9 turning left towards Dalum and the Odense Campground (on Odensveg). Look for Den Fynske Landsby signs (near the train tracks, south edge of town). After touring the open air folk museum drive into the center. There is a large parking lot right next to the pedestrian zone where you'll find H.C. Andersen's house.

Leave Odense following signs for E-66. Stay on the freeway driving past Nyborg, and butting right up to the Knudshoved-Halsskov ferry (165 kr per car and driver, 35 kr per passenger, always call for free reservation: Svendborg—09/210682,

Copenhagen—01-148880 or any other DSB office, one-hour crossing, boats leave every 30 minutes). Leave E-66 at Ringsted, following route 14 to Roskilde. Set your sights on the twin church spires and park somewhere between there and the water where you'll find the Viking ships.

Copenhagen is just 30 minutes from Roskilde. If you're returning your car to the airport, stay on E-66 and follow the signs to Kastrup. From there Bus #9 or #31 will take you downtown and to the hotel you reserved about 22 days ago.

Sightseeing Highlights

▲Odense—1988 is the 1,000th anniversary of Odense. Hometown boy Hans Christian Andersen once said, "Perhaps Odense will one day become famous because of me and perhaps people from many countries will travel to Odense because of me." Today Odense is one of Denmark's most visited towns. Denmark's third largest city, with 170,000 people, it's big and industrial. But its old center retains some of the fairy tale charm it had in the days of H.C.A. and it has plenty to offer. Park your car and hoof it. It is well connected to Copenhagen by train-boat-train (sixteen 3-hour trips each day). The T.I. is in the town hall right downtown (Tel. 09/127520, open daily in summer 9:00-19:00, Sunday 11:00-19:00, off season Mon-Fri 9:00-17:00, Saturday 9:00-12:00.) They run daily city bus tours (50 kr, two hours, at 15:00) and a "Meet the Danes" program.

▲Den Fynske Landsby—The Funen Village Open Air Museum is a sleepy gathering of 24 old buildings preserving the 18th century culture of this region. There are no explanations in the buildings because the many school groups who visit play guessing games. So pick up the 10 kr guidebook. 10 kr admission, open June-August daily from 9:00-18:30; April-May and September-October daily from 9:00-16:00. Off season, only Sundays from 10:00-16:00. From mid-July to mid-August there are H.C. Andersen plays in the theater every afternoon (the 30 kr ticket includes admission 90 minutes early to see the museum).

▲Hans Christian Andersen's Hus—This HCA museum is packed with momentos from the popular writer's life, his many letters and books, and hordes of children and tourists. It's fun if you like his tales. At 39 Hans Jensensstraede, open daily in summer 9:00-18:00, shorter hours off season. 20 kr. Across the street is the popular Flensted shop—full of imaginative mobiles and Danish arts and crafts.

Brandt's Klaedefabrik—In 1977 a huge textile factory (18,000 sq. meters) was shut down. Rather than demolish it, they turned it into a cultural center. Today it houses several modern art and graphics museums, shops and cafes. The people-watching is great from its outdoor cafes.

Egeskov Castle—One of Denmark's most impressive castles is newly opened to the public. Egeskov shows off its royal and very lived-in interior and its fine gardens. If you're a fan of fuchsias, old cars, or hunting trophies, this place is thrilling. Expensive—45 kr, open May-September 10:00-17:00, just off the Odense-Svendborg road. Bad bus connections but very easy by car.

▲▲Roskilde Cathedral—Denmark's roots—Viking and Royal—are on display in Roskilde, a pleasant town 20 miles west of Copenhagen. 500 years ago, Roskilde was Denmark's leading city. Its imposing twin-spired cathedral houses the tombs of 38 Danish kings and queens. It's a stately, modern-looking old church with great marble work, paintings (notice the impressive 3-D painting, with Christian IV looking like a pirate, in the room behind the small pipe organ) and wood carvings (in and around the altar). It's all surrounded by an impressive sea of clean cobbles (except for rice in the cracks). The 20 kr guidebook is very good. April-September 9:00-18:00, off season 10:00-16:00, 5 kr admission.

▲▲▲Viking Ship Museum—This award-winning museum displays five different Viking ships—one is like the boat Leif Ericsson sailed to America a thousand years ago. The descriptions are excellent—and in English. It's the kind of museum where you want to read everything. Request the English movie introduction as you enter. These ships were deliberately sunk to block a nearby harbor and recently excavated, preserved and pieced together. The museum cafeteria serves the original Vikingburger (23 kr)—great after a hard day of pillage, plunder—or sightseeing. Open June-August 9:00-18:00, a little shorter hours off season. 18 kr entry.

Roskilde is an easy side trip from Copenhagen on the S-Tog commuter train. Its tourist office (02/352700) can find you a room in a private home and give you an old town walking tour brochure.

▲Ancient Sights near Roskilde—One of the best ancient sights in Denmark is the 5000-year-old passage grave near the village of Ove, (just off route 14). Bring a flashlight—or matches for the candles people have put on the walls. You'll actually be able to stand up in this grave site surrounded by 15 wall stones and under 4 large ceiling stones.

Lejre Research Centre—This well publicized "Iron Age Community" is an intriguing prehistoric "camp" but not worth the time or steep admission price.

Chieftains Tomb—Near the town of Lejre is a desolate burial ground consisting of two rows of stones that form a Viking ship. Take the very tiny road at the edge of Gamle Lejre where you see the "Skibsaetningen." All of these sights and others are explained with a good map in the "Surroundings of Roskilde" brochure, available at tourist offices.

Copenhagen

It'll feel fine to be back "home" in Copenhagen. Depending on how much time you have left, there's lots more to do in Copenhagen. For departure and airport tips refer back to the pages on the first day when you landed.

Congratulations! You've completed the circle. Soon you'll be home, browsing through your photos, and this trip will be stored away in the slide carousel of your mind. But before too long you'll find yourself scheming about another far away adventure.

SCANDINAVIA IN 22 DAYS BY TRAIN

Scandinavia in 22 days by train is most efficient with a little reworking as shown in the following itinerary. You also have a few options that drivers don't. If you sleep on the very comfortable Nordic trains, places not worth driving to on a short trip become feasible. Consider a swing through Finland's eastern lakes district or the scenic ride to Trondheim.

I'd go overnight whenever possible on any ride six or more hours long. Consider streamlining your plan by doing North Zealand sights as a side trip from Copenhagen, skipping the Vaxjo-Kalmar day and spending the night on the very efficient Copenhagen-Stockholm train (there is no Copenhagen-Kalmar overnight train). The Bergen-Setesdal-Arhus-Copenhagen leg is possible on public transit, but getting from Bergen to Kristiansand will really test your patience and Setesdal is not worth the trouble if you don't have the poke-around freedom a car gives

Scandinavia in 22 Days by Train

Day	Place	Overnight in
1	Arrive in Copenhagen	Copenhagen
2	Sightsee Copenhagen	Copenhagen
3	Copenhagen, North Zealand	Copenhagen
4	Roskilde, Odense, Aero	Aeroskobing
5	Aeroskobing	Aeroskobing
6	Aero-Cop.-Vaxjo, Sweden	Vaxjo
7	Vaxjo, glass country, Kalmar	night train
8	Stockholm	Stockholm
9	Stockholm, Uppsala side trip	boat
10	Helsinki	Helsinki
11	Helsinki, Turku	boat
12	Stockholm	night train
13	Oslo	Oslo
14	Oslo	Oslo
15	Lillehammer, Gudbrandsdal	Andalsnes
16	"Golden Route," Geiranger Fjord	Hellesylt
17	Fjord country to Flam	Aurland
18	"Norway in a Nutshell"	Aurland
19	Scenic Sognefjord cruise	Bergen
20	Bergen	Bergen
21	Bergen-to-Oslo scenic train	night train
22	Copenhagen	

you. A flight straight home from Bergen would be wonderfully efficient.

The suggested train itinerary is heavy on fjord scenery (my kind of problem). You'll find the Andalsnes-Flam segment trying but worthwhile. The Aurland-Bergen boat, which is too expensive for drivers, is a great fjord finale.

Below are the basic connections you'll need to do Scandinavia by train, bus and boat (they work in both directions). Some lines make fewer runs or even close in the off season. This information is all you need to plan your trip. Pick up exact schedules as you travel, available free at any tourist office. The trip I've laid out easily justifies the purchase of a 21-day Nordtourist pass ($340 first class, $230 second class, buy at any Scandinavian station) or a 21-day Eurailpass ($370, first class only, from travel agents in U.S. only).

	Trips/day	Hours
Kobenhavn to:		
Hillerod (Frederiksborg)	40	½
Louisiana (train to Humlebaek)	40	½
Roskilde	16	½ , on Odense train
Odense (via Roskilde)	16	3
Helsingor (ferry to Sweden)	40	½
Stockholm	6-8	8
Vaxjo via Alvesta	6	5
Oslo	4	10
Berlin via Gedser	2	9
Amsterdam	2	11
Frankfurt/Rhine castles	4	10
Hamburg	5	5-½
Stockholm to:		
Kalmar	2	8
Helsinki	2	14 by boat
Turku	2	10 by boat
Uppsala	30	3/4
Oslo	3	7
Vaxjo to Kalmar	9	1-½
Helsinki to Turku	7	2-½

Oslo to:

Lillehammer	4	2-½
Andalsnes	3	66
Bergen	4	7-8
Trondheim	3	7-8

Norway's Mountain and Fjord Country

Lillehammer to:

Andalsnes	4	4
Lom (change at Otta)	3	4
Andalsnes to Alesund by bus	2	½
Andalsnes over Trollstigvegen to Geiranger Fjord	4	early a.m.
Lom to Sogndal (bus dep 8:50, 15:50)	2	4 (summer)
Sogndal to Kaupanger	10	½
Sogndal to Gudvangen	4	3
Flam to Bergen via Myrdal	3	3-½
Flam to Bergen by boat (dep 6:00, 15:05)	2	6-½ , $50
Flam-Aurland-Gudvangen by boat	3	2
Gudvangen to Voss (stop at Stalheim)	7	1¼ by bus

Kaupanger to:

Gudvangen (dep 8:50, 11:40, 14:45, 17:40)	4	2¼
Revsnes	16	¼
Flam/Aurland	4	2

Bergen to:

Haukelegrend, one trip possible daily, several changes, complicated

Alesund	1	10

South Norway

Setesdal Valley, Hovden to Kristiansand	2	5
Kristiansand to Oslo	6	4-5
Hirtshals, Denmark by ferry	4	4

Denmark

Hirtshals to Arhus	16	2½
Arhus to Odense	16	2
Odense to Svendborg	16	1
Svendborg to Aero, ferry	5 (summer)	1¼
Aero to Kobenhavn	5	5
Halsskov-Knudshoved	26	1

The Eurailpass covers all the train rides listed plus the boats
from Stockholm to Helsinki and Turku, the Denmark-Sweden
ferry and the Halsskov-Knudshoved ride. The Nordtourist pass
is good on all of these (except the Stockholm-Helsinki ride, only 50%), plus all Danish state ferries and the Kristiansand-
Hirtshals trip. Your travel agent has brochures and more info.

Scandinavia: Main Train Lines

TELEPHONING & TOURIST INFORMATION

Too many timid tourists never figure out the phones. They work and are essential to smart travel. Call hotels in advance to make a reservation whenever you know when you'll be in town. If there's a language problem, ask someone at your hotel to talk to your next hotel for you.

Public phone booths are much cheaper than using the more convenient hotel phones. The key to dialing direct is understanding area codes. For calls to other European countries, dial the international access code, followed by the country code, followed by the area code without its zero, and finally the local number. When dialing long distance within a country, start with the area code (including its zero), then the local number. (In Denmark, all numbers—local or long distance—require the area code.)

Telephoning the USA from a pay phone is easy. Gather a pile of large coins ($2 per minute) and find a booth that says international. The best budget approach is to call with a coin and have that person return your call at a specified time at your hotel. From the USA they'd dial 011-country code-area code without zero-local number. Collect, person-to-person and credit card calls are more expensive and complicated. Calls from midnight to 8:00 am are 20% cheaper, but Scandinavia to USA calls are twice as expensive as direct calls from the USA.

Country Codes
USA and Canada—1
Great Britain—44
Germany—49
Denmark—45
Finland—358
Norway—47
Sweden—46

International Access Codes
(to call out of. . .)
Denmark—009
Finland—990
Norway—095
Sweden—009
USA—011

U.S. Embassies or Consulates
Copenhagen—01-423144
Helsinki—90/171931
Oslo—02/566880
Stockholm—08/630520

Emergency Telephone Numbers
Denmark—000
Oslo (only)—000
Sweden—90000
Helsinki—002 or 000

Tourist Information Numbers

City/Country	Area Code	T.I.
Denmark	01	111415
Copenhagen	01	111325,156518
Sweden	08	223280 7892000
Vaxjo	0470	41410
Kalmar	0480	15350
Stockholm	08	7892000, 240880
Finland	90	650155
Helsinki	90	171133,174088
Uppsala	018	427044
Norway	02	427044
Oslo	02	416221,427170
Lillehammer	062	51098
Lom	062	11286
Gaupne (Nigard)	056	81211
Andansnes	072	21622
Aurland (Flam)	056	33313
Bergen	05	321480
Setesdal (Hovden)	043	39630
Setesdal (Valle)	043	37312
Kristiansand	042	26065
Arhus	06	121600
Odense	09	127520
Aeroskobing	09	521300
Roskilde	02	352700

Tourist Information (T.I.)

Each of these countries has an excellent network of tourist information offices both locally and in the USA. Before your trip, send a letter to each country's National Tourist Office (listed below) telling them of your general plans and asking for info. They'll send you the general packet, and if you ask for specifics (calendars of local festivals, good hikes around Bergen, castle hotels in Jutland and so on) you'll get an impressive amount of help. If you have a specific problem, they are a good source of assistance.

During your trip, your first stop in each town should be the tourist office, where you'll take your turn at the informational punching bag smiling behind the desk. This person is rushed and tends to be robotic. Prepare. Have a list of questions and a proposed plan to double-check with him or her. They have a wealth of material that the average "Duh, do you have a map?" tourist never taps. If you'll be arriving late, or want to arrange a room, call ahead.

In the USA, write to Norway, Sweden, Denmark or Finland c/o **Scandinavian Tourist Board**, 655 3rd Ave., New York, NY 10017, or call (212) 949-2333.

SCANDINAVIAN YOUTH HOSTELS

This is a list of most of the youth hostels that lie along our proposed tour route. I've listed their town, name, address, phone number, and number of beds—in that order. Each country has many more hostels and publishes a much more informative and complete national youth hostel handbook and the International Youth Hostel Handbook, Volume 1 comes out annually listing all 2,000 of Europe's hostels. These books are available at most hostels.

DENMARK
Kobenhavn (Copenhagen): 1) Bellahoj, Herbergvejen 8, 2700 Kobenhavn-Bronshoj, 01/289715, 308 beds. 2) Amager Sjaellandsbroen 55, 2300 Kobenhavn S, 01/522908, 448 beds. **Roskilde:** Horgarden, Horhusene 61, 4000 Roskilde, 02/352184, 114 beds. **Lyngby (Raadvad):** Raadvad, 2800 Lyngby, 02/803074, 94 beds. **Helsingor:** Ndr Strandvei 24, 3000 Helsingor, 02/211640, 200 beds.

SWEDEN
Sodra Ljunga: STF Vandrarhem, Sodra Ljunga 341 00 Lujungby, Smaland,0372/16011, 10002, 10324, 49 beds. **Vaxjo:** STF Vandrarhem, Evedal, 355 90 Vaxjo, Smaland, 0470/63070, 55 beds. **Kosta:** STF Vandrarhem, Storavagen 2, 360 52 Kosta, Smaland, 0478-50835, 50512, 44-110 beds. **Orrefors:** STF Vandrarhem, Silversparregatan 14, 380 40 Orrefors, Smaland, 0481/30020, 30513, 42 beds. **Nybro:** STF Vandrarhem, Brunnsgatan 2, 611 32 Nykoping, Sodermanland, 0155/11810, 60 beds. **Kalmar:** STF Vandrarhem, Rappegatan 1, 392 30 Kalmar, Smaland, 0480/12928, 71 beds.**Olands Skogsby:** STF Vandrarhem, Olands Skogsby, 386 00 Farjestaden, Oland, 0485/38395, 38032, 60 beds. **Ottenby:** STF Vandrarhem, Ottenby, 380 65 Degerhamm, Oland, 0485/62062, 96 beds. **Vastervik:** STF Vandrarhem, Johannesbergsskolan, Lysingsvagen 8, 593 00 Vastervik, 0490/10390, 45 beds. **Soderkoping:** STF Vandrarhem, Mangelgarden,614 00 Soderkoping, Ostergotland, 0121/10213, 30 beds. **Uto:** STF Vandrarhem, Skargarden, 130 56 Uto, Sodermanland, 0750-57600, 40 beds. **Eksjo:** STF Vandrarhem, Osterlanggatan 31, 575 00 Eksjo, Smaland, 0381/11991, 13305, 50 beds. **Stockholm:** 1) STF Vandrarhem, "af Chapman", Skeppsholmen, 111 49 Stockholm, 08/103715,205705, 130 beds. 2) STF Vandrarhem, Skeppsbholmen Vastra Brobanken, 111 49 Stockholm, 08/202506, 140 beds. 3) Zinken, Pipmakargrand 2, 117 41 Stockholm, 08/685786, 268 beds.

FINLAND
Helsinki: 1) Stadionin maja, Pohj Stadiontie 3B, 00250
Helsinki, 90/496071, 231 beds. 2) Vantaan retkeilymaja, Tik-
kurilan Urheilupuisto, Valkoisenlahteentie, 01300 Vantaa,
90/8393310, 50 beds. 3) Retkeilymaja Academica,
Hietaniemenkatu 14, 00100 Helsinki, 90/440171, 190 beds. 4)
Dipoli YH, Jamerantaival 5, 02150 Espoo, 90/460211, 158 beds.

SWEDEN
Sigtuna: STF Vandrarhem, Gula Skolan, 193 00 Sigtuna, Uppland, 0760-51861. **Uppsala:** 1) Sunnersta herrgard, Sun-
nerstavagen 24, 752 51 Uppsala, Uppland, 018/324220, 80 beds.
2) Glantan, Norrbyvagen 46, 752 39 Uppsala, Uppland,
018/108060, 50 beds. **Karlstad:** STF Vandrarhem, Ulleberg,
653 42 Karlstad, Varmland, 054/166840, 113 beds. **Fryksta:**
STF Vandrarhem, Fryksta, 665 00 Kil, Varmland, 0554/11350,
41 beds. **Varmskog:** STF Vandrarhem, c/o Fam Calvert, Varmskog, 670 24 Klassbol, Vrml. ,0570/61134, 61147, 30 beds.
Nysater: STF Vandrarhem, Lagergarden, 660 30 Varmlands-
Nysater. (Route E 18, Karlstad, 56 km), 0533/30308,
054/161124, 50 beds.

NORWAY
Oslo: 1) Haraldsheim UH, Haraldsheimvn 4, 0409 Oslo 4,
02/222965, 02/155043, 300 beds. 2) Bjerke, UH, Trondheimsvn
271, 0589 Oslo 5, 02/648787, 141 beds. **Lillehammer:** Birke-
beiner'n UH, Sigrid Undsetsvei, 2600 Lillehammer, Oppland,
062/51994, 52496, 88 beds. **Sjoa:** Sjoa UH, 2653 Sjoa, Oppland, 062/36037, 80 beds. **Dombas:** Dombas UH, 2660 Dombas, Oppland, 062/41045, 85 beds. **Aandalsnes:** Setnes UH,
6300 Aandalsnes, More og Romsdal, 072/21382, 70 beds.
Hellesylt: Hellesylt UH, 6218 Hellesylt, More og Romsdal,
071/65128, 102 beds. **Skjak:** Bismo UH, Mogard, 2692 Bismo,
Oppland, 062/14026, 44 beds. **Boverdalen:** Boverdalen UH,
2687 Boverdalen, Oppland, 062/12064, 38 beds. **Skjolden:**
Skjolden UH, 5833 Skjolden, Sogn og Fjordane, 056/86615, 30
beds. **Sogndal:** Sogndal UH, 5800 Sogndal, Sogn og Fjordane,
056/71061, 90 beds. **Laerdal:** Laerdal UH, 5890 Laerdal i Sogn,
Sogn og Fjordane, 056/66101, 40 beds. **Flam:** Heimly UH, 5743
Flam, Sogn og Fjordane, 056/32241, 21 beds. **Mjolfjell:** Mjolfjell UH, 5729 Mjolfjell, Hordaland, 055/18111, 140 beds. **Voss:**
Voss UH, 5700 Voss, Hordaland, 05/512017, 512205, 160 beds.
Bergen: Montana UH, 5030 Landas, Bergen, 05/292900, 250
beds. **Odda:** Odda UH, Eidsbratet 1, 5750 Odda, Hordaland,
054/42005, 110 beds. **Sauda:** Sauda UH 4200 Suada, Rogaland,
047/92678, 20 beds. **Vinje i Telemark:** Grungebru UH, 3893
Vinjesvingen, Telemark, 036/72765, 42 beds. **Drammen:**

Drammen UH, Korsvg62,3000 Drammen, Buskerud, 03/822189, 180 beds. **Hovden:** Triangel Feriesenter, 4695 Hovden i Setesdal, Telemark, 043/39501, 48 beds. **Kristiansand:** Roligheden UH, Marviksvn 98,4600 Kristiansand, 042/94947, 135 beds. **Hirtshals:** Kystvejen 53, 9850 Hirtshals, 08/941248, 88 beds. **Hjorring:** Thomas Morildsvej, 9800 Hjorring, 08/926700, 112 beds. **Alborg:** "Fjordparken", Skydebanevej 50, 9000 Alborg, 08/116044, 114 beds. **Hobro:** Nedre Strandvej 21, 9500 Hobro, 08/521847, 08/525666, 64 beds. **Randers:** Ved campingpladsen i Fladbro, 8900 Randers, 06/429361, 95 beds. **Arhus:** "Pavillonen", Ostre Skovvej, 8240 Risskov, 06/167298, 126 beds. **Skanderborg:** Dyrehaven, 8660 Skanderborg, 06/520673, 120 beds. **Ry:** "Knudhule", Randersvej 90, 8680 Ry, 06/891407, 96 beds. **Horsens:** Flintebakken 150, 8700 Horsens, 05/616777, 140 beds. **Ribe:** Ribehallen, Hovedengen, 6760, Ribe, 05/420620, 120 beds. **Vejle:** Vandrerhjem, Gl Landevej 80, 7100 Vejle, 05/825188, 116 beds. **Odense:** Kragbjerrggarden, Kragsbjergvej 121, 5230 Odense M, 09/130425, 230 beds. **Faborg:** Gronnegade 72, 5600 Faborg, 09/611203, 612133, 89 beds. **Aeroskobing:** (Island/Ile/Insel/Isla), Smedevejen 13, 5970 Aeroskobing, 09/521044, 73 beds. **Marstal:** Faergestraede 29, 5960 Marstal, 09/531064, 57 beds.

SCANDINAVIAN PHRASES

English Engelsk	Danish Dansk	Norwegian Norsk	Swedish Svensk
Do you speak	taler De	snakker De	taler ni
Yes/No	ja/nej	ja/nej	ja/nej
Thank you	tak	takk	tack
You're welcome	vaersagod	vaersagod	vaersagod
Excuse me	undskyld	unnskyld	forlat
Hello	dav	hi	hej
Good day	god dag	god dag	god dag
Good morning	god morgen	god morgen	god morgen
Good night	god nat	god natt	god natt
Goodbye	farvel	farvel	adjo
Man	herre	herre	herre
Woman	dame	dame	dame
Where is	hvor er	hvor er	var ar
The road to	vejen til	veien til	vagen til
When	hvornar	nar	nar
Open	abnet	apent	oppet
Town hall	radhuset	radhuset	radjuset
Post office	posthuset	postkontoret	postkontoret
Station	banegarden	jembane	jarnvag
Hotel	hotel	hotell	hotell
I'd like	jeg vil	jeg vil	jag skulle
A room	et vaerelse	et vaerelse	ett rum
Single	enkelt	med en seng	med en badd
Double	dobbelt	med to senger	med tva baddar
With bath	med bad	ned bad	med bad
Key	noglen	nokkelen	nyckeln
Toilet	toilette	toalettet	toaletten
Old/new	gammel/ny	gammel/ny	gammel/ny
Tourist office	Turistbureau	Turist Informasjon	Turistbyra
To the right	til hojre	til hoyre	til hoger
To the left	til venstre	til venstre	til vanster
Straight ahead	lige ud	rett fram	rakt fram
Stop	stop	stopp	stopp, halt
Caution	pas paa	se opp	se upp
Slow	langsom	sakte	sakta
One-way street	ensrettet	envegskjoring	enkelriktad

No entry	ingen indkorsel	gjennom-kjoring forbudt	infart forbjuden
Brake	bremse	bremse	broms
Breakdown	motorskade	motorstopp	motorstopp
Car	bil	bil	bil
Fuse	sikring	sikring	sakring
Garage	autovaerk-sted	bilverksted	bilverstad
Oil change	skifte olie	skifte olie	byt olja
Parking place	parkering-splads	parkering-splass	parkering-splats
Gas station	benzintank	bensinstasjon	bensinstation
Tire	daek	ring	tack
Mountain	bjerk	berg	berg
Valley	dal	dal	dal
Lake	vand	vann	vatten
Beach	strand	strand	strand
Town	by	by	stad
Church	kirke	kirke	kyrka
Castle	slot, borg	slott	slott
Street	gade	gate	gata
Road	vej	vei	vag
Square	torv, plads	torg, plass	torg, plats
Bridge	bro	bru	bro
Railway	jernbane	jembane	jamvag
Ferry	faerge	ferje	farja

1	en	en	en
2	to	to	tva
3	tre	tre	tre
4	fire	fire	fyra
5	fem	fem	fem
6	seks	seks	seks
7	syv	sy v	sju
8	otte	atte	atta
9	ni	ni	nio
10	ti	ti	tio
11	elleve	eleeve	elva
12	tolv	tolv	tolv
13	tretten	tretten	tretton
14	fjorten	fjorten	fjorton
15	femten	femten	femton
16	seksten	seksten	sexton
17	sytten	sytten	sjutton
18	atten	atten	aderton
19	nitten	nitten	nitton
20	tyve	tjue	tjugo
21	en og tyve	tjue en	tjugo en
22	to og tyve	tjue to	tjugo tva
30	tredive	tretti	trettio
40	fyrre	forti	fyrtio
50	halvtreds	femti	femtio
60	tres	seksti	textio
70	halvfjerds	sytti	sjuttio
80	firs	atti	attio
90	halvfems	nitti	nittio
100	hundrede	hundre	hundra
200	to hundrede	to hundre	tva hundra
1000	tusind	tusen	tusen

Breakfast	morgenmad	frokost	frukost
Lunch	middagsmad	middagsmat	middags-maltid
Dinner	aftensmad	koeldsmat	kvallsmat
Eat	spise	spise	spisa
Drink	frikke	frikke	dricka
Many	me get	mye	mycken
A little	lidt	lite	litet
The bill	regning	regning	rakning
Pay	betale	betale	betala
Menu	spisekort	spiseseddel	matsedel
Fried	stegt	stekt	stekt
Boiled	kogt	kokt	kokt

Soup	suppe	suppe	soppa
Meat	kod	kjott	kott
Calf	kalv	kalv	kalv
Lamb	lam	lam	lam
Reindeer	ren	rein	ren
Ham	skinke	skinke	skinka
Pig	svin	svin	svin
Sausage	polse	polse	korv
Fish	fisk	fisk	fisk
Cod	torsk	to rsk	torsk
Salmon	laks	laks	lax
Shrimp	reje	reke	raka
Trout	orred	orret	forell
Bread	brod	brod	brod
Cake	kage	kake	kaka
Vegetables	gronsager	fronnsaker	gronsaker
Beans	bonne	bonne	bona
Cauliflower	blomkal	blomkal	blomkal
Green salad	gron salat	hodesalat	huvudsallat
Peas	aert	ert	arta
Potatoes	kartoffel	potet	potatis
Fruit	frugt	frukt	frukt
Apple	aeble	eple	apple
Cranberry	tyttebaer	tyttebaer	lingon
Strawberry	joldbaer	jordbaer	jordgubbe
Beer	ol	ol	ol
Coffee	kaffe	kaffe	kaffe
Cream	flode	flote	gradde
Milk	maelk	melk	mjolk
Mineral water	mineralvand	mineralvann	mineral-vatten
Tea	te	te	te
Water	vand	vann	vatten
Wine	vin	vin	vin

The Months: januar, febrar, marts, april, maj, juni, juli, august, september, oktober, november, december.
The Days (Sunday-Saturday): sondag, mandag, tirsdag, onsdag, torsdag, fredag, lordag.

Finnish/Suomalainen: Yes—niin; No—en; Thanks—kiitos; Goodbye—nakemiin; Hello—hyvaa paivaa; What does it cost?—Paljonko maksaa?

HOLIDAYS & FESTIVALS

Denmark
Tivoli, May 1-September 15, always a festival, Copenhagen.
Midsummer Eve, June 23 & 24, big festivities all over Scandinavia, bonfires, dancing, burning of tourists at the stake.

Norway
Constitution Day, May 17, Independence parades and celebration, Oslo.
Midsummer, June 23-24, "Jonsok Eve" celebrated nationwide with bonfires, beer, open-air dancing, boating.
Horten Festivalen, 1st Sunday in July, small festival features all kinds of music, especially rock; located 50 mi S of Oslo in Horten, reached by train & bus from the Oslo West station.

Sweden
Midsummer, Friday and Saturday nearest June 24, dancing, games, music during height of summertime when days are longest, nationwide and throughout Scandinavia.
Asele Market, 2nd or 3rd weekend in July, Laplanders' most important folk festival for 200 years, Asele (400 mi N of Stockholm).
Ancient Gotland Athletic Games, 2nd Saturday and Sunday in July, ancient sports contests between Norsemen, Stanga (Gotland), 25 mi SE of Visby.

These are just a few of Scandinavia's countless folk and music festivals. The Scandinavian Tourist Board office in the USA will send you free calendars of events.

BACK DOOR CATALOG
ALL ITEMS FIELD TESTED, HIGHLY RECOMMENDED,
COMPLETELY GUARANTEED AND DISCOUNTED BELOW RETAIL.

The Back Door Suitcase/Rucksack $60.00

At 9"x21"x13" this specially designed, sturdy functional bag is maximum carry-on-the-plane size (fits under the seat). Made of rugged waterproof Cordura nylon, with hide-away shoulder straps, waist belt (for use as a rucksack), top and side handles, and a detachable shoulder strap (for toting as a suitcase). Lockable perimeter zippers allow easy access to the roomy (2200 cu. in.) central compartment. Two outside pockets are perfect for books and other frequently used items. Over 8,000 Back Door travelers have used these bags around the world. Rick lives out of one for 3 months at a time. Comparable bags cost much more. Available in navy blue, black, grey, or burgundy.

Moneybelt $6.00

Required! Ultra-light, sturdy, under-the-pants, nylon pouch just big enough to carry the essentials comfortably. I'll never travel without one and I hope you won't either. Beige, nylon zipper, one size fits all, with instructions.

Catalog . . . . Free

For a complete listing of all the books, products and services Rick Steves and Europe Through the Back Door offer you, ask us for a copy of our 32-page catalog. It's free.

Eurailpasses

With each Eurailpass order we offer a free taped trip consultation. Send a check for the cost of the pass you want along with your legal name, a proposed itinerary and a list of questions and within two weeks we'll send you your pass, a taped evaluation of your plans, and all the train schedules and planning maps you'll need. Because of this unique service, we sell more train passes than anyone on the West Coast.

Back Door Tours

We encourage independent travel, but for those who want a tour in the Back Door style, we do offer a 22-day "Best of Europe" tour. For complete details, write to us at the address below.

All orders will be processed within one week and include a one year's subscription to our Back Door Travel newsletter. Add $1.00 postage and handling to each order. Washington state residents add 7.8% sales tax. Sorry, no credit cards. Send checks to:

Europe Through the Back Door
120 Fourth Ave. N. • Edmonds, WA 98020 • (206) 771-8303

Other Books from John Muir Publications

22 Days Series
These pocket-size itineraries are a refreshing departure from ordinary guidebooks. Each author has an in-depth knowledge of the region covered and offers 22 tested daily itineraries through their favorite destinations. Included are not only "must see" attractions but also little-known villages and hidden "jewels" as well as valuable general information.

22 Days Around the World by R. Rapoport and B. Willes (65-31-9)
22 Days in Alaska by Pamela Lanier (28-68-0)
22 Days in the American Southwest by R. Harris (28-88-5)
22 Days in Asia by R. Rapoport and B. Willes (65-17-3)
22 Days in Australia by John Gottberg (65-40-8)
22 Days in California by Roger Rapoport (28-93-1)
22 Days in China by Gaylon Duke and Zenia Victor (28-72-9)
22 Days in Dixie by Richard Polese (65-18-1)
22 Days in Europe by Rick Steves (65-05-X)
22 Days in Florida by Richard Harris (65-27-0)
22 Days in France by Rick Steves (65-07-6)
22 Days in Germany, Austria & Switzerland by R. Steves (65-39-4)
22 Days in Great Britain by Rick Steves (65-38-6)
22 Days in Hawaii by Arnold Schuchter (28-92-3)
22 Days in India by Anurag Mathur (28-87-7)
22 Days in Japan by David Old (28-73-7)
22 Days in Mexico by S. Rogers and T. Rosa (65-41-6)
22 Days in New England by Anne Wright (28-96-6)
22 Days in New Zealand by Arnold Schuchter (28-86-9)
22 Days in Norway, Denmark & Sweden by R. Steves (28-83-4)
22 Days in the Pacific Northwest by R. Harris (28-97-4)
22 Days in Spain & Portugal by Rick Steves (65-06-8)
22 Days in the West Indies by C. & S. Morreale (28-74-5)
All 22 Days titles are 128 to 152 pages and $7.95 each, except *22 Days Around the World*, which is 192 pages and $9.95.

"Kidding Around" Travel Guides for Children
Written for kids eight years of age and older. Generously illustrated in two colors with imaginative characters and images. An adventure to read and a treasure to keep.
Kidding Around Atlanta, Anne Pedersen (65-35-1) 64 pp. $9.95
Kidding Around London, Sarah Lovett (65-24-6) 64 pp. $9.95
Kidding Around Los Angeles, Judy Cash (65-34-3) 64 pp. $9.95
Kidding Around New York City, Sarah Lovett (65-33-5) 64 pp. $9.95
Kidding Around San Francisco, Rosemary Zibart (65-23-8) 64 pp. $9.95
Kidding Around Washington, D.C., Anne Pedersen (65-25-4) 64 pp. $9.95

Asia Through the Back Door, Rick Steves and John Gottberg (28-76-1) 336 pp. $13.95

Buddhist America: Centers, Retreats, Practices, Don Morreale (28-94-X) 400 pp. $12.95

Bus Touring: Charter Vacations, U.S.A., Stuart Warren (28-95-8) 168 pp. $9.95

Catholic America: Self-Renewal Centers and Retreats, Patricia Christian-Meyer (65-20-3) 325 pp. $13.95

Preconception: Preparing for Pregnancy and Parenthood, Brenda E. Aikey-Keller (65-44-0) 256 pp. $13.95

Complete Guide to Bed & Breakfasts, Inns & Guesthouses, Pamela Lanier (65-43-2) 520 pp. $14.95

Elderhostels: The Students' Choice, Mildred Hyman (65-28-9) 224 pp. $12.95

Europe 101: History & Art for the Traveler, Rick Steves and Gene Openshaw (28-78-8) 372 pp. $12.95

Europe Through the Back Door, Rick Steves (65-42-4) 404 pp. $14.95

Floating Vacations: River, Lake, and Ocean Adventures, Michael White (65-32-7) 256 pp. $17.95

Gypsying After 40: A Guide to Adventure and Self-Discovery, Bob Harris (28-71-0) 264 pp. $12.95

The Heart of Jerusalem, Arlynn Nellhaus (28-79-6) 312 pp. $12.95

Indian America: A Traveler's Companion, Eagle/Walking Turtle (65-29-7) 424 pp. $16.95

Mona Winks: Self-Guided Tours of Europe's Top Museums, Rick Steves (28-85-0) 450 pp. $14.95

The On and Off the Road Cookbook, Carl Franz (28-27-3) 272 pp. $8.50

The People's Guide to Mexico, Carl Franz (28-99-0) 608 pp. $15.95

The People's Guide to RV Camping in Mexico, Carl Franz with Steve Rogers (28-91-5) 256 pp. $13.95

Ranch Vacations: The Complete Guide to Guest and Resort, Fly-Fishing, and Cross-Country Skiing Ranches, Eugene Kilgore (65-30-0) 392 pp. $18.95

The Shopper's Guide to Mexico, Steve Rogers and Tina Rosa (28-90-7) 224 pp. $9.95

Ski Tech's Guide to Equipment, Skiwear, and Accessories, edited by Bill Tanler (65-45-9) 144 pp. $11.95

Ski Tech's Guide to Maintenance and Repair, edited by Bill Tanler (65-46-7) 144 pp. $11.95

Traveler's Guide to Asian Culture, Kevin Chambers (65-14-9) 224 pp. $13.95

Traveler's Guide to Healing Centers and Retreats in North America, Martine Rudee and Jonathan Blease (65-15-7) 240 pp. $11.95

Undiscovered Islands of the Caribbean, Burl Willes (28-80-X) 216 pp. $12.95

Automotive Repair Manuals

Each JMP automotive manual gives clear step-by-step instructions together with illustrations that show exactly how each system in the vehicle comes apart and goes back together. They tell everything a novice or experienced mechanic needs to know to perform periodic maintenance, tune-ups, troubleshooting, and repair of the brake, fuel and emission control, electrical, cooling, clutch, transmission, driveline, steering, and suspension systems and even rebuild the engine.

How to Keep Your VW Alive (65-12-2) 424 pp. $19.95
How to Keep Your Rabbit Alive (65-21-1) 420 pp. $19.95
How to Keep Your Subaru Alive (65-11-4) 480 pp. $19.95
How to Keep Your Toyota Pickup Alive (28-81-3) 392 pp. $19.95
How to Keep Your Datsun/Nissan Alive (28-65-6) 544 pp. $19.95

Other Automotive Books

The Greaseless Guide to Car Care Confidence: Take the Terror Out of Talking to Your Mechanic, Mary Jackson (65-19-X) 224 pp. $14.95

Off-Road Emergency Repair & Survival, James Ristow (65-26-2) 160 pp. $9.95

Road & Track's Used Car Classics, edited by Peter Bohr (28-69-9) 272 pp. $12.95

Ordering Information

If you cannot find our books in your local bookstore, you can order directly from us. Your books will be sent to you via UPS (for U.S. destinations), and you will receive them approximately 10 days from the time that we receive your order. Include $2.75 for the first item ordered and $.50 for each additional item to cover shipping and handling costs. UPS shipments to post office boxes take longer to arrive; if possible, please give us a street address. For airmail within the U.S., enclose $4.00 per book for shipping and handling. All foreign orders will be shipped surface rate. Please enclose $3.00 for the first item and $1.00 for each additional item. Please inquire for airmail rates.

Method of Payment

Your order may be paid by check, money order, or credit card. We cannot be responsible for cash sent through the mail. All payments must be made in U.S. dollars drawn on a U.S. bank. Canadian postal money orders in U.S. dollars are also acceptable. For VISA, MasterCard, or American Express orders, include your card number, expiration date, and your signature, or call (505)982-4078. Books ordered on American Express cards can be shipped only to the billing address of the cardholder. Sorry, no C.O.D.'s. Residents of sunny New Mexico, add 5.625% tax to the total.

Address all orders and inquiries to:
> John Muir Publications
> P.O. Box 613
> Santa Fe, NM 87504
> (505)982-4078

MEN OF IRON

MEN OF IRON

HOWARD PYLE

Adapted by
William Kottmeyer
St. Louis Public Schools

Illustrated by
CLARK B. FITZGERALD

Phoenix Learning Resources
New York

The Phoenix Everyreaders

The EVERYREADERS were selected from the great literature of the world and adapted to the needs of today's children. This series retains the flavor of the originals, providing mature content and dramatic plot structure, along with eye appeal designed to motivate reading.

This approach was first developed in the renowned St. Louis Reading Clinic by Dr. Kottmeyer and is the direct outgrowth of wide and successful teaching of remedial reading.

A high interest level plus the carefully controlled vocabulary and sentence structure enable pupils to read the stories easily, confidently, and with enjoyment.

ISBN 0–7915–1361–0

1   3   4   5   6   7   8   9   0   99   98   97   96   95   94   93

CONTENTS

1.

*I*n the year 1400 Myles Falworth was only eight years old. Myles was too young to understand what was happening in England then. But later he found out. Then he understood what he had seen as a little boy.

Richard II had been king. But Richard was a weak king. He had many strong enemies. These enemies killed him. And so Henry IV became the new king.

Every king has friends. The new King Henry did not like Richard's friends. Richard had given them castles and lands. Henry took the castles and lands away and gave them to his own friends. So Richard's friends soon became King Henry's enemies. They plotted to kill him. But Henry found out about this. He got his army together and went after them. One by one he caught and killed them.

Myles' father, the blind Lord Falworth, had been Richard's friend. Lord Falworth had not been in the plot to kill King Henry. He lived quietly in his fine castle with his wife, his son, and his servants.

One night little Myles heard a horse come galloping in. The boy looked out the window. The horse was smeared with sweat and was panting. The rider threw himself at the door and beat on it. Myles knew him well. He was Sir John Dale, Lord Falworth's dear friend.

Even Myles knew something was wrong. Sir John was pale and could hardly stand up.

"Let me in!" he panted. "They're close behind me."

"John!" cried Lord Falworth. "Come in. Who is after you?"

"The King's men. They'll kill me. Can you hide me?"

Myles heard no more. His mother put him to bed then. But early the next morning he saw the horsemen ride in. A knight in black armor led them.

Myles crept downstairs. The black knight was sitting at a table. He was asking questions. Myles could hear his men going through the rooms.

Myles' father stood before the fireplace. The big scar on his face was red. That was the wound that had made him blind. Myles knew his father was angry. The scar always got red then. The boy came closer. He slipped his hand into his father's. Lord Falworth held the little hand tight. He said nothing.

2

Suddenly there was a noise in the hall. Voices called. Men ran here and there. The black knight got up. Sir John Dale came walking in, pale as death.

"Here I am," he said. "I give myself up."

The black knight pulled out his great sword. Sir John raised his arm over his head. The black knight swung. Myles hid his face. He heard the heavy blow — and another. Sir John gave a last loud cry. Then his body crashed to the floor. Myles looked again. Sir John lay dead. The black knight's sword dripped blood.

That night Lord and Lady Falworth and Myles left the castle. Myles always remembered that night. Old Diccon Bowman wrapped him in a sheepskin. Then he carried him down to the castle yard. A stranger was warming his hands over a fire. His riding boots were covered with mud. He had been riding hard. Years later Myles found out who he was. His father's friend at the King's castle had sent him.

"Fly for your life!" he said. "The King will kill you. He knows you hid Sir John."

The horses were waiting. Myles saw Father Edward, Lord Falworth's old friend. Diccon Bowman picked Myles up. He held the boy on his saddle. All night long they rode. At last Myles fell asleep. When he woke up, the sun was shining.

2.

*F*or eight years the Falworth family lived in Father Edward's little farm house. Lord Falworth had often helped Father Edward. Now Father Edward was paying him back. The King's men looked everywhere for the Falworths. They never found them. Father Edward kept them too well hidden.

Myles had a hard life. Every morning he walked six miles to school. At night his mother taught him French.

"Why must I learn French?" he asked.

"You will grow up soon," said the blind father. "England is no place for a Falworth. You may have to go to France to live."

Every afternoon Diccon Bowman took over. In those days a boy had to learn to fight. Old Diccon had followed Lord Falworth to war. He had been a great fighter himself. Now he taught Myles. Myles had to learn to use the big broadsword, then the short sword. He had to fight with the long wooden poles called cudgels. Diccon taught him to shoot, too. Soon Myles was a good shot with the long bow and cross bow. Every day he had to use the long battle lance. Then came throwing the knife and dagger.

These things a knight had to learn. Knights did not learn to wrestle. But Myles did.

"He will fight with sword and lance," said Lord Falworth. "But the wrestling will make him strong."

"It makes him quick, too," said Father Edward.

So every Sunday a champion wrestler came to the little farm house. Myles was strong and he learned quickly. Soon he could throw any lad under twenty.

Myles' life was hard, but he had fun, too. Other boys lived near by. He could swim in the river. There were the hills and woods. Sometimes there was a fair in the little town not far away.

Here Myles had his first fight. He beat a young fellow of twenty with the cudgel. He was then only fourteen.

Old Diccon had gone to the fair with him. The old man met some friends and Myles went off alone. Soon Diccon saw a crowd gathering. He guessed a fight had started. He ran to look. There he saw Myles fighting a big strong fellow. Diccon pushed through to pull Myles away. But he saw Myles was doing well. So he stood and watched. Soon Myles landed a hard fast blow. The other lad went rolling in the dust. Diccon never told Lord Falworth about the fight, but he was proud of the boy.

A little later Myles became a squire. When boys were about fifteen they could be squires. Then they trained hard to become knights. Myles was now a big strong boy. He had brown curling hair and laughing blue eyes. His shoulders were broad and he was tough as an oak.

On the day he was sixteen, Old Diccon met him coming home from school.

"Myles," he said sadly, "go see your father. He wants to talk to you. Oh, Myles, you must go away tomorrow."

Myles stopped. "Go away?" he cried.

"Yes," said Diccon. "You go to some fine castle. You must learn to be a knight. You must live in a lord's castle."

"Are you joking, Diccon?"

"No, lad," said Diccon. "Your father will tell you. I hate to see you go."

It was true. Myles was to leave next day. His father, mother, and Father Edward were waiting.

"We have talked it over, Myles," said Lord Falworth. "It's time you left. You must make your way. I'll give you a letter to my friend, the Earl of Mackworth. He is the King's friend. Once we were very close. We swore we would always help each other. I think he has not forgotten. He will help you rise in the world. Tomorrow Diccon takes you to his castle. Give him this letter. It asks him to give you a place there."

"But why, Father?" asked Myles. "Why must I go?"

"We have taught you what we can here, my boy. We cannot make you a knight. You must live in a great lord's castle. You must learn to fight. You must fight for your lord. You must see battle and war."

He turned away. Now Father Edward spoke.

"Myles," he said, "you will need some money. Here are forty silver coins. You can pay them back some time. God bless you."

Early the next morning Myles and Diccon rode away. Myles' eyes were wet. He turned his head so Diccon would not see. Myles was on his way to become a man of iron — a knight.

3.

The Mackworth castle looked like a town. Tall chimneys and roofs rose high above the ground. The castle stood on a high hill. A river ran around three sides. On the fourth side was a deep ditch, or moat. The road ran along this moat. Myles looked up at the great castle. He knew now what a great lord the Earl must be. Myles felt a little homesick.

They rode over the moat bridge and up the hill. Diccon spoke to the gate keeper. He let them in. A guard took them to the castle. Here a house servant met them. He led Myles and Diccon to a great waiting room. They sat down to wait.

People came and went, laughing and talking. He had never seen such a busy place. Here and there stood men in armor. Near a door sat three or four young squires. Myles poked Diccon.

"Are they squires, Diccon?" he asked.

"Yes."

"And will I be with them?"

"Yes, if the Earl takes you."

Myles looked at the boys again. They were looking at him and laughing. Poor Myles knew he looked like a country boy. His face got red.

Suddenly one jumped up and came over.

"Hello," he said. "What's your name? Can I help?"

"My name is Myles Falworth," said Myles. "I have a letter here for the Earl."

"A letter?"

"Yes. I want to be a squire here."

"Have you ever been a castle squire?"

"No, but I can fight with the sword and lance."

"Who gave you the letter?"

"My father. He was once the Earl's friend."

"Well, maybe that will help. My name is Francis Gascoyne. I'll help you. Get your letter ready. The Earl will come out soon. He's going on a trip. We squires here are to go along. Do you know him?"

"No," said Myles, "I don't."

"I'll tell you when he comes out. Listen! I hear the horses outside. Get ready."

Myles got his letter out. A tall thin squire came out. He spoke to the other squires. They jumped up and got in line. The men in armor stood stiff and straight. Everyone was quiet.

"He's coming," whispered Francis.

Two men suddenly came through the door. One was a priest. The other was the Earl of Mackworth.

9

4.

The Earl of Mackworth was a tall man. He had a thin face, thick, bushy eyebrows, and a hawk nose. He wore a long gray beard. His coat was black velvet, trimmed with fur. Under his coat was a shirt of armor. His riding boots came to his knees. A golden collar hung from his neck.

Myles just looked. Then he heard Francis whisper.

"That's the Earl. Give him the letter."

Myles hardly knew what he was doing. He walked forward, his heart pounding. When he came near, the Earl stopped. He looked hard at Myles. Myles kneeled and held out the letter. The Earl took it. He looked at it, then at Myles.

"Who are you?" he said. "What do you want?"

"I am Myles Falworth. I come to be a squire."

The Earl shot a keen look at him.

"Falworth?" he said. "I know no Falworth."

"The letter will tell you," said Myles. "My father was your friend."

The Earl opened the letter.

11

"You may stand," he said. He read quickly. Then he put the letter in his pocket.

"That's the way it is," he said to the priest. "We who rise in the world pay for it. I knew this man a long time ago. Now he loads his son on me. I've got to take him, I guess." He looked around. "Here," he called to Francis. "Take this boy to the kitchen. Get him something to eat. Then take him to Sir James Lee. Tell Sir James to put his name on the castle books. Tell him to train him for fighting. He's not to be a castle squire. He seems too rough and husky to help women."

The men laughed. Then Francis pulled him back. The Earl and his men went out. Myles, Diccon, and Francis were alone. Francis looked put out.

"I lose my fun," he said. "I don't go along. I wish you had come this morning."

"I guess I bring trouble to everybody," said Myles bitterly. "I wish I had never come here."

"Never mind," said Francis. "It's not your fault. Come on. We'll get you something to eat."

5.

The Earl of Mackworth, like other lords, kept a small army of knights and squires. These knights and squires fought for him. When the King was fighting a war, the Earl sent his men to help. So the Earl trained many boys as squires. The squires became knights. The more knights he had, the greater was the lord.

There were about eighty squires at Mackworth Castle. They were from eight to twenty years old. Those under fourteen were called pages. They helped the women. After fourteen they became real squires. The big squires were eighteen to twenty years old. These big squires ruled the younger ones.

Often the big squires made the younger ones work for them. When Myles came, there were only thirteen big squires. But they were big and strong. The sixty-four other squires and pages did what the thirteen told them. Often the big squires were cruel.

Sir James Lee trained the squires. Sir James was an old one-eyed knight. Many wounds marked his

13

tough old body. He had fought for King Henry until he was badly wounded. Now he could fight no more. So the King had sent him to Mackworth Castle to train squires. He was a fierce, tough old fighter.

But Sir James did his job well. He ruled the squires with an iron hand. He lived near them. Whenever they started a fight or made too much noise, he would roar "Shut up!" Then every squire was as quiet as a mouse.

Francis now took Myles to Sir James' room. The old man sat at a table. Walter Blunt, leader of the big squires, was there. Walter was about twenty, a head taller than Myles.

"Sir," said Francis, "here is a new squire. My Lord the Earl sends him."

"Another one?" snarled the old knight. "I've got enough trouble now. He doesn't look very smart, either."

"Sir," said Francis, "my Lord said he should not help in the castle. He should learn to fight."

"He did, did he? I'll try him first. You, what's your name?" He did not wait for Myles' answer. "Blunt, have you got room for him?"

"Yes, sir. One boy is sick. There's an empty cot."

"All right. Put him there. Write his name in the books. Now get out."

Francis and Myles got out quickly.

"The old boy is tough today," said Francis. "Come on. I'll show you around."

Francis took Myles through the castle and the yards. Before long they were great friends. At last they came to the armor maker's shop.

"The Earl sent a piece of his armor in," said Francis. "Would you like to see it?"

"Yes, I would," said Myles eagerly.

The armor maker was a big friendly man. He showed the boys the armor. Myles could not take his eyes off it.

"Say, Francis," said the man, "did I show you my new dagger?"

"No," said Francis.

He opened a big box. He took out a beautiful dagger. The boys looked with open mouths. Francis asked to hold it.

"For whom did you make it?" he asked.

"A knight in London. And, what do you think? He died before I finished it. Nobody has enough money here to buy it. I must keep it myself — and I'm a poor man."

"How much do you want for it?" asked Francis.

"Seventeen silver coins buys it."

"Ah, yes," said Francis. "I'd love to have it. But I haven't got nearly that much. I don't get that much in a year."

"Francis," said Myles, "you've been a good friend to me. I've got forty silver coins. I can spend them as I want to. Will you take the dagger as a present from me? I want you to have it."

Francis' eyes opened wide. He could hardly talk.

"Do you mean it?" he said at last.

"I mean it," said Myles. "Take it."

The armor maker first thought Myles was joking. But then Myles got out the money.

"Now I call that a fine present, don't you, Francis?" said the armor maker.

"Yes, sir," said Francis. "It's a wonderful present." He suddenly threw his arms around Myles and kissed him. "Myles," he said, "I liked you when I first saw you. Now I love you like a brother. I'll always be your true friend. Maybe you'll need a friend here. New boys often do. Well, you've got one."

"Thanks," said Myles. "I'd like you as my friend, Francis."

And so Myles made himself a good friend. Arm in arm the boys walked across the castle yard.

6·

*W*hen Walter Blunt called the roll next morning, he stopped Myles.

"The Earl talked to Sir James Lee," he said. "Sir James won't take you until he sees what you can do. He wants to see you at the posts." The posts were wood, about six feet high. Squires learned to use the sword by swinging at these posts. "Have you ever practiced at the posts?" asked Blunt.

"Yes," said Myles. "Every day the last four years except Sundays."

"With shield and broadsword?"

"Yes. And sometimes with the short sword."

"All right. Use that stuff there. That's number seventeen. That will be your number."

So Myles got down the armor. It was rough and heavy. The squires wore it to get used to fighting armor. There were an iron breast plate, shoulder plates, arm and leg plates, and a helmet. The big shield was covered with leather and iron. The heavy broadsword was dull.

Five mornings a week the squires marched out to the posts. Sir James Lee and two other knights worked with them. They showed them how to hit and guard themselves. After five minutes the boys began to sweat. Then they began to pant. But Sir James kept them going until they were ready to drop. Then they rested while others practiced.

Sir James watched Myles hacking at his post. Myles did his best. He practiced every blow he had learned. Sir James said nothing for a while. Then he spoke.

"You fight like an ox," he said. "There! You got back too slowly. Do it again. Get back quicker."

Myles did it again. "Bah!" cried Sir James. "You're a week late. Here, swing at me."

Myles looked at Sir James. The old man had no sword. He carried only a heavy stick.

"Swing, I say!" said Sir James. "What are you waiting for? Are you afraid?"

"No," said Myles, "I'm not afraid. I don't fear you or any man." Myles swung as hard as he could. Crack! A shock ran up Myles' arm. He nearly dropped the sword. Then — crack! Sir James rapped him on the helmet. Myles saw stars.

"There," said Sir James. "If I had a sword then, I'd have knocked your brains out. Now, swing again — if you're not afraid."

Myles' eyes watered but he spoke up bravely. "All right," he said, "I will." This time he got back fast. He took Sir James' stick on his shield.

"Good!" said the old man. "Remember that. When you cut at the legs, get back fast. Now do it at the post."

Francis and the other squires had watched and heard it all. They had never heard anybody talk back to Sir James before.

"Say, you've got your nerve, Myles," said Francis later. "I never heard anybody talk that way to Sir James."

"Well," said another squire, "I think he liked it. But, say! He cracked you hard, Falworth. I'm glad he didn't hit me. Did it hurt?"

"A little," said Myles. But his head was still ringing.

7.

*A*ll the squires talked about Myles that night. They told how the new boy Falworth had spoken back to Sir James Lee.

"What did he say, Falworth?" asked Walter Blunt.

"Nothing," said Myles. "He showed me how to guard myself quickly."

"I don't know why he should," said Blunt. "You must be very fast — or very slow."

"He's fast," said Francis. "The second time he couldn't hit Falworth. Myles caught the stick on his shield."

But Myles' bravery soon got him into trouble. The big squires made the others work for them. They soon saw that Myles would not be easy to handle. Myles got angry when they tried it.

"I tell you, Francis," he said, "I won't do it. I'll not do their work. Why should we?"

"Why fuss about it?" said Francis. "All the others do it. They'll beat you if you don't. I'd rather do it than get beaten."

"Well, I won't do it. Maybe you're used to it. I don't care how many there are."

"Then you're a fool," said Francis.

The smaller squires washed in the yard every morning. Walter Blunt had had a big wooden tub made for the big squires. They put the tub inside where it was warm. Every morning two younger squires had to carry water. That made Myles angry.

"I'll die before I carry water for them," he said.

One night, soon after this, the squires were wrestling and playing in their big hall. Myles and Francis were trying to keep three others off their cots. Just then Walter Blunt came by. He was going to the castle. He stopped on his way through.

"I'll be back late, I guess. Falworth and Francis, you carry water tomorrow morning."

Then he was gone. Myles stood looking after him, his mouth open. Francis laughed. But then he put his hand on Myles' shoulder.

"Myles," he said, "you won't make trouble, will you?"

Myles did not answer. He sat down on his cot.

"I said I'd die before I'd get their water," he said.

"Yes," said Francis, "but you didn't mean it."

Myles said nothing more.

The next morning Francis shook him awake. Still half asleep, Myles got his clothes on. He stumbled

21

after Francis, still dressing. He did not wake fully until he saw Francis filling the buckets.

"Say!" cried Myles. "What are you doing? I'll carry no water."

"All right," said Francis, "don't. I'll carry them myself." He picked up two buckets and started off. Myles did not want Francis to do all the work himself. He grabbed the other bucket. And so he did carry the water after all.

The boys poured the water into the tub. A big squire sat on his cot, watching.

"Why so late?" cried the big squire.

"We haven't got wings," shouted Myles. His voice rang through the hall. Everybody looked up. Walter Blunt came forward.

"What's this?" he cried. "What do you mean, talking like that? I ought to crack your head for you." He picked up a wooden club and looked hard at Myles. Myles looked straight back at him. Trouble was coming fast. Then Francis dragged Myles away.

"Myles, Myles," said Francis. "Why look for trouble? Every big squire will have it in for you."

"I don't care," said Myles. "Did you hear him? He talked to me like a dog."

And so Myles made himself some enemies, too. He soon found out that enemies mean trouble.

8 •

*M*yles was still boiling as the squires marched to morning prayers. Francis tried to talk to him again.

"Why look for trouble, Myles?" he asked. "It's foolish. You wanted to come here. Why don't you do what we all do?"

"You're no friend to say that," said Myles. He pulled his arm away from Francis.

"You're wrong," said Francis. "If I were not your friend, I would say nothing. It doesn't hurt me when you get beaten." They got to the chapel just then, or they would have quarreled.

Myles soon saw the big squires were still angry. He had to ask Blunt a question about his armor. Blunt gave him a short cold answer. Myles' face got red.

"I'll show him," he said. "I'm as good as he is. He's trying to shame me."

The storm was ready to break.

The day was hot and sticky. The squires asked to go swimming in the river. Sir James said they could go after they had practiced at the posts. Myles was putting his armor away when a page came in.

"Sir James wants you, Falworth," he said.

"Just my luck," said Myles. "Now I can't go swimming."

"Wilkes and I will wait for you, Myles," said Francis. "Won't we, Edmund? You hurry and go to Sir James."

Sir James Lee was waiting in his room.

"Well, boy," he said, "I've watched you. I think you'll do. We'll make a knight out of you yet."

"Thank you, sir."

"Are you going to write home soon?" he asked suddenly.

"Why — yes," said Myles in surprise.

"When you do, remember me to your father. I knew him well. We were good friends and we often fought together. For his sake I'll try to help you as much as I can."

"Thank you, sir."

Sir James held up his hand. "Never mind. I must tell you something else. Do you know your father is an outlaw?"

"No!" cried Myles. "You lie!"

"Don't lose your head, boy," said Sir James quietly. "Sometimes it's no shame to be an outlaw. He is in

great danger. You don't know how great it is. If the King knew where he is, your father would die to-morrow. I tell you this to warn you. Say nothing about him to your friends. Tell no one who he is."

"But why is he an outlaw? What did he do?"

"I cannot tell you now. I must tell you only this. Your father has an enemy. This enemy is as strong as the Earl himself. All your father's bad luck comes from him. He blinded your father. If he finds out where your father is, he will kill him."

"Sir," cried Myles, "tell me his name. I will kill him."

Sir James smiled. "You talk like a boy. Wait till you grow up. This man is the champion knight of England. He is a great lord and the King's dear friend."

Myles was silent for a long while. Then he spoke. "Will the Earl not be my friend now? He was once my father's friend."

Sir James shook his head. "The Earl can do nothing now. He cannot help your father openly. If the King found it out, that would be the end. No, boy. You must fight your own way."

Myles' eyes flashed. "Then the Earl is a coward! He is no true friend. He turns his back on my father."

"You are a foolish boy," said Sir James. "You

know nothing. The Earl will lose all he has by helping your father openly. Don't be a fool. The Earl is like everybody else. He has many enemies. He must save himself first."

Myles could say no more. But his heart was bitter. Sir James saw it.

"You will have hard knocks, lad," he said. "Don't get into too many fights yet. Try to get along quietly here. Else people will want to know who you are. You will help your father by keeping quiet."

And just five minutes later Myles had the first great fight of his life.

Francis and Edmund Wilkes were still waiting. Six or eight other squires were there. Walter Blunt and three other big squires were dressing.

"Why so long, Myles?" said Francis. "We thought you would never come."

"Where are you going, Falworth?" called Walter Blunt.

"I'm going swimming," said Myles.

"No, you're not," said Blunt. "You don't leave the castle today. Remember how you talked back this morning? You're going to shine my armor."

Now, everything had gone wrong with Myles that day. He was still bitter about the Earl. Blunt's words were the last straw. Francis and Edmund got ready to leave.

"Stop, Francis," cried Myles. "I'll not do that dog's dirty work. I'm going along."

Everybody looked up surprised.

"Are you crazy?" cried Blunt.

"No, I'm not. You can't make me do your work."

"I'll break your head," said Blunt angrily. He stooped and picked up a wooden club. He came at Myles.

Francis stepped between them. "Don't hurt him, Blunt," he begged. "He's new here. He doesn't know our ways."

"Get back, Francis," said Blunt. He pushed Francis away. "I'll teach him our ways."

Myles looked around. He saw another club lying on the floor. He picked it up and backed against the wall. His heart was beating hard. His face was white, but his blue eyes had a hard look. Blunt stopped.

"Tom! Wat! Ned!" he called. "Come here. Give me a hand with this fellow."

"Don't touch me," panted Myles. "I'll brain you."

Francis slipped away. Out the door he ran for help.

The battle was sharp and short. Blunt rushed. Myles struck, hard and wild. Blunt turned the blow with his club. Then he dropped his club. He grabbed Myles around the body, holding his arms.

Myles dropped his club, too. He pulled his right arm loose. He smashed Blunt full in his face. He hit him again. Blunt fell back. Then the three big squires were on Myles. They held his legs and arms. Suddenly they all crashed to the floor together.

Myles fought like a wild cat. He scratched, kicked, and bit. He got one by the collar and ripped his clothes off to his belt. He kicked another in the stomach. The younger squires stood on the benches, watching. But they feared the big squires too much to help. Myles fought his battle alone.

But four to one was too much. Slowly they wore him down. Blunt now picked up the club again. He stood over them, waiting his chance. The blood ran from his mouth. He had murder in his eyes.

"Hold him a little," he cried. "I'll stop him."

Then he got his chance. Myles' head came up. Blunt swung. Myles got his arm partly up. The club smashed against arm and head. Myles cried out.

"They'll kill him!" cried Wilkes.

Blunt struck two more times. Both blows got Myles on the body. At last they got him down. They held his arms and pushed his face to the floor. Blunt smiled. He raised the club for one terrible blow to end the fight.

9.

"What is this?" roared a loud voice. There stood Sir James Lee. The fight stopped. The big squires jumped to their feet.

The older boys stood quiet. But Myles was deaf and blind with anger. He looked wildly around him, breathing hard.

"Who hit me?" he cried. "Who hit me when I was down? I'll kill him!" Then he saw Blunt. "You did it! You coward!" He jumped at Blunt like a tiger.

"Stop!" cried Sir James Lee. He caught Myles' arm.

Myles still did not see Sir James. "I won't stop!" he cried. He swung blindly at the old knight. "Let me go! I'll kill him!"

Sir James pinned him against the wall. Only then did Myles see him.

"Do you know who I am?"

Myles stopped then. His arms fell. "Yes," he said, "I know you." He stood still.

Sir James took Blunt and Myles by the arm. Off they marched to his office. The other squires followed, saying nothing. Sir James shut the door, leaving the others outside.

"Now, Walter Blunt, what does this mean?"

"Why," said Blunt, "this fellow won't obey us. I was just teaching him a lesson. He's been making trouble since he got here."

"You're a liar!" cried Myles. "I make no trouble."

"Shut up, you," said Sir James. "I'll tell you when to talk."

"I won't shut up," said Myles. "I have no friend here. Everybody is against me. I won't let him tell lies about me."

Even Blunt was surprised at Myles' boldness. He had never heard anybody talk so to Sir James. Sir James just looked at Myles. Myles began to cool off.

"Boy," said the knight, "you know no rules or laws. It's time you learned them. Now listen. Don't open your mouth again. Don't say one word before I tell you to. If you do, I'll lock you up for a week. You'll go on bread and water." Sir James turned to Blunt. "Now, Blunt, tell me your story."

This time Blunt's story was fairly true. Then Myles had a chance to tell his.

"Now, Blunt," said Sir James, "I said the boys could go swimming. Why did you say no?"

"I thought we older squires were the leaders."

"You are. But you don't go against my orders. Do you get that?"

"Yes, sir."

"All right. You may go. Let me hear no more of beating with clubs. You may fight your battles, but there will be no killing. This is twice, now. I've got enough. Shake hands, now, and be friends."

Blunt held out his hand. Myles held his behind him.

"No," said Myles. "He hit me when I was down. I won't shake his hand."

"All right, if that's the way you want it," said Sir James. "You may go, Blunt. Falworth, stay. I have more to say to you."

Blunt went out. "Now tell me this, Falworth. Why won't you work for the big squires? The other squires do it. They always have."

"I just can't stand it," said Myles. "They can't make me. If you tell me to, I'll do it."

"No," said Sir James, "I won't tell you to. You do as you want. But how can you hope to get away with it? They're older and stronger than you."

"I don't know," said Myles. "But they won't make me. I don't care if there are a hundred big squires."

"You're a fool," smiled the knight. "You're not being brave. You're being foolish. You're butting your head against a wall. Be smart. Strike when you're ready. If I were you, I'd get my friends behind me. Then —" Here he stopped. But Myles knew what he meant.

"Sir," said Myles, "I thank you. You've been good to me. I ask your pardon."

"I give it," said Sir James. "But don't forget. Do this again and I'll lock you up. Now go."

Only one boy was there when Myles came out — faithful Francis. He had given up his swimming to stay with his friend.

"It was good of you, Francis," said Myles. "I don't know why you love me so."

"Why," said Francis, "because you're the bravest and best fighter of all the squires."

Myles laughed. But he was glad Francis said so. "I'll not fight for a while," he said. Then he told Francis what Sir James had said.

Francis gave a surprised whistle. "Say, Myles," he said, "I think he's on your side. Well, so am I. And we'll get others."

"Good," said Myles. "We'll soon be strong enough to stand against the big squires."

10·

$\mathcal{E}$very boy likes a secret hiding place. Myles and Francis found theirs one summer afternoon. They called it the Nest.

Behind the stables lay the oldest part of the Mackworth castle. It had great thick walls. From one part rose a tall round tower. The green ivy grew thick on the walls. Pigeons lived on the top. Here and there were windows.

Myles had often wondered about the old tower. One day he pointed to it and said, "Francis, what is that place?"

"That's the old Roman tower. It's hundreds of years old. They say you can get lost in it."

"Who lives there now?"

"Nobody — not for more than a hundred years. They say that the Earl then was Earl Robert. Somebody murdered the Earl's brother there. Some say the Earl did it himself. Since then the tower has been shut tight."

Myles looked at the tower. "It looks strange. I

wonder what it's like inside. Have you ever been inside, Francis?"

"No. It's been locked since Earl Robert's time."

"Why haven't you gone inside?"

"Why, I never thought of it." He turned and looked at it carefully. "How would you get in?"

"Look," said Myles. "See that hole in the ivy? That's a window. You could get from the wood pile to the hen house roof. You can climb from there to the stable roof."

Francis looked again. "Do you want to try it?"

"Yes."

"All right. Lead the way. I'll follow you."

They got to the stable roof easily enough. But the window was ten feet too high to reach. Myles looked up and down. The ivy branches were thick and strong. But below lay a stone walk.

"I think I can climb up there," said Myles.

"You'll break your neck."

"No," said Myles. "I don't think so. Here goes."

"You're crazy," said Francis. "One day you'll get me into trouble. But if you go, I'll follow."

It was a dangerous climb. Myles made it, though, and Francis followed. Soon they were sitting in the window. The old shutter was locked, but they broke it. They climbed inside. There they found themselves near a stone stairs.

At the bottom was a great oak door hanging on one hinge. Myles pushed it open. They heard soft footsteps.

"Ghosts!" whispered Francis. Myles felt a cold chill. But then he laughed.

"Rats!" he said. "Look there. He's big as a cat." He picked up a stone and threw it. Hundreds of tiny feet ran off.

The boys looked around them. The room was round, about twenty feet across. There were old chairs, tables, and chests. Piles of old clothes and leather lay near the wall. There was another pile of old armor, helmets, spears, pots and pans.

"Look at that!" said Francis. "Old — I've never seen such old things. Look at that bow. They haven't used those for years."

They pulled the stuff apart, raising clouds of dust. Now and then a big rat ran to his hole.

"Come on," said Myles, brushing his coat. "It's getting late. Let's see what else there is."

Another stairway led upward through the thick wall. The room above was like the one they had left. Then came two more. Steps led from the third floor to a closed door. The boys pushed against it. The lock gave way. They tumbled outside and looked in wonder. It was the top story. The roof had fallen in and the ivy grew on the inside walls.

"Look," said Myles. "There's another room over there."

They went through the open door. Now they found themselves in a beautiful little chapel. The boys looked down through the windows. Far below lay the castle and other buildings. They could see the tiny people at their work. It was like a show. The cool wind fanned their hot faces.

"We'll call it our nest," said Francis. "We'll come here like the hawks."

The next day Myles got the armor maker to make him some spikes. He and Francis drove them into the tower wall. Now they could safely climb to the window when they wanted.

11·

The two friends kept their secret a little while. Sometimes they looked through the old armor. Other times they went to the tower top and just talked. Myles told Francis stories he had read in his school books. Francis told him about the life in the castle. Myles was eager to hear.

"Francis," he said, "I have never talked with a girl. I don't think I could. You must be pretty brave. I'd rather fight three men than talk to a girl."

Francis laughed. "Why, they're nothing to fear. They're very gentle and kind."

"I could never face one," said Myles.

It was in the tower that Myles first told Francis his family secret. This is how it happened. The two friends were alone one day in the chapel.

"Say," said Francis, "you've been here a month or more. The Earl has never had you at work in the castle. I wonder why, Myles."

"He would rather have a dog there than me," said Myles bitterly.

"Why, Myles?"

"Because he's a coward. He's afraid to have me there."

"Afraid? Why afraid of you?"

Myles remembered what Sir James had said. He knew he should keep quiet. But Francis was his best friend.

"I'll tell you," he said. And so he told Francis the whole story. "Now," he said, "see what the Earl does? He leaves me alone. He won't help his old friend, my father. He won't help me. Don't you think he's a coward?"

"I don't know, Myles," said Francis. "The Earl

has many enemies. He's been in trouble, I know. He knew many of the King's enemies. Maybe he knows best. Maybe he can't help you right now."

"I didn't think you'd stand up for him," said Myles bitterly. "I'll never forgive him. I thought you were my friend. I thought you would stand by me."

"I do, Myles, I do. I like you better than anybody. But I think the Earl and Sir James will help you."

"Then why don't they do it now?"

Francis did not answer. After a while he said, "Do you know who your father's enemy is?"

"No," said Myles. "My father never said anything. Sir James won't tell me. But this I know. Some day I'll kill him." He stopped. Francis looked at him. Myles' eyes were full of tears. Francis looked away.

"You won't tell anybody, will you, Francis?"

"No, Myles. You know I won't."

After this the boys were closer friends than ever before.

Myles never forgot what Sir James had told him. Now, a month later, he was the leader of the young squires. So one day he told his new plan to Francis. Myles wanted to form a club of young squires. They would call themselves "Knights of the Rose." They would meet in the old tower.

"But what will we do?" asked Francis.

"We'll stick together and fight the big squires."

Francis shook his head. He did not like to fight. "Why ask for trouble?" he said. "They don't bother us much. Let's let them alone." But Myles would not stop. "Now listen, Myles," said Francis. "This means a fight. Are you going to do it? I don't want to fight them."

"Yes, I'll fight them. I'll fight alone if I have to."

"All right. If you want a beating, you can have it. I'll pick you up when they are through with you."

"Don't joke about it," said Myles angrily. "I mean it. If you won't help, say so. I'll get somebody else."

"Now, Myles, don't get angry. I'm your friend. I'll stick with you."

They talked to two other young squires and Edmund Wilkes. All three wanted to join the club. Myles and Francis showed them the tower rooms. The five then picked fifteen more boys to join.

And so the twenty Knights of the Rose came to be. They had secret pass words and signs. Myles became the Grand Commander. They held their secret meetings in the old tower.

12.

*F*or a week everything went well. Then one morning Myles, Francis, and Edmund sat in the castle yard. Myles was shining his armor. The other two watched. Just then a page named Robin came by. He had been crying. Myles looked up.

"Here, Robin," he called. "What's the matter?"

"Mowbray beat me with a strap," he said.

"Beat you? Why?"

"The big squires sent me to get them a drink. They said I took too long."

"Now, see there," said Myles. "They beat him for that. I'm sick of it. I won't stand it any longer."

"Myles," said Francis, "cool off. You know Robin would make anybody angry. He always fools around and never works. A beating will do him good."

"How you talk, Francis! You know you don't want to see him beaten. How many of our Knights are here today?"

"Seventeen," said Wilkes. "Three are gone today."

"Seventeen are enough," said Myles. "Let's meet

42

this afternoon. We have had enough of the big squires."

Francis looked at Edmund. "This is it," he whispered.

So that afternoon they met in the tower. Myles did most of the talking. "Let's have it out with them now," he said. "We've taken enough."

The boys looked at each other. Myles soon saw they did not want to fight.

"What do you want, Myles?" said one. "Do you want us to jump them?"

"No," said Myles. "I thought you would all pitch in. I can see you don't want to. But I'll tell you this. I've had enough. I won't ask you to fight. But do this. Stand by me. Don't let five or six of them get on me."

"Well, there's Walter Blunt. He's strong. He can beat any two of us."

"No, he can't," said Myles. "You're too much afraid. I tell you I don't fear him. I'll fight him myself. But you fellows must back me up."

"If you fight him, I'll back you up, Myles," said Francis.

"I will, too," said Edmund Wilkes.

"And I, and I, and I," cried the others.

So they agreed that Myles would have a fair chance. If a fight started they would stand by him.

13.

*S*omehow the news of the coming fight leaked out. That evening the squires talked eagerly among themselves. Before long the big squires heard about it too. Some put their knives near their beds. They were careful to let the younger squires see them do it. Many young hearts beat harder to see the shining blades. But nothing happened that night. The lights went out early.

As the sun arose, they got up. Myles put his clothes on. He sat on his bed and waited.

Then it happened. Two young squires started to bring the big squires' water. As they crossed the room Myles called:

"Stop! We get no more water. Set those buckets down. Get back to your places."

The two boys stopped. Then everybody began to talk. The Knights of the Rose came over to Myles. They gathered behind him.

The big squires were not ready for trouble.

"What's the matter here?" cried one. "Why aren't you getting the water?"

"Falworth says we shouldn't," said the squire.

"What do you mean, Falworth?"

Myles' heart beat hard, but he spoke up bravely. "I mean you carry your own water."

"Say, Blunt!" called the big squire. "Falworth says they won't carry our water."

Blunt had heard it all. He was just dressing. Now he came forward. "Now, Falworth," he said, "you're making trouble again. You won't carry water? I'll see if you won't!" He kept coming. Two or three big squires were close behind. Then Francis spoke up.

"Look here, Blunt. You better stop or you'll get hurt. We will not let you bang Falworth again. Stand back."

Blunt stopped. He looked at the boys behind Myles. They were pale, but they stayed there. Blunt turned suddenly and walked back to the other big squires. He said a few words. Now the thirteen big squires picked up the wooden clubs. Some got out their knives. The little squires and pages ran to get away.

Myles was pretty sure he could throw any one of the big squires. He knew some of his friends would get hurt in a big fight. Now he stepped forward.

"Look here, Blunt," he called. "You hit me when

45

I was down last time. This is our fight. Will you fight me alone? Look, I'll throw my club away. I'll fight you bare handed." He threw his club down.

"All right," said Blunt. He threw his club down too.

"Don't go, Myles," cried Francis. "He's a dirty liar. He's got a knife. I saw him hide it. It's in his shirt."

"You lie!" said Blunt. "I swear I have no knife. Your friend knows you're afraid of me, Falworth."

"You're a liar," cried Myles. "Swear you have no knife, and I'll meet you."

"You heard me say so. What more do you want?"

"All right. Come on."

Francis tried to hold Myles back. "He has a knife, Myles. I saw it." But Myles was hot for the fight. He pulled loose.

The two stopped and looked each other over. Blunt was taller, stronger, and older. But that did not seem to bother Myles.

The boys saw Blunt slip his hand toward his shirt. Myles saw it, too. He knew what that meant. Francis had been right. Myles jumped like a flash. He caught Blunt's hand. He felt the dagger.

"You dog! Help, Francis, he has a knife!" cried Myles.

Now Myles' friends started to help. But the big

squires pushed forward. "Stand back," they cried. "Let them fight it out alone. Get back or we'll knife you, too." They pulled out their knives and held them ready.

Myles' friends stopped just a moment. But that quickly the fight ended. Blunt tried to get his knife loose. Myles hung on, holding his wrist. Blunt twisted and pulled, but he could not get it free.

"You won't get it out," panted Myles. "You won't stab me!"

Blunt suddenly let go the knife. He threw his arms around Myles, trying to throw him down. In that moment he lost his battle.

Nobody saw just what happened. Myles moved fast as lightning. Walter Blunt came flying over Myles' shoulder. He landed on the stone floor — on his head. He lay very quiet.

The big squires now ran forward to pick him up.

"You'll pay for this, Falworth," cried one. "He's dead."

Myles started for him, but he ran. Francis now took him by the arm. "Come on, Myles. You might have killed him."

"I don't care," said Myles. But he let Francis and Edmund lead him away.

Blunt's friends carried him off. They laid him on a bench. Some rubbed his hands. Others poured water on his face. At last Blunt opened his eyes. He sat up. They had to hold him up. His face was white as death.

"Ah," said Edmund. "I'm glad you didn't kill him."

"So am I," said Myles.

14·

*B*ut Myles' victory did not end the fight. It was the beginning. More bitter battles lay before him.

The day after the fight the water tub was gone. The big squires made a show of looking for it.

"Ho! Ho!" roared Edmund Wilkes. "They have stolen their own water tub. They don't want another fight."

No one ever carried water again. But the war was not over. One morning, a week later, Myles and Francis were crossing the yard. They passed a few big squires.

"Ah, Falworth!" they cried. "Do you know Blunt is nearly well again?"

"No," said Myles, "but I'm glad he is."

"You won't be glad very long. He will get you."

"Yes," said another, "I wouldn't want to be in your shoes. He will have your blood. He's coming back next Wednesday or Thursday."

"Myles," said Francis a little later, "I think he will try to get you."

"I don't know," said Myles. "I don't care much. I'm not afraid of him."

Blunt came back one morning after chapel. All the squires were in the big hall. Blunt read the names of those who were to work in the castle that day. Myles stood with the others. Blunt finished reading the names. Then he walked straight up to Myles. Nobody made a sound. All could hear him.

"Falworth," he said, "you tricked me. I'll never forget it. I'm going to get you. You're going to remember me as long as you live."

Myles faced him boldly. "All right," he said. "I'm not afraid of you."

"You're not?" said Blunt. "Well, you will be when I get through." He laughed and walked away.

The big squires started again that very night. They ordered the young squires about as they used to.

"They're as bad as ever," said Myles to the others a few days later. The Knights of the Rose were together in the old tower. "If we don't stop it now, we will never stop it."

"You had better quit, Myles," said Edmund Wilkes. "They will kill you yet. They all have it in for you now."

"I will not quit. It isn't right. I'm going to tell them again tonight."

And he did. That night the squires were playing and running as they always did before bed time. Myles jumped on his cot.

"Quiet!" he shouted. "Listen to me." The boys stopped playing. "I want those big squires to hear this. We will do their work no more. There are twenty of us who won't work."

He jumped down. The big squires said nothing that night. But the next day they made their plans.

Myles and Francis were throwing their daggers at a target. Some other squires were watching. Suddenly little Robin, the page, stuck his head around a corner.

"Ha, ha, Falworth," he said. "Blunt is going to get you today. I heard him. He's going to cut your ears." He ducked back and ran.

Myles went after him and caught him. He brought him back by the neck, squealing and kicking. "There!" said Myles. He threw him on the bench. "Sit there, you little runt. Now tell me what you mean. And quit crying — or I'll cut your ears off."

At last it all came out. A big squire had sent

Robin to clean his boots. Robin had fallen asleep on a cot instead. Voices awakened him. Some big squires came in. Robin hid under his cot.

Those who came in were Walter Blunt and three big squires. The others were trying to talk Blunt out of something. Blunt would not listen. He wanted to lie in wait for Myles. When they caught him they were going to cut his ears. Myles boiled to hear it. People cut the ears of robbers and thieves in those days.

"He would not dare!" cried Myles, his eyes flashing.

"Yes, he would," said Francis. "His father is Lord Blunt. He is a great lord. The Earl would not do anything to him. But, Robin, where will they wait for Myles?"

"Behind the gate as he goes to get his armor," said Robin.

"Are they there now?" asked Wilkes.

"Yes, nine of them," said Robin. "I heard Blunt tell Mowbray to get the others. They know Myles will go that way this morning."

The boys looked at each other a while. "Well, boys," said Myles, "what shall we do?"

"Go tell Sir James," said Francis.

"No," said Myles. "That's a coward's way. They want a fight. Let's give it to them."

51

Myles had his way. They agreed to fight. Francis made the plan. Wilkes went to get the Knights of the Rose. Myles and Francis went to the armor maker. They wanted knives — a foot long.

"No, no," said the armor maker. "You are wrong, Myles. If I give you knives, somebody will be killed. The boy's family will get you into trouble. You might even hang. I'll tell you something better. Go to Old Tom and get yourselves cudgels. Those long wooden cudgels are better than knives. You can crack a head with them. They are better than knives or daggers. You can hit them before they get close."

Myles thought a minute. "I think you are right. Come on, Francis. Let's get the cudgels."

15.

At the end of the castle yard was a picket gate. This gate opened on a narrow passage. The passage led to another yard. The big squires were waiting in the passage. Francis had made a plan. The Knights of the Rose would hide near the picket gate. Myles was to go into the passage. When the big squires jumped him, Myles' friends would rush in and save him.

So Myles walked in alone. He looked here and there, but saw no one. He held his cudgel tight. Suddenly he saw the big squires come running. Myles turned and ran to his friends. "Come on! Come on!" he cried.

"Get him!" cried Walter Blunt. "He's getting away! Hit him with a rock!" He picked up a stone and threw it. It sailed past Myles' head, just missing him.

"Charge!" cried Myles' friends. They came tearing through the gate. Myles now turned and ran with them.

The surprised enemy stopped. They held their knives ready. Then they saw the cudgels. They turned and ran.

One big squire stopped and threw his knife at Myles. His aim was deadly. But Myles ducked like a cat. The knife rattled on the stones. The big squire turned to run again. But he was a moment too late. Myles reached him with his cudgel. He went over like a bottle and rolled senseless on the ground.

The big squires banged the gate shut. The Knights of the Rose were left outside. They shouted and beat on the gate.

"Watch out!" cried Myles. "Here they come.

Run! They've got stones." They scattered around the yard, hiding behind the walls.

The gate flew open. The big squires threw the stones at the running boys. One hit Edmund Wilkes on the head. He dropped like a log. Another hit Myles' shoulder. His whole arm went dead.

The big squires would not come into the yard. The Knights of the Rose would not charge because of the stones. So each side stayed where they were.

The lad whom Myles had hit sat up. He rubbed his head. Wilkes now came to and crawled behind a wall. Myles looked around a corner. The big squires were talking it all over.

"Ho, Falworth!" cried Blunt. "We want to talk."

"What do you want?"

"No fighting until we talk?"

"All right. Talk."

"Look! We throw our stones down. We lay down our knives. You put your cudgels down."

Myles laid his cudgel down and stepped out. Francis and the others followed.

"Now," said Myles, "what do you want?"

"Listen," said Blunt. "You asked me to fight you your way last time. Then you played a dirty wrestling trick. Well, I met you as you asked."

"Yes," said Francis, "and you had a knife. You would have stabbed him."

"You lie," said Blunt. "I had no knife. Now listen, Falworth. I fought you, didn't I?"

"You ought to know," said Myles. His friends laughed. Blunt bit his lip.

"Well," he said, "I dare you to fight me now. You and I alone. We fight with sword, shield, and helmet. That's the way knights would fight."

"You coward, Walter Blunt!" cried Wilkes. "You know you can beat him with swords. You are four years older. You've had three times as much practice."

Blunt said nothing. He just looked at Myles and smiled. Myles looked at the ground. He knew Blunt could beat him with swords.

"You're afraid to fight me, Myles Falworth," said Blunt. The big squires began to laugh.

Then Myles looked up. His face was white. "No," he said, "I'm not afraid. I'll fight you, Blunt."

"Come on, then. The men are all eating dinner. Nobody will stop us."

"You shall not fight him, Myles!" cried Francis. "He will kill you. You shall not fight him, I say."

Myles turned but said nothing.

"What's going on?" called a knight from a window.

"Blunt and Falworth are going to fight it out," said a squire. The man laughed. But it was no joke for poor Myles.

16·

*M*yles did not seem to have a chance. Fifteen minutes fighting, and Blunt did not have a scratch. Poor Myles was bleeding in five or six places. Twice Francis and Edmund had tied up his wounds.

He was not badly hurt yet. He carried a shield and wore a steel helmet. But Myles' friends saw how it would end. The big squires cheered Blunt and laughed at Myles.

Once Myles pulled back panting. He leaned on Francis' shoulder. Francis' eyes were wet with tears. "Dear Myles," he whispered, "fight no more. Give up. You have not hurt him yet. He will kill you."

Blunt heard him. "You're hurt, Falworth," he said. "I don't want to kill you. Say I've beaten you. You fought a good fight. Give up now."

"Never!" cried Myles. "I'll never give up. You can kill me first. I won't give up."

Everybody there knew Myles meant it.

"No," said Blunt, "I'll fight you no more, Falworth. You have had enough."

56

"By heavens!" cried Myles. "You shall fight me, you coward! You wanted this fight. Now go on. Let go, Francis. I say he shall fight me."

And then Blunt began to lose his head. Myles was like a bulldog. He kept coming, kept swinging. Blunt backed up. Then Myles' friends gave a shout. Blunt pulled back. He put his hand to his shoulder. He looked at it. It was bloody. The blood began to run down his sleeve. He looked at it, then at his friends.

"I will fight no more," he said.

"Then give up!" cried Myles.

The shouts of Myles' friends stung Blunt. The fight started again. Blunt suddenly cut at Myles' legs. But Myles had learned that lesson from Sir James Lee. Myles met the blow as Sir James had met it. He struck as Sir James had struck him — full and true. Blunt's helmet helped. Myles felt his sword bite through the steel cap. Blunt's sword fell. He stumbled back. His eyes rolled. The blood shot down his cheek.

Blunt turned and fell flat. Myles stood there panting. He had won again. But what a victory! "Is he dead?" he whispered.

"I don't know," said Francis. He led Myles away.

A little later a big squire passed Myles' cot. Myles lay there, his cuts burning hot.

"Sir James wants you, Falworth," he said.

By now Myles knew Blunt was not dead. It hurt him to move, but his heart was light. He walked into Sir James' office. Sir James sat alone. Myles told him the whole story. Sir James listened.

"I never saw such a boy," he said. "Always fighting, Falworth! Did you try to kill him?"

"No, sir, I did not."

"Well, you almost did. You were lucky. Now, sir, I'll stop this. You fight no more with swords. Get to your cot. Stay there a week — and don't come out. You get bread and water twice a day. We'll cool you off a little."

Myles wiped his eyes. Sir James looked keenly at him. "You look pale," he said. "Are you hurt bad?"

"No, sir, not much. I'm sick in my stomach."

"Yes," said Sir James, "I know that feeling well. That's from losing blood. Go on, now. I'll send somebody to patch you up. Lie down and rest."

Myles never knew it, but Sir James went straight to the Earl. He told him the whole story. The Earl laughed. "Good," he said. "The boy is brave. But let's get this Blunt away. He'll kill Falworth or Falworth will kill him."

So Blunt never troubled the squires again. The big squires did their own work ever after. Myles had won the first great fight of his life.

17.

The months passed, but still Myles did no castle work like the other squires. By this time he got to know more about the Earl's family. Lady Mackworth was a thin, middle-aged woman. Lady Anne was the daughter. She was tall, thin, and dark. She looked like her father, the Earl. The squires all said she was beautiful, but quiet and proud. Lady Alice was the Earl's niece. She was a very pretty black-eyed girl of fourteen.

There was also Lord George Beaumont, the Earl's brother. Myles soon got to know Lord George well. Lord George had heard about Myles' fight and liked him. He often talked to Myles about his adventures and hopes. He himself had fought his own way and felt friendly to Myles. So Myles felt more friendly to the Mackworth family because of Lord George. Still, he was bitter about the Earl himself.

Even in those days boys played ball. Myles and the other squires played a game called trap ball. During the spring they played every day in the big castle yard. They batted the ball much as we do today. One windy spring day Myles was batting. The wind was blowing behind him. He had already hit three or four balls to the end of the yard. There stood the wall of the Earl's garden. The castle ladies used this garden to walk in. No one else could come in.

The boys backed up to the wall to catch any ball that might go so far. Once more Myles hit the ball hard and high. The wind caught it and carried it. Over the garden wall it sailed.

The boys' shouting stopped. "Now you've done it, Myles," said Francis. "It's the only ball we have." The boys all came in.

"I couldn't help it," said Myles. "How did I know the ball would fly so far? Well, I lost it. I can go get it. I'll climb the wall."

"No, you won't, Myles," said Francis quickly. "Don't be crazy. Do you want an arrow in your ribs?"

Now the Earl's garden was the one place outsiders never saw. Only Lady Mackworth and her family used it. Just before Myles came to the castle, a cook's helper had climbed the garden wall. The soldier had shot him with his cross bow. The poor fellow had dropped into the garden, an arrow in his side.

The other squires remembered him well. But

Myles just shook his head. "I'll climb the wall and get it," he said.

A pear tree grew near the wall. Some of the branches hung over into the garden. Myles looked to see if any one were watching. Telling the boys to keep watch, he climbed the tree. Now he crawled out on a big branch until he was over the wall. He let himself down and hung by his hands. He looked down. His feet were a few feet above the wall.

He saw that the wall was pointed like a house roof. Thick green moss grew over it. "I'll slip," he said to himself. But it was too late to go back. He had to jump.

He let go. The branch flew back up. Myles hit the wall and tried to hold on. The moss slid under his feet. He made a grab with his hands. His fingers slipped. With a sharp cry he pitched into the garden below!

He saw green leaves before his eyes. Then, with a crash, he broke through a wooden frame that formed a little garden house. He landed heavily.

He heard a scream — and another. He sat up. The world was whirling around him. He closed his eyes, then opened them. He was looking straight at the Lady Anne and Lady Alice. They were holding each other tight, looking at him with wide, scared eyes.

18·

*L*ady Anne spoke first. "Who are you? Where are you from?" Her voice shook.

"My name is Myles Falworth," he said. "I am a squire here."

"Ah, yes," said Lady Alice. "I thought I knew your face. Did I not see you with Lord George?"

"Yes, lady," said Myles bashfully. "I am sometimes with him."

"And what are you doing here?" asked Lady Anne angrily. "How dare you come into our garden?"

"I didn't mean to," said Myles. His face was hot and red. "I slipped and fell. Lady, I did not mean to frighten you."

Lady Anne looked at him. His clothes were torn and dirty. His face was red. He looked down at the ground. Lady Anne could not stay angry. She looked at Lady Alice. They had to smile.

"But why did you climb the wall?"

"I came to find our ball. I hit it over the wall."

"You came for only a ball?"

"Well, we have only this one ball. I lost it, so I thought I ought to get it."

The two young ladies were no longer frightened. Lady Alice laughed. Myles' face got still redder.

"Well, Master Myles," said Lady Anne, "I think you mean no harm. But you should not have come. My father would be angry if he knew. Do you know no one may come here? Even Lord George may not. The soldiers will shoot any one who does."

"Yes," said Myles, "I know. But we wanted to play some more."

"Well, you are a bold fellow, Myles. You were brave to come, so I'll help you. Where did the ball go?"

"Over there," said Myles, pointing. "If you will let me, I'll get it and go."

"No!" cried Lady Anne. "Stay where you are. Some one may see you. I'll get it."

So she left Myles and her cousin. Myles did not know what to say or do. He twisted a little twig he had in his hands. Lady Alice watched him. "Did you hurt yourself?" she said.

"No," said Myles. "I've had worse falls than this."

"You have? Well, you did scare me."

"I'm sorry," said Myles. "I would not scare you for all the world."

The young lady laughed and blushed. She looked

toward the garden. "My cousin can't find it," she said.

But soon Lady Anne came back carrying the ball. Myles thanked her.

"Did you hurt yourself?" said Lady Anne.

"No," said Myles. "I've had worse falls. Once I thought I'd broken my ribs. And once, long ago, I fell from a windmill. I caught the blade and tried to get a ride. The fall was much worse than this."

Now the squires had been whistling to Myles from the yard. They had seen him fall. "I would like to stay," said Myles. "But do you hear my friends? They think I may be hurt. If I whistle and throw the ball back they will know I'm all right."

"Go ahead," said Lady Anne. "Then tell us about that windmill. We young ladies never hear such stories. They won't let us talk to boys. We would like to hear your adventures."

So Myles threw the ball back and whistled. Then he told them about the windmill. The girls laughed. He told of other adventures. Soon he was bashful no longer. He found he liked to talk to them. But at last he had to go.

"Well," he said, "I never had such a good time! I have never talked to ladies before — except my mother. I would rather talk to you than anybody. I wish I could come again."

The young ladies laughed. "You are a bold lad to ask such a thing," said Lady Anne. "How could you come? Would you fall from the wall again?"

"No," said Myles, "but if you say yes, I'll get here."

"No," said Lady Anne, "I don't dare tell you to come. But if you are brave enough —"

"Yes!" said Myles eagerly. "I'm brave enough."

"Then we will be here next Saturday at this time. I'd like to hear more of your adventures. What did you say your name is?"

"Myles Falworth."

"Then we will call you Sir Myles. You shall be our knight. How would you like the Lady Alice to be your true lady?"

"Yes," said Myles eagerly, "I would like that." Then he blushed again.

"I need no knight," said Lady Alice, blushing too. "You stop teasing, Anne! Let him be your knight."

"No," laughed Lady Anne. "You shall be his lady. He shall be your knight. Maybe some day he will do a brave deed for you. But now, Sir Myles, you had better go. I'll let you out the back gate. If you come again, be careful. The Earl may clip your ears if he catches you."

That evening Myles told Francis of his adventure. His friend listened with open mouth.

"But, Myles," he said, "did Lady Anne not seem proud and cold?"

"No," said Myles. "Only at first. And, Francis, think of it! She said Lady Alice should be my true lady! And I am to go again, next Saturday. Lady Anne said I could."

About this time Myles wrote home again, telling of his strange adventure. He told also about going back to the garden. Then he wrote this:

"So Francis and I got some big spikes. We drove them into the garden wall. On Saturday I climbed up the wall. The two ladies were there waiting. They said they were angry that I came, but they were not. They thought I was brave to come again."

During the next month Myles climbed the wall six times. Lady Anne would not let him come oftener. And so the three became good friends.

19.

But suddenly it all ended. One Saturday afternoon he climbed the wall again. The three talked for about half an hour. Then it was time for Myles to go. He was telling a joke the squires had played on a watchman.

The young ladies listened with laughing faces. Myles was looking at Lady Alice. Suddenly he saw her smile fade away. Her eyes got wide and frightened. She gave a cry and jumped up.

Myles turned quickly. His heart seemed to stop beating. There, with a terrible look, stood the Earl of Mackworth.

Myles never knew how long they just sat there. Lady Anne got up slowly. She and Lady Alice just stood there, pale and shaking. The Earl pointed to the castle. Myles could see his finger shake.

"You girls!" he cried with a hard voice. "You girls! What does this mean? Why are you here with this fellow? Get to your rooms. Don't come out until I tell you to. Go, I say!"

"Father," said Lady Anne, "do not hurt this young man." She was pale as death. "Please do not hurt him. I asked him to come. He would not have come had we not asked him."

The Earl stamped his foot. "Did you not hear me?" he cried. "I told you to go. I'll settle with this fellow."

"Father," began Lady Anne again.

But the Earl roared, "Go!"

The Earl watched until they were gone. Myles stood there, his eyes on the ground. He knew the Earl was looking at him. Suddenly the Earl spoke. "What have you to say?"

Myles raised his eyes. "I have nothing to say."

"Did you hear what my daughter said? She said you came because they told you to. Is that true?"

Myles' throat was dry. "No," he said at last. "It is not true. I came here looking for a ball. Then I asked them if I could come again. I have. No, I did not come because they told me. I came because I wanted to. I asked them to let me come."

The Earl grunted. "How many times have you been here?" he asked.

Myles thought a moment. "This is the seventh time."

"You know no one is to come here, don't you?" said the Earl. "Do you know what I'll do to you?"

"Maybe you will kill me," said Myles slowly.

"No," said the Earl. "I will not kill you. You come from a good family. But what if I cut off your ears? What if I have you beaten in the castle yard?"

The blood rushed to Myles' face. He looked up quickly. "No," he cried boldly. "You shall not shame me. My family is as good as yours. You can kill me, but you shall not shame me."

"Well," said the Earl, "who do you think you are? A young lord? Or a prince? Are you to tell me what to do?"

Myles began to get angry. "No," he said, "I'm not a lord or a prince. But I'm as good as you are. I'm the son of your old friend. You know my father is blind and helpless. You know he is an outlaw. But I'd rather be in his place than yours. He has nothing, but you —"

"Go on," said the Earl. "Finish it — or show yourself a coward. What's the matter with me?"

"You have shamed yourself," said Myles. "You will not help a true friend."

"Myles Falworth," said the Earl, "you are a bold fool. How do you dare say that to me? Don't you know that will make it worse for you?"

"What else could I do?" cried Myles. "You told me to say it or be a coward. I am no coward."

"That I believe," said the Earl. "You're as bold

71

as anybody. But listen to me. You say I do nothing for my old friend, your father. You lie. I'll take your talk because of him. And I will forgive your coming here — for his sake. There's the gate. Get out! But wait. How did you get in here?"

Myles told him about the spikes. The Earl looked sharply at him.

"But you did not drive the spikes in alone," he said. "Who helped you?"

"I cannot tell you," said Myles.

"All right," said the Earl. "I won't ask you to. Now go. Knock the spikes out. No more tricks, now. Get out."

20·

*M*yles was glad he had got off so easily. But as he thought it over, he began to worry. He had not said anything while Lady Alice was there. What did Lady Alice now think of him? He talked to Francis.

"I know I'm not a knight, Francis," he said. "Still, some day I would like to be her knight. I just stood there and said nothing to help her."

72

"I would not worry," said Francis. "I think you're lucky. The Earl was kind to you. He must like you."

"Yes," said Myles, "he was good to me. But I said I'd never go back to see her. A knight would not give up so easily. I've got a plan, Francis. I need your help. You work in the castle. I want to write her a letter. You can slip the letter to her."

"Oh, no, I won't. I'll keep out of trouble, thank you. You give her your own letter."

But Myles kept after Francis to do it. At last he agreed. He knew a girl who often saw Lady Alice. So he gave her the letter to give Lady Alice.

Myles felt better then, but not very long. That night as the squires were getting ready to go to bed, a call came for Myles.

"Myles Falworth! Myles Falworth!"

"Here I am," cried Myles. "Who wants me?"

It was the Earl's own man. "The Earl wants to see you, Myles Falworth. Get ready and come on."

Myles quickly changed his clothes. What could the Earl want? Myles could guess it was about his letter. He followed the man to the Earl's rooms. The man opened the door of the Earl's bedroom. Myles went in.

The Earl was eating his evening meal in bed. Myles saw him sitting up against two red silk pillows. He had a white cloth over his knees. He held

73

a silver tray of bread and cheese on his lap. Two pages and three men were waiting on him. Near by were a dozen candles to light the room.

At last the Earl finished. He washed his hands and mouth from a silver bowl. He leaned back and waved Myles to come. The Earl sent the others away. Myles came up to the bed. The Earl looked at him a moment.

"I guess you know why I sent for you," he said. "I got the letter you sent Lady Alice. I have it here. I just finished reading it." He took it out and read it again. "I see no harm in it, but write her no more letters."

"I meant no harm," said Myles.

"I believe you. You may go."

Myles still stood there.

"Well, what is it?" asked the Earl.

"Lady Alice did say I could be her knight."

"Don't be a fool," said the Earl. "You are not even a knight yet."

"I know you think I'm a fool," said Myles.

"Listen, Falworth. I've been as good to you as I can. If you were anybody else I would run you out of here. I've forgiven you everything. What more do you want?"

Myles began to see the Earl was right. He had been his friend. Francis had always said so. Myles

74

stood thinking it over. The Earl lay back on his pillows.

"How old are you?" he said.

"Seventeen last April."

"Then you are old enough to have some sense. Lady Alice is rich. She will be a very rich woman. She can marry the best man in England — an earl or a duke. You are just a poor boy. Your father is an outlaw. One word to the right man and his head would come off. He has a great enemy. This man is greater than I. This enemy is watching for your father. You raise your head and he will kill you. Myles Falworth, how can you talk of being Lady Alice's knight?"

Poor Myles stood still. "Sir," he said, "you're right. I have been a fool. Sir, I will not do it again. I will forget about Lady Alice."

"I don't say that, boy. But you must first raise yourself and your family. Until you do, do not trouble her. Now go."

21·

 he very next day Sir James Lee called Myles in.
"Sit down," he said.

Myles sat down, wondering. The old knight
looked at him a long time. His one eye was bright
and steady as a hawk's. At last he spoke.

"How old are you?"

"Seventeen last April," said Myles.

"Well," said Sir James, "you are big for your
age. I wish you had a man's sense. You're still a
boy though." Again he looked at Myles.

"You have a friend," said Sir James. "You have
a real friend. Ever since you came he has been
watching you. Do you know who he is?"

"Lord George, I guess," said Myles.

"No," said Sir James, "I don't mean Lord George.
He likes you, I know. Can you keep a secret, boy?"

"Yes," said Myles.

"Will you, if I tell you who he is?"

"Yes."

"It is the Earl himself."

76

Myles looked at the gruff old knight in surprise.

"Yes, he has watched you since you came," Sir James went on. "He knows about your fights, too. What do you think of that, Myles Falworth?"

"Sir," said Myles, "did he know I was going to the garden?"

"No," said Sir James. "He knew nothing until your mother wrote and told him. Your father told her to."

"My father!" cried Myles.

"Yes," said Sir James. "When your father found out about it he wrote the Earl. He wanted him to stop you."

"Sir," said Myles, "I don't know if I'm awake or dreaming."

"You're awake all right," said Sir James. "But I must tell you some other things. The Earl thinks you are ready. Boy, a lot depends on you. The Earl thinks you will be a great knight. Next Monday Sir Everard and I will begin to train you. You must learn to fight with the long lance. You must learn to ride. Go to Ralph Smith. He has a suit of armor ready for you. Tell nobody the Earl is your friend."

Myles turned to go. When he got to the door, Sir James spoke again.

"Wait," he called. "I nearly forgot to tell you this. The Earl has given you a present. It is a great strong war horse. Any knight would be proud to have him. Myles Falworth, you are a lucky lad."

"Sir," cried Myles and then stopped. "Sir, did you say the horse is *mine?*"

"Yes, it is yours."

"My very own?"

"Your very own."

Myles never knew how he left. It was all a wonderful dream. He could hardly keep from shouting. He thought of Francis. He ran to find him.

"Come, Francis," he cried. "I have a wonderful story to tell you."

They climbed to the old tower again. "Sit down, Francis," said Myles. "Oh, this is great!" Then he told Francis the whole story. He said nothing about the Earl, though.

Francis sat still. He loved Myles and was glad for him. But his heart was heavy. He feared they would soon have to part.

22.

The next three years were hard ones. Myles worked until he thought he would drop. Day after day he trained. Sir James Lee was hard as iron and cold as stone. Myles used to hate hacking at the posts with his sword. Now he was glad to do it. The rest was riding, riding, riding in the castle yard. He held his shield ready. He held his lance up. He charged his horse forward. Then he bent over, swung his lance down, brought it back up. Practice and more practice.

Now and then Sir James let him practice against other knights. Sometimes, too, Sir Everard worked with him. Sir Everard would ride to one end of the yard, Myles to the other. Sir James would give the signal to start. They would ride straight at each other, lances pointing up. At the last moment each swung his lance down at the other. Then the shield must save the rider. If the rider did not set himself and hold on, he crashed to the ground. The lances usually broke. If you did it right, you were not hurt.

"Sir James," Myles said one day, "tell me the truth. Am I getting any better? Will I ever be a knight?"

"You are a fool," said Sir James. "Do you think you can learn in a year? Wait. I'll tell you if you will become a fighter or not. Wait till you are ripe."

"You're an old bear!" said Myles to himself. "I'll show you yet. I'll learn to fight as well as you."

The last year the work got easier. Now Myles often rode against other castle knights. They practiced with sword, lance, and war club. In these battles Myles always did well. He himself did not know how strong he was or how well he fought. Maybe that was why the others liked him so well.

He was by now leader of the big squires. He did the work Walter Blunt once did. The squires and pages all loved him. He was their greatest hero. Still, Myles did little work inside the castle. Usually he worked for Lord George. The Earl always spoke to him, though, when he saw him. Myles saw how much the Earl had done for him. He would have been glad to die for him.

Myles often saw Lady Anne and Lady Alice. Sometimes, when the Earl was there, he talked with them. The Earl did not seem to mind. Myles felt easy and friendly with Lady Anne. But he still hoped to become Lady Alice's knight some day.

He was by now a tall, handsome lad. His eyes were blue as steel, quick and sharp. He had broad, strong shoulders. Lady Alice saw these things. Often she watched Myles when no one was looking. It is no wonder she often thought about him.

* * *

In 1411 there came five great days for the Mackworth family. King Henry IV himself would visit the Earl. The King was traveling with a French count. The Count had come from France to get help for the French King.

At last the great day came. That morning Myles had his list of squires and pages. He read the names and gave each boy his work to do. Just as he started, Lord George's man called him.

"Myles Falworth! Lord George wants you quick."

Myles gave his list to Francis and hurried to the castle. He found three men helping Lord George put on his armor.

He smiled as Myles came in. "My boy," he said, "I've talked to Mackworth about you. How would you like to be my squire today and go meet the King?"

"Oh, sir," cried Myles eagerly, "I would like nothing better. I hope I'm not too clumsy."

Lord George laughed. "You are easily pleased," he said. "But clumsy! Myles, you are not clumsy.

Go get your armor. I have a coat for you with my colors."

Five minutes later Francis was helping Myles put his armor on. "Just think, Myles," he said. "Lord George picked you over all the castle knights and lords."

"Yes," said Myles, "I don't know why he picked me."

"Why, I know that. He knows what we all know. You're the best fighter and rider here."

Myles laughed. "Don't make fun of me, Francis. I'll rap you one. Say, who rides with the Earl?"

"I heard Wilkes say it was Sir James Lee."

"Good," said Myles. "He will show me what to do. I'm afraid I'll make a fool of myself. Lord George would never forgive me."

"Don't worry," said Francis. "You won't do anything wrong."

At last the Earl, Lord George, and the others were ready. They all got on their horses. The bugle sounded and away they rode. The autumn sun shone on the bright armor and shields.

The Earl and Lord George rode first. Each had on a full suit of armor. Over their armor they wore velvet with the family colors. Behind the two brothers and their squires rode the other knights and soldiers. There were about two hundred and fifty. The spears and lances pointed up. Banners and flags waved in the wind.

For ten miles they rode before they met the King and his men. When they came close, they stopped. Myles saw a man dressed in a plain blue riding suit. He sat on a beautiful white horse. Myles knew he must be the King. Now Sir James nodded to Myles. He jumped from his horse, so Myles did, too. Sir James ran to help the Earl get down. Myles helped Lord George.

The Earl and Lord George took off their helmets. Myles took Lord George's and held his horse. The two brothers now walked to meet the King. The Earl kneeled before him and bowed his head. The King reached out his hand. The Earl got up and then kissed the King's hand. Lord George did the same.

Myles could not hear them, but he saw they were talking. The King now turned and called a knight to him. The knight rode forward. The King spoke a few words. The knight took off his iron glove and shook the Earl's and Lord George's hands. Myles knew he must be the famous French Count.

They talked a few minutes longer. Then the French Count rode back to the King's men. Now they all moved forward. The Earl and Lord George walked beside the King.

While this was happening the Earl's men lined up along the road. As they came to these people, the King spoke a few words. He stood near Myles. Myles saw a plain, stout man. His face was smooth and fat. The eyes were a pale blue. Myles had thought he would see a great handsome man. But King Henry was just fat and looked a little sick.

The Earl and Lord George now put on their helmets again. In a moment they were all riding back to Mackworth Castle.

23.

$\mathcal{T}$he squires all were excited and eager to see the King. But that very afternoon they got even more excited. At one o'clock they saw the Earl and Lord George walk toward their hall. What could it mean? The Earl himself coming to the squires' hall! They watched the two go into Sir James Lee's office.

The playing and shouting stopped. The boys sat quietly, asking one another what would happen. At last Sir James came out. He called a page and sent him running. A few minutes later the page came back with Myles Falworth. Myles went into Sir James' office. The boys looked at one another with wondering eyes.

Myles was pale when he came in. He knew something important was going to happen. The Earl sat at Sir James' table. Lord George sat in a window. Sir James stood before the fireplace. All looked very serious.

"Good day, Myles Falworth," said the Earl. Myles bowed to him and the others. "I'll get right to the point. You know we have been training you hard these three years. We want you to make your way in the world. But we want more than that. We have always known that some day you must fight your father's enemy. We have been quietly getting you ready. Myles, you must be a great knight or nothing. The time has come to prove you. I wish we had another year to train you. But now we have a chance that may never come again. Have you ever heard of Sir Montaine?"

"Yes, my lord. I have heard of him often," said Myles. "He won the great prize in France last year."

"I see you know him," said the Earl. "He's the one I mean. He is the champion knight of France. He has won three first prizes lately. I am glad you know him. Do you know that Sir Montaine is here with the French Count?"

"No," said Myles. "I heard he was in England. I did not know he was here."

"Yes," said the Earl, "he is here. Tell me this, Myles Falworth. If you were a knight would you dare fight Sir Montaine?"

Myles just stared at the Earl. The Earl looked back calmly, stroking his beard. Then Sir James spoke.

"You heard your Lord speak," he said. "Have you no tongue to answer?"

"Be quiet, Lee," said the Earl. "Let the lad think before he speaks."

"My Lord — my Lord," he said. "I do not know what to say. I am almost afraid to answer."

"What?" cried Sir James. "Afraid? If you are afraid, speak no more to me."

"Lee, be quiet," said the Earl. "I don't think you know what he means. Speak up, Myles. Why are you afraid?"

"Only because I am so young, sir. I don't want to make a fool of myself."

"No, Myles," said Lord George. "You don't know how good you are. We think you can hold your own with him."

"Hold my own?" cried Myles, turning to Lord George. "Sir, you can't mean that! Hold my own against Sir Montaine?"

"Yes," said Lord George, "that's what we mean."

"Come, Myles," said the Earl. "Tell me. Will you fight Sir Montaine?"

"Why, yes," said Myles. "If you ask me, I will fight anybody."

"That's a brave lad!" cried Lord George.

"Good, Myles!" cried the Earl, reaching out his hand. Myles took it and kissed it. "I have talked to the King about you this morning. He has agreed to make you a knight if you will fight Sir Montaine. He is taking a nap now. Be ready. I'll bring you to him when he wakes."

Myles had always dreamed of being a knight some day. But that had always seemed far off. Now, to be made a knight by the King himself! And with the Earl's help! And to fight the great French champion!

"I'll see that you have the right clothes, Myles," said Lord George.

"You may go now, Myles," said the Earl. "Be at George's rooms at two o'clock. You must be dressed right to meet the King."

The squires all gathered around him when he came out. They questioned him eagerly. He looked around for Francis. He could not say a word, so he walked away. He hardly knew where he was walking. The wonderful news was too much for him.

He threw himself down on the grass. How long he lay there he never knew. At last someone touched his shoulder. He jumped to his feet. It was Francis.

"What's the matter, Myles?" asked Francis. "What are they all talking about?"

"Oh, Francis!" cried Myles, his voice choking. "They are going to make me a knight. The King himself will do it. I am to fight Sir Montaine."

He reached out his hand. Francis took it. They stood quietly a while. Then Francis spoke.

"You are going to be a great man, Myles," he said. "I always knew it. Now the time has come. You will go away and live somewhere else. You will leave me. Soon I'll not see you any more. You will soon forget me."

"No, Francis, I will never forget you," said Myles. "I will always love you better than anybody else."

Francis shook his head and looked away. He had a big lump in his throat. Suddenly he turned to Myles. "Will you do something for me?" he asked.

"Yes," said Myles. "What is it?"

"Take me as your squire."

"Francis," said Myles, "why do you want to be a squire? You too will be a knight some day."

"Because I'd rather be your squire than a knight," said Francis.

Myles threw his arm around his friend's neck.

"You shall have your wish," he said. "Knight or squire, you are my true friend."

Together they went back to the castle. At two o'clock Myles went to Lord George's rooms. There Lord George gave him the clothes he needed. He put on a fur trimmed coat of green velvet and a black velvet cap. His trousers were red silk. The shoes were black velvet with gold thread. Myles had never worn such fine clothes. Lord George laid his hand on Myles' shoulder.

"You are a handsome lad, Myles," he said.

"You are very good to me, sir," said Myles.

About three o'clock a page came. "The King and the Earl are waiting," he said.

"Come, Myles," said Lord George. They walked to the Earl's rooms. "Myles," said Lord George, "watch yourself. For your father's sake be careful. Don't speak your father's name."

Lord George led him to the King. The Earl and the French Count were there. Myles knelt down. The King smiled kindly. He reached out his hand. Myles kissed it. Then the King raised him to his feet.

"Well," said the King, "you are a strong, handsome lad. I like your looks. They tell me you are ready to fight Sir Montaine. There is a tough old lion. You dare to fight him, boy?"

"Yes, my Lord," said Myles. "I know I cannot beat him. But I will gladly try anything you wish."

The King looked pleased. "You are a fine young man," he said. "Do you speak French?"

"Yes, my Lord," said Myles.

"I am glad of that," said the King. "I want you to meet Sir Montaine."

He turned and waved to a big, thick, black-haired knight. The knight came forward. The King had the two shake hands. Myles looked him over, and he looked Myles over. Myles was young and fresh, not much more than a boy. Sir Montaine was a brown, scarred fighter of many battles.

"So," said the King. "Now you know each other. Come, Mackworth, I wish to talk to you. We need some men to send to France."

Myles left. The King walked up and down, talking to Mackworth and the French Count.

That night was the last for Myles and Francis in the squires' hall. The next day they moved to Lord George's rooms. Myles' days as a squire were over. He was ready to become a man of iron.

24·

*I*n Myles' day it was a great thing to be made a knight by the King. Most men were made knights by other knights. But the Earl wanted Myles to have this great honor. The Earl had his reasons, too. So he made his plans carefully.

You could become a knight on the battlefield by great fighting. Then they did not make a big fuss about it. But when the king made a knight, they usually held a big celebration.

Myles had to have two squires of honor. These men had to be knights themselves. Lord George was one, and Sir Montaine was the other. Sir James Lee asked Myles questions about the laws of knights. Then they led him into the chapel. Here he had to stay up all night, keeping watch over his armor. He laid his armor, helmet, sword, and lance before the altar. In the morning he lit a candle and put it on the altar.

Myles then slept. Francis wakened him about noon and brought him food. Next the two squires of honor came in. A servant brought his clothes. Lord George came forward.

"Hurry, Myles," he said. "The King is coming. Get ready."

The great castle hall was filled with people. At one end stood a platform covered with red satin. Here the King would sit. A carpet lay down the middle, running to the platform. On one side were the seats for the castle people. On the other side sat the town people.

A whisper ran around that the King was coming. Then everybody was quiet. They heard the horses before the door. The horns blew. Then in marched the King and the others.

First came twenty knights. Then followed the nobles. Last came King Henry. The Earl walked on his right, the French Count on his left. Slowly they marched to the platform.

Now Myles and his friends came in. First came Francis, carrying Myles' sword. The sword was in a red leather cover. The sword belt was leather and silver. The gold spurs of a knight hung from the sword handle. Behind Francis came Myles. He wore a white wool robe and a silvered leather belt. Under the robe he wore his shining new armor, a present from the Earl. Next came five or six squires. As they came in, the crowd clapped their hands.

"I never saw such a handsome lad," whispered Lady Anne.

Lady Alice nodded, her eyes on Myles.

Myles knew his face was pale. He kept his eyes on King Henry. He walked forward slowly. Then Lord George touched his arm. Myles stopped. He was just before the platform.

He saw Francis go up the steps. Then he kneeled and gave the sword and spurs to the King. King Henry laid the sword across his knees. Francis bowed and stepped aside. The King took the spurs, looked at Myles, and smiled. Then he turned and gave one spur to the Earl.

The Earl took it and bowed. He came slowly down the steps. He knelt down and lifted Myles' foot. Then he put the spur on Myles' foot, arose, bowed to the King, and stepped aside.

The King gave the other spur to the French Count. He put the other spur on Myles' foot and also stepped aside. Then the King slowly arose. He opened the leather sword belt. The Earl and the Count each took Myles by the hand. They led him up the steps to the King. The King put the sword belt around Myles' waist. He raised his hand and struck Myles on the shoulder. Then he cried:

"Be a good knight!"

Everybody cheered and clapped hands. The King

laid both hands on Myles' shoulders and kissed his cheek. That ended it. Myles was no longer Myles Falworth. Now he was Sir Myles Falworth — a man of iron.

25.

*U*sually a great feast was held for a new knight. But for Myles there was to be no such feast. The Earl had wanted the King himself to make Myles a knight. He wanted Myles to be as good as any other knight in England. He wanted Myles to fight a famous knight. All these things he had been able to do.

But the Earl wanted to keep Myles away from the King. There was one thing King Henry must not know now. That was that Myles was Lord Falworth's son. "Falworth?" the King had said. "I seem to know the name. Who is this Myles Falworth?" The Earl had held his breath then. But the King had other things to think about. Soon he forgot about the matter. The Earl did not want to take any more chances. Having a big feast might spoil everything. The King would talk with Myles and find everything out.

The King was worried about helping the French King just then. The French Count had come to ask him for help. The Earl could help King Henry with men. So, it was easy to keep the King's mind off the feast. He was eager to see the fight, though. Nobody loved a good fight better than Henry.

The Earl had set the next morning for the fight. All day long the workmen were busy building the stands. The two knights were to fight in the great castle yard.

That afternoon the Earl sent for Myles. He talked for about half an hour. He told Myles many things he had not known. Some things Myles had guessed already.

"You want to know who your father's enemy is," said the Earl. "The time has come to tell you. He is the Earl of Alban."

Myles closed his fists, but said nothing.

"Yes," said the Earl, "he is your father's bitter enemy. He is my enemy, too. Have you heard of him?"

"Only that he is a great knight and lord. I have never seen him," said Myles.

"Yes, you did," said the Earl. "When you were a child he once came to your castle."

"I know," cried Myles. "He's the one who killed Sir John Dale, isn't he?"

"The same," said the Earl. "He blinded your father. There was a great tournament at York. Your father was a good knight. He was in it. His horse threw him during the fight. Alban saw him lying helpless. Twice he rode his war horse over him. Your father's squire pulled him away. But the wounds made your father blind."

"He tried to do it? He wanted to kill my father?"

"He did. I myself heard him boast he had done it."

"But why?" cried Myles.

"Because of your mother," said the Earl. "Alban had wanted to marry her. When your father won her, Alban swore he would kill him."

The Earl told Myles how Alban had kept on. First he got the King to make Lord Falworth an outlaw. Then he got the Falworth castle and lands. The blind Lord's friends had tried hard to save him. But Alban had won out.

"I've got his fat lands," he said. "I'll never stop till I find him. When I do, I'll kill him."

"Ever since," said the Earl, "he has been hunting your father. Some day he may find him. Then —"

Now Myles knew why the Earl had trained him. He knew, too, why the Earl had been so careful. Some day he must be his father's champion. Some day he would fight the great Earl of Alban. He must clear his father's name. He must get back his lands and castle. He must kill the Earl of Alban!

"He is your enemy too, my Lord?" asked Myles.

"He is," said the Earl. "I helped your father win your mother. Alban knows that. He has sworn to get me, too. He plots against me now. If he finds your father, off comes your father's head. Mine will go, too, for I helped him get away."

"I see," said Myles.

"I have taken the trouble to have the King make you a knight. I want you to fight this French knight. Why do you think I am doing this? Now you are as good as Alban himself. You are the King's knight. I want to see if you will be a great fighter. You will have to be great to beat Alban. I am trying you out against Montaine. If you can handle him, you have a chance with Alban. I wish we could have waited longer. I am not ready for Alban yet. But the King was here, so we had to move. He wants soldiers to help France. I am going to send you. I want to keep you away till we are ready. Lord George goes to France with two hundred men. You go, too. Stay till I send for you."

Myles got up to go. "May Francis go, too?" he asked.

"He may," said the Earl.

Myles wanted to say more. He waited, not knowing how to start.

"What do you want?" asked the Earl.

Myles' heart beat hard. "Sir," he said, "I guess you forgot. I never have. Long ago I asked to be Lady Alice's knight. You laughed then. You said I was not even a knight. Now I am. May I be her true knight and fight for her?"

"I don't know just what you mean," said the Earl. "Just what do you want?"

"Not much right now," said Myles. "I would like to ask her for something to wear tomorrow. I want her to be my true lady. All knights serve a lady. I want to serve Lady Alice."

The Earl stroked his beard a while. "All right," he said. "You may ask her. I will not say no. But Lady Anne must be there when you ask her. Go to the long hall. I shall send them."

Myles waited in the hall. At last the door opened. Lady Alice and Lady Anne came in. Lady Anne gave him her hand. Myles bowed and kissed it.

"I am glad you are a knight, Sir Myles," she said. "I am sure you will be a good one."

Lady Alice hung back, saying nothing.

"Come, Alice," said Lady Anne. "Don't you wish Sir Myles joy and good luck?"

Lady Alice held out her hand bashfully. Again

Myles bowed and kissed her hand. "I wish you joy, Sir Myles," she said softly. Lady Anne stepped back so Myles could talk to Lady Alice alone. Myles did not know how to begin.

"Lady," he said — "I — have a favor to ask."

"What is it, Sir Myles?"

"Lady," he said, "I've always hoped to be your true knight some day." He stopped. "Have I made you angry?"

She shook her head.

"Now the time has come," said Myles. "Tomorrow I fight a famous knight. I am a nobody. But I fight for England, and Mackworth — and — and you. You are not angry?"

Again Lady Alice shook her head.

"In battle knights always wear something of their lady's. I wish you would give me something to wear. Will you?"

He waited, but still Lady Alice said nothing.

"I guess I should not have asked," said Myles sadly. "If I have made you angry, I am sorry."

Then she turned quickly to him. "No, Sir Myles," she said. "I did not know what to say. I am proud to have you serve me." She took a gold chain from her neck. "I give you this chain," she said. "I shall be happy if you will wear it. I wish you good luck." Then she turned and ran.

26·

*A*nd now the great day came. If Myles failed, all hopes were gone. If he did well — many things could happen.

It was a fine, clear September day. A fence about five feet high cut the castle yard in half. On one side was a grandstand. The best place was kept for the King. Below the King's seat were places for the castle knights and ladies. The stands were covered with bright cloth. Flags and pennants waved in the breeze.

At each end were tents for the two fighters. Over Myles' tent hung the Mackworth colors, black and yellow. A great wooden shield was nailed to the tent top. On the shield were painted the three hawks which meant the Mackworth family. Myles stood in his tent watching the crowd gather. The ladies were already there. Pages ran here and there, leading people to their seats. Many town people crowded around the fence. Myles felt his heart beat hard to see so many people.

Suddenly the horns blew. A great gate opened. Into the yard rode the King, the Earl, and the French Count. Behind them came other castle lords. Then Francis called Myles to get his armor on.

Wilkes and Francis fitted the last piece on as Lord George and Sir James came in. Lord George took Myles' hand. "Good luck, boy," he said.

Sir James seemed worried. He said nothing. Now Francis set the big helmet in place. Sir James tried each piece of armor to be sure it was right.

Just then a page came in. "The King is ready," he said.

"Come on, Myles," said Lord George.

"Francis," said Myles, "hand me my bag."

Francis handed it over. Myles took out the chain Lady Alice had given him. "Tie it around my arm," Myles said. Francis tied it fast. Lord George watched and smiled.

"Why, Myles," he said, "have you picked out a lady already?"

"Yes, my Lord," said Myles.

"Who is she? A castle girl?"

"My Lord," said Myles, "Lady Alice gave me the chain."

Lord George looked surprised. "Well," he said, "you aim pretty high."

At that moment two squires led Myles' horse to

the tent door. Francis and Wilkes helped him mount. He rode slowly along the fence to the King. Sir Montaine came riding up from the other tent. A squire now called out the fighters' names. Myles had to say a few words, asking to fight Sir Montaine. Sir Montaine had to answer. Then a squire read out the rules for fighting. When it was over, the squires led their knights back to the tents. The crowd clapped their hands and cheered.

Sir James Lee met Myles at his tent. He looked up into Myles' face.

"You will not fail, will you?" he said. "You will not shame me?"

"No, my dear master," said Myles. "I will do my best."

"I believe it," said Sir James. "I think you will do well. I talked to Montaine this morning. I think he will just break three lances with you. I don't think he will try to throw you hard. Remember what I have always told you. Dig your toes in hard. Bend forward. Keep your elbow in close. Hold your lance a foot above his helmet. When you get close, drop it square on his shield. So, Myles, good luck!"

Francis tied the helmet fast. Sir Montaine was ready. Myles took Sir James' hand and shook it. He put on his glove, took the lance, and turned his horse to face Montaine.

27.

*A*s Myles turned his horse he saw Sir Montaine was ready. He could see straight ahead through the peep hole in his helmet. Sir Montaine sat like an iron statue. His lance pointed up. The sun flashed on his shining armor.

Myles clamped his teeth shut. He said a quick prayer. He raised his lance high. There was a moment of dead quiet. Myles saw the King raise his hand. The bugle sounded loud and clear. Myles drove his spurs into his horse. The great war horse leaped forward.

Myles saw Montaine rushing at him, coming closer, closer. Myles dug his toes in and bent forward. As they came close, Myles dropped his lance square against the moving shield. There was a crash like thunder. Myles heard wood splinter. His horse staggered, then rushed on. As Myles slowed up he heard the crowd clapping and cheering. He saw he was still holding his broken lance. His heart was beating hard.

Only then did he know he had done well. He turned to ride back to his place. Montaine was riding toward him, also holding a broken lance. As they passed each other, a voice came from Montaine's helmet. "Well done, Sir Myles. Well done." Myles threw the broken lance aside. Francis brought another.

"Oh, Myles!" cried Francis. "You did it! You did it! I never saw a better ride. Oh, Myles, knock him off this time!"

Myles laughed. He took the new lance. He walked his horse up and down so he would not cool off. Then he mounted again. Once more the King waved his hand. Once more the horn blew. Again the two rushed together with a crash. Again the lances broke. Once more the people cheered.

This time Montaine stopped on the way back. "Sir Myles," he said, "I did not know you were so good. I was going to let you break three lances. Now watch out. This time I am going to throw you. I warn you."

"Thank you, my Lord," said Myles. "I will do my best. But pardon me. Your saddle seems a little loose. I would tighten it if I were you."

"No," laughed Montaine, "do not worry about me. I have fought too often to need advice. If you think you can throw me, go ahead."

Myles called for a drink. Francis took off Myles' great helmet. Myles wiped the sweat from his face. Sir James came up and took his hand.

"My dear boy," he said, "I am a happy old man today. You ride like a knight of twenty battles."

"I am glad you say so, dear master," said Myles. "I shall need all my skill. Montaine says he will throw me this time."

"He does?" cried Sir James. "Then he will aim for your helmet. You have one chance. Strike for his helmet. Is your hand shaking?"

"Not now," said Myles.

"Then keep cool. Maybe you will come out all right."

Francis put the helmet back on and tied it. What Sir James had said was true. A blow on the helmet would tear a rider off his horse. But most knights could strike a perfect helmet blow only once in fifty tries. The big helmets had only one flat spot. That spot was where the helmet was welded together. Here two little bands crossed each other. If the lance point hit here, the rider went rolling. If it hit anywhere else on the helmet, the lance would slide off. This blow Myles had to try.

Wilkes came running to hand Myles a new lance. Sir James himself had picked it out. It was oak, tough, thicker than the others. Myles held it in place. He looked at Montaine. Now he forgot the crowd. He saw only his enemy.

The people seemed to know what would happen. Everyone stopped talking. Myles said a quick prayer.

Then, for the third time, the King raised his hand. The bugle blew the third time. Again Myles dug his spurs into his horse. Once more the iron enemy rushed nearer, nearer, nearer. Myles saw only one thing — the little helmet cross. He set himself for the crash. In a flash he dropped his lance straight and true. The next moment the crash came. There was a blaze of blinding light. Sparks flew before Myles' eyes. He felt his horse stagger. He drove his spurs deep into its sides. Then he heard another crash. Once more his horse sprang forward. Myles looked up in surprise. His helmet was gone! He heard a great shout. For a moment he felt sick. He had lost! He turned his horse. Then his heart gave a leap. He could hardly believe what he saw. There, in tangled harness and saddle, lay Sir Montaine. His horse was trotting loose. Two squires ran to help him up. The castle people were waving their hats and shouting. Myles rode slowly back to the fallen knight.

The squire pulled out his dagger and cut the helmet loose. Montaine's face was white as death. His eyes flashed.

"I was not thrown right!" he cried. "I tore his helmet off. My saddle came loose. I am the winner. I knocked his helmet off."

"Sir," said the man who was judge of the fight, "you are wrong. Surely you know that losing a helmet does not lose the fight."

"I fell because my saddle straps broke."

"That is true," said Myles. "I saw the saddle was loose. I told him so before we charged."

"Sir," said the judge to Montaine, "what more do you want? This knight warned you himself. Was it not fair that he did?"

Montaine stood still a little while, leaning on his squire. He looked down at the ground. At last he turned and walked off. The squires picked up his shield and helmet.

Francis picked up Myles' helmet. Lord George and Sir James Lee came walking to Myles. They led him before the King.

Even the French Count praised Myles. Everybody had a good word for him. Myles looked up and saw Lady Alice watching him. He bowed and smiled.

Back in the tent now, Sir James Lee burst in. He threw his arms around Myles' neck and kissed both his cheeks.

"My own dear boy," he said. "This is a great day for me. I am happier than if you were my own son.

110

I am happier than when I won my own first fight."

"Sir," said Myles, "his saddle was loose."

"Bah!" cried Sir James. "He knew it, didn't he? He went down because you hit him fair and true. The world champion would have gone down under that blow."

28.

Lord George was not ready to go to France until three weeks after the King left Mackworth Castle. So Myles had a chance to visit his father and mother. He had not seen them for years. Now he could see how low they had fallen. Their little farm house was a poor place. But Myles knew now what a great friend Father Edward was. If Lord Falworth were found, Father Edward would lose his head. Father Edward knew this. Yet he had hidden his outlaw friend for years.

Myles had many talks with him. Father Edward told him many things he had not known. Myles asked why the King was so bitter against his father.

"Your father was King Richard's friend, Myles,"

he said. "He wanted Richard to stay as king. You cannot blame King Henry too much. Your father was ever Henry's enemy. Then your father helped Sir John Dale. That was the last straw."

"His enemy, yes," said Myles. "But my father did nothing after Henry was king, did he?"

"No," said Father Edward. "I know your father well. He is a good man. He would not fight his own king."

"Is it right for me to fight Alban?" asked Myles.

"I cannot say it is wrong," said the old man.

And so Myles went to France with Lord George. He was there only six months. But those six months made a great change in him. He fought in the fierce Paris battles. In six months Myles changed from boy to man. Then one day the Earl's man came with a letter. Myles was to come back. He must go to the Mackworth House, near London. Myles knew his time had come.

On a bright April day he and Francis rode through London. It was the first time Myles had seen the great city. He and Francis rode through the dirty streets calmly. He had seen too much lately to get excited.

The Earl of Mackworth looked the same as ever. But the Earl hardly knew Myles. The six months had made a new Myles Falworth. The smooth boy face was burned almost black. A white scar ran over his right eye. The two stood looking at each other.

"My Lord," said Myles, "you sent for me. Here I am."

"When did you land, Sir Myles?" asked the Earl.

"Last Tuesday."

"You are changed," said the Earl. "I can hardly believe it is you."

Myles smiled. "I have seen many things in Paris and France," he said. "They make a boy become a man quickly."

"I see you have had many adventures. That is why I sent you," said the Earl. "Do you know why I asked you to come back?"

"Yes," said Myles calmly. "You would want me for only one reason. You want me to fight Alban."

"You talk very boldly," said the Earl. "I hope you fight as boldly as you talk."

"No man can say I am afraid."

"Well, that I believe. But you are right. You must fight Alban. The time is ripe. I am sending for your father to come to London. It will not be safe for you and me to be together now. I have talked to the King's son, the Prince of Wales. He is on our side. He will take you in. You will stay with him until everything is ready."

Myles bowed but said nothing. The Earl waited.

"Well, sir," he said at last, "have you nothing to say? You are pretty cool about all this."

"Sir," said Myles, "I have thought this all over in France. I want to ask you a plain question."

"Ask it," said the Earl.

"Sir, you have something to gain if I kill Alban, have you not?"

"Did George tell you that?"

Myles did not answer.

"All right," said the Earl, "I won't ask you to tell. And I'll give you the answer. Yes, it will help me if you kill him."

"That makes no difference to me," said Myles. "I fight this battle for my father. But if I help you, you can do me a favor."

"What is the favor, Sir Myles?"

"That I may ask Lady Alice to be my wife."

The Earl started up from his seat. "Sir Myles Falworth —" he began. Then he stopped. Myles looked at him calmly. The Earl walked over to the window. He looked out a long time. Suddenly he turned. "Sir Myles," he said, "your family is a good family. Just now it is poor. If you raise it back again, your chance is as good as anybody's. That is my answer. What do you say?"

"I could ask no more," said Myles.

29.

*T*hat night Myles stayed at Mackworth House. Next morning the Earl, Francis, and Myles went up the river to the Prince's palace. The Earl's men rowed the big boat. Past the London palaces and gardens they went. At last they came to Scotland Yard, the Prince's own palace. Broad marble steps led up from the river.

The Earl, Myles, and Francis stepped ashore. The Earl led them up into the Prince's garden. Soon they heard laughing voices. Turning a corner they came suddenly upon some young men. They were sitting at a table. Some were eating a late breakfast. Servants were carrying food.

Myles knew the Prince as soon as he saw him. He was three or four years older than Myles. His face was frank and open. The eyes were dark and blue. He wore his thick yellow hair to his shoulders.

"Aha!" cried the Prince. "Here comes the Old Fox. What brings the Old Fox this morning? I'll bet he will catch himself a goose."

All faces turned to the Earl. He bowed and smiled.

"Your Highness is joking, I am sure," he said smoothly. "Sir, I bring you the young knight we spoke about. This is Sir Myles Falworth. You were going to take him in, you remember."

"Sir Myles," said the Prince, "I have heard great things about you. The Earl and others tell me you fought bravely in France. I shall be glad to have you live here." He smiled and looked at the Earl. "I will get you away from the Old Fox, too. Our side cannot do without this clever Earl. But he will always take care of himself. Well, enough of this. My Lord, will you have breakfast?"

"Pardon me, your Highness," said the Earl. He smiled a smooth smile Myles had never seen before. "I must go. Your Uncle Winchester waits. We must talk this business over. You will like Sir Myles better than an old fox. I leave him in your good care."

And this was how Myles met the Prince who later became Henry V. For a month he lived with the Prince. The two were soon fast friends. The Prince liked the quiet young knight. Wherever the Prince went, Myles went, too. Often the Prince talked to Myles about his own troubles. The King and the Prince did not get along well. The King thought the Prince was getting too much power.

The Prince also talked of Myles' coming battle. He told him how the Earl had planned the fight. He told him why they wanted to get Alban. He said that only Myles could strike him down.

Then, at last, came the time to move. One morning the Prince called Myles. With the Prince were his brother and his uncle.

"Poor Myles," said the Prince. "Here we are, the greatest lords of England. To get rid of our enemy we use Myles and his blind father. It is not right."

"Pardon me, your Highness," said Myles. "It does not matter. I fight for my father."

"Yes, Myles, I know. Do you know why I called you? Today you must face Alban before the King. The Earl has made his plans. The time is ripe. Do you know your father is at Mackworth House?"

"No," said Myles, "I did not know."

"He has been there two days," said the Prince. "The Earl has sent for us. First we go to Mackworth House, then to the palace. We have the time set to see the King. Alban will be there. The Earl will see to that. Let's go."

30.

*P*art of the King's palace was an old building called the Painted Room. Painted on the wall were war pictures. These pictures told the story of all England's wars.

The King liked to spend his time here. He was often sick and liked to rest. The cold walls and floors were covered, and the big room was bright and cheerful. They brought Myles here to face the great Alban.

They met just outside the door. Myles and his father waited with a few knights. The others went in. Myles could hear voices inside. He thought he heard the King's voice. Suddenly the Earl came back out.

"Everything is ready," he whispered. "Alban is inside." He turned to Myles. "Sir Myles," he said, "remember what I told you. You know what to say and do." He took Lord Falworth's hand and led him inside. Myles followed.

The King sat leaning against his pillows. Near

him stood his two sons, the Princes, and other nobles. Myles looked at only one man — the Earl of Alban. He had not seen that face since he was eight years old. He could still see Alban standing over Sir John Dale, his sword dripping blood. Alban still had the same black eyebrows, hooked nose, and dark cheeks.

Alban had just been talking to another lord. A smile still hung on his lips. He looked up. The smile died away. His eyes got wide. His face turned white. In a flash he saw his danger. He saw the others look at him. His hand closed on his sword.

The Earl led the blind Lord Falworth up to the King. They both kneeled.

"What is this, my Lord?" said the King. "I thought to see the young knight, Falworth. You bring an old blind man."

"I have taken this chance, my Lord, to bring him to you. You have not been fair to him. There stands the young knight. This is his father, Lord Falworth. He asks mercy of his King."

"Falworth," said the King. "I seem to know the name, but I cannot place him. My head bothers me. I cannot remember."

Now Alban came forward. "My Lord, pardon me. I know him. He is Lord Falworth, the outlaw. He hid Sir John Dale from us. He wanted to kill you years ago. He is my enemy, too. My enemies

119

have brought him here. They want to harm me. I put myself into your hands."

The King's sickly face flamed red. He got to his feet.

"Yes!" he cried. "I remember now. I remember the man and the name. Who dares bring him here?"

The Earl shot a quick look at Winchester, the King's brother. He came forward.

"My Lord," he said, "here I am, your own brother. I beg you not to judge too quickly. It is true this man was made an outlaw. But he had no chance to talk. I ask you to listen."

The King looked at Winchester angrily. He bit his lower lip. Alban stood calm and quiet. At last the King turned to the blind Lord.

"What have you to say?" he asked.

"My Lord," said the blind man, "I come to tell you the truth. I am no traitor. I had no chance to say so before. I was blind and helpless. My enemies were strong. Now I have help. I say the Earl of Alban is a foul liar. I have a champion to prove me right. I ask for a trial by battle."

The Earl flashed a look at Myles. He came forward and kneeled beside his father. The King looked at him angrily.

"My Lord and King," said Myles, "I am this man's son. I come as his champion. You made me

121

a knight yourself. I may fight any man in England."
Now he got up and pulled off his iron glove. He
threw it crashing on the floor. Then he cried,
"William of Alban, I call you a liar. I throw down
my glove. If you dare fight me, pick it up."

Alban moved to pick it up. But the King stopped
him. "Stop!" he cried. "Do not touch it. Let it
lie. Let it lie, I say." He turned to the others. "Now
tell me this. What does this mean? Who brought
this man here?"

He looked from one to the other. No one spoke.

"I see," said the King. "You all have done it.
Alban is right. You are all his enemies. You are my
enemies, too. This is a foul plot. I made this boy a
knight. He can fight anybody — even Alban. But I
say the courts shall judge. Let us see what the judges
say. Until we hear, throw this outlaw lord in prison.
Take him away to London Tower. Keep the glove
until the court speaks."

The King stood still a moment. Then he looked
at the Earl. "I know I am a sick man," he said.
"Some people have been my friends many years.
They are plotting now. My Lord Mackworth, I
see your hand in all this. You got me to make young
Falworth a knight. You brought him here today.
You are working with my sons and my brother."
Then he turned to Alban. "Come, my Lord. I am

tired. Lend me your arm." And so he left, leaning on Alban's arm.

"Your Highness," said a soldier, "I must do as the King said. I must take Lord Falworth to the Tower."

"Do so," said the Prince. "We knew this would happen. See that he gets good care. I shall visit him myself this afternoon."

31.

The High Court did not speak until July. Some things were against Lord Falworth, some for him. The Earl had found good lawyers, though. So the Court finally asked the King to settle the case by battle. In those days, cases were often settled that way. If one knight had a case against another knight, they could fight it out. The winner of the fight won the case.

Sick King Henry was angry. He had tried to get the judges to rule against Lord Falworth. But the judges knew the King could not live long. The Prince and the Earl would rule when the King died.

So the Court ruled for the Falworths. That old fox, the Earl, had known what would happen long before. The King hoped to save Alban if he could. If the fight went against Alban, he hoped to stop it in time. If Alban was winning, he meant Myles to die. A friend of the Prince heard the King say this.

"That means you must win or die, Myles," said the Prince.

"I want it that way," said Myles.

The King set the date for September 3. The place was much like the Mackworth Castle yard. A six-foot fence ran around the battle ground. The ground itself was sixty yards long and forty yards wide.

One day Myles and the Prince visited the place. They met Alban and his friends just leaving. The Earl spoke to one of his friends.

"There's that young Falworth fool," he said. "His father is going to die as a traitor. This boy I will kill. I have beaten far better knights than he."

Myles heard him. He looked calmly ahead. He knew Alban wanted him to hear. He said nothing.

"Are you afraid, Myles?" asked the Prince.

"I am afraid for my father," said Myles. "Alban I do not fear."

"But Alban is about the best knight in England. He is a killer. If he can, he will surely kill you."

"I am not afraid, my Lord," said Myles calmly.

"I'm not afraid for you, either!" cried the Prince.

At last the day came. Early in the morning the Prince came to get Myles. Francis was getting the armor ready. They went to eat at Scotland Yard.

The Earl and others were there. All were nervous. If Alban won, he would be stronger than ever. And Alban never forgot an enemy.

After they had eaten, the Prince got up. "The boat is ready," he said. "Myles, you will want to see your father and mother. I'll go along. Do you want anyone else?"

"I want Sir James Lee and Francis," said Myles.

"All right," said the Prince.

They went up to the Tower. Lady Falworth met them, her eyes red and her face pale. Myles kissed her hand, and she burst into tears. She knew Myles must win or die. The Earl and Myles then talked with Lord Falworth.

"What about my mother if I lose?" asked Myles.

"I will see that she is cared for," said the Earl. "As for your father —"

Lord Falworth smiled. "If Myles loses, you need not worry," he said. "I know what will happen."

Myles took his father's hand. "I'll do my best," he said.

"I know, my son. God bless you."

32.

*M*any years before, the rules had been made for trial by battle. Knights ever since had fought under those rules. So Myles had to come to the east gate with Francis and two knights. There the Falworth lawyer met him. He led Myles inside. The battle judges were there. The Chief Judge had to follow the rules also.

"Stand, Sir Knight," he cried. "Tell why you come. What is your name?"

Myles answered, "I am Myles Falworth. King Henry IV made me a knight. I come to fight William, Earl of Alban. He says my father, Lord Falworth, is a traitor. I call Alban a liar. May God show us who is right."

The Chief Judge now looked into Myles' helmet. "This is Sir Myles Falworth," he said. "Open the gates. Go in, Myles Falworth."

The stands were like those at Mackworth Castle. There was a place for the King. Flags blew in the breeze. But there was no laughing or cheering.

Myles rode his horse up to the King. Here he stopped. The judge called out his name and said he was ready.

"Then call the Earl of Alban," said the King. "It is time to begin."

Myles looked up at the faces in the stands. He saw the Prince and his friends. Mackworth and other nobles were there, too. Next to the Earl sat his father. Sir James Lee was on his other side. The blind man's face was pale. The Earl was, too, but he kept looking keenly at Myles.

Then the judge cried, "Hear, hear, hear! William, Earl of Alban, come to do battle. We call you to fight Sir Myles Falworth, champion of Lord Falworth. Hear, hear, hear! Let Alban come."

Myles saw the Earl come riding in the other gate. The Chief Judge met him and asked the same questions he had asked Myles. The Earl wore a full suit of beautiful new armor. He rode up next to Myles.

At last everything was finished. Then Francis led Myles' horse back to the east gate. Francis looked the armor over carefully. Then the judges looked over the arms. Each knight could have a long sword, a short sword, a dagger, a battle ax, and a thick broad sword.

For this fight they were not to use lances. Instead,

they had the thick broad sword. This sword could strike a terrible blow. It was heavy and clumsy, and not good against a fast fighter. But Alban had asked the King to use it instead of a lance. The King had ruled for him. The younger knights no longer used this short broad sword. Myles had never practiced fighting with it. Alban had used it for years and often fought with it. The King knew he would help Alban by ruling to use it and not the lance.

Now the judges got everybody out of the way. Myles took off his glove and shook Francis' hand. Poor Francis' face was white as death. The others now got out of the fighting grounds. The judges locked the gates. Myles was alone, face to face with his enemy.

33 •

$\mathcal{T}$he judge took his seat just below the King. The King then leaned forward and spoke to him. The judge called out:

"Let them go! Let them go! Let them go!"

The two knights had been sitting still as iron statues. When the judge called the third time, they started forward. They both rode slowly, but neither stopped. They met in the middle of the battle ground.

Myles fought with the long sword, Alban with the short broad sword. They began swinging as soon as they got close. For a time nothing could be heard but the thunder of crashing blows. They spurred their horses together, charged, turned, and pulled away. Sometimes great clouds of dust hid them.

The people in the stands were quiet, watching eagerly. Now and then Myles' friends raised a cheer. From the beginning Myles seemed to have the better of the fight. He kept forcing Alban back.

Myles' father sat as though he could see. The

Earl leaned until his lips were close to Lord Falworth's ear. He told the blind man every time a blow landed.

"Don't be afraid," said the Earl. "Myles is holding his own." Then, after a while: "God is with us. Myles has wounded him twice. Alban's horse is wearing out. A little longer and we win."

Myles now drove Alban before him fiercely. The mighty blows were more than Alban could stand. Back, back, back he went. Just as he had him, Myles stopped.

"Why does the boy spare him?" cried the Earl. "Three times he had him! That time he had him against the wall."

What the Earl said was true. Myles could have ended the fight three times already. Three times he had spared Alban. He knew he had the fight won. He wanted to show the King that Alban was getting a fair chance. But Myles paid high for what he did.

Alban sat upon his panting, sweating war horse. He sat still as a rock, holding his short broad sword before him. He had been wounded twice. One wound was under his armor. No one knew how bad it was. The other wound was on his shoulder. A thin stream of blood ran down his side. Myles was about ten steps away.

"My Lord," said Myles, "you are badly wounded.

You are going to lose this battle. Will you give up?"

"Never, you dog!" cried Alban. "Never!"

Then, quick as a flash, he drove his horse straight at Myles. He swung one last terrible blow. Myles pulled his horse back and raised his shield. The sword slipped off the shield and landed on his horse's neck. The horse staggered and fell on his knees. Alban charged again and crashed into the horse. The horse went over and over in the dust. As his horse went down, Myles got one foot loose. The other caught for a moment. Myles crashed flat and hard. In the cloud of dust no one could see what happened. Alban dug his spurs in his horse and rode straight over Myles' body. He stopped, turned, pulled the horse high into the air. The horse's front hoofs crashed down. Alban had ridden over the father years before. Now he did the same thing to the son. Myles, half gone, saw him come, but was helpless. A fallen knight in armor cannot rise. Myles closed his eyes. There was a roaring crash, then another.

The men in the stands were shouting and screaming. Only the King sat still. Alban turned his horse and looked at the King. He had not fought fair, and he knew it. A knight could not ride his horse over his enemy. The King said nothing. He wanted Myles to die. Alban turned and rode up to Myles.

Myles looked up. He saw Alban above him, raising his sword for the death blow. Down flashed the heavy sword. Myles jerked his shield over. He caught the blow and turned it aside. But that made it last only a little longer.

Once more Alban raised the sword. He swung it twice around his head before he struck. Myles tried to get the shield up again. The sword crashed through the armor and bit deep to the bone. Myles pulled the shield weakly over his face. Alban swung the third time. The blade fell straight and true, just under Myles' left arm. The sword cut through the steel and stuck fast. Myles groaned and grabbed the sword with both hands. Had Alban let go, he could have taken his time killing Myles. Instead, he tried to pull the sword loose. The horse dragged Myles to his knees. He held on with one hand and grabbed the saddle with the other. The next moment he was on his feet. Alban tried to beat him off. Myles caught him by the belt. Alban beat him on the head. He spurred and reared his horse back trying to shake Myles loose. Myles held him in a death grip.

He did not feel the blood run. He felt no pain. With his free hand he got hold of the heavy, spiked iron battle ax tied to Alban's saddle. He gave it a yank and tore it loose. Then, grinding his teeth,

he struck as he never struck before. Crash! Crash! Crash! Once — twice — three times he smashed into Alban's helmet. The third terrible blow split the helmet wide open. Myles saw the awful, broken face a moment — and then the saddle was empty. Alban crashed to the ground.

Myles, panting, dizzy, sick to death, held tight to the horse. He felt the hot blood fill his armor and saw it spill on the ground. He dimly saw the judges and squires gather around him. He heard a judge ask if he were badly hurt. He did not answer. Francis yanked his helmet open. Myles' face was like ashes. The lips had no color. Great drops of sweat stood on his head.

"Water! Water!" he cried. He started blindly toward the gate. A shadow seemed to fall on him. "It is death," he said. He stopped, swayed, and fell to the ground.

THE END

*B*ut Myles was not dead. Those who saw his face had thought so at first. He fainted because he had lost so much blood. The Prince's doctor took care of him and had him carried to Scotland Yard. The Prince and the Earl watched the doctor wash and bandage the great open wound. Myles lay still, eyes closed, weak as a child. At last he opened his eyes.

"What has happened to my father?" he asked faintly.

"You have saved his life, Myles," said the Prince. "He is a free man again."

Myles closed his eyes. Two tears ran down his cheeks.

Myles' wound was a bad one. The weeks grew into months before he could get up. Then one day the Earl came to see him. They talked a while and then were quiet.

"My Lord," said Myles suddenly, "do you remember what we spoke of when I came back?"

"I remember," said the Earl.

135

"And have I won the right to ask for Lady Alice?"

"You have won it," said the Earl.

There is little else to tell. In January King Henry died. The Prince became king and all went well for the Falworths and Mackworths. The new King gave the Falworths their castles and lands back. Myles married Lady Alice. Sir James Lee and Francis, now a knight, too, came to live at Falworth Castle.

Myles was rich and happy after his hard fighting.